SAVING SEX

SAVING SEX

SEXUALITY AND SALVATION IN AMERICAN EVANGELICALISM

AMY DeROGATIS

OXFORD
UNIVERSITY PRESS

OXFORD
UNIVERSITY PRESS

Oxford University Press is a department of the University of Oxford.
It furthers the University's objective of excellence in research, scholarship,
and education by publishing worldwide.

Oxford   New York
Auckland   Cape Town   Dar es Salaam   Hong Kong   Karachi
Kuala Lumpur   Madrid   Melbourne   Mexico City   Nairobi
New Delhi   Shanghai   Taipei   Toronto

With offices in
Argentina   Austria   Brazil   Chile   Czech Republic   France   Greece
Guatemala   Hungary   Italy   Japan   Poland   Portugal   Singapore
South Korea   Switzerland   Thailand   Turkey   Ukraine   Vietnam

Oxford is a registered trademark of Oxford University Press
in the UK and certain other countries.

Published in the United States of America by
Oxford University Press
198 Madison Avenue, New York, NY 10016

All quotations from the Bible are from THE HOLY BIBLE, NEW INTERNATIONAL
VERSION®, NIV® Copyright © 1973, 1978, 1984, 2011 by Biblica, Inc.® Used by
permission. All rights reserved worldwide.

Cataloging-in-Publication data is on file at the Library of Congress
ISBN 978-0-19-994225-1

3 5 7 9 8 6 4 2
Printed in the United States of America
on acid-free paper

For Chris, Emma, and Joe

CONTENTS

PREFACE

The idea of this book began as the result of a classroom conversation. About ten years ago in my Religion and Gender course at Michigan State University a student asked me a question. We had been discussing a reading on sexual purity practices within Orthodox Judaism and she asked, "Where do Christians go to read about the proper ways to have sex?" Hoping not to go too far off topic, I responded by saying, "I can tell you what they read to find out how NOT to have sex," and then I brought the conversation back to our reading. But as I walked to my office after class I remembered conversations I had with married graduate student friends who were raised in evangelical households and had complained about what they viewed as the "kitschy" and out-dated marital advice literature they had been given as wedding gifts, often from pastors. In graduate school these texts became the topic of jokes, not research. I never would have considered this topic if it hadn't been for the student's question. In my office I ran an online search for "Christian sex manuals," and I was delighted to find that Special Collections in the Main Library of Michigan State University had a vast holding of these texts, thanks to an intrepid librarian who had bought up remaindered books at Eerdmans and Zondervan warehouse sales. At that moment, when I saw the number of manuals devoted to biblical sex, I started reading and imagining this book.

From the start I wanted to write a book that would be read by my peers and also a general audience, including the undergraduates who take my classes and continue to raise questions that enrich my experience as a teacher and a researcher. I knew that this type of writing would be a challenge for me because it is different from the strictly academic

ix

mode I have worked in for many years. I underestimated how difficult. Throughout this book I have tried to write in an accessible manner, keeping in mind my primary audience. I hope that I have succeeded in a small part to accomplish that goal. For readers who relish more technical writing, please read my articles published in the *Journal of the American Academy of Religion* 77, no. 2 (June 2009): 275–302 and *Church History: Studies in Christianity and Culture* 74, no 1 (March 2005): 97–137. I thank those two journals for giving me permission to use revised versions of the published articles in this book.

Like any study on popular forms of literature in American culture it is difficult to know where and when to stop. In my case, every day that I worked on this book I found new sources to ponder, and more than once I worried about what new book or newsworthy item would surface while I was trying to complete a chapter. Rather than hunting down a limited group of source materials in distant archives as I did in my first book, for this project I have been sorting through what often seemed to be an endless amount of primary data readily available in local bookstores and via the Internet. Eventually I had to stop collecting and start writing. When I did, I sifted through material and made choices about which sources were the most representative and interesting to use in my study. I regret that I have not been able to include all the sources that I wanted to, and I acknowledge that many more will be produced during and after the publication of this book. That, I have come to understand, is both the benefit and drawback of writing about popular texts focused on sex.

This is a book on evangelicalism and sexuality that I hope will be read in many contexts and inspire conversations in both classrooms and coffee shops. I look forward to future research that takes up questions raised in this study and pursues new texts and different approaches not covered in this book. To my mind, this is a topic that continues to be relevant, and there is always room for new voices in the conversation. What follows is my contribution to the question of the relationship between sexuality and salvation in American evangelicalism.

ACKNOWLEDGMENTS

Two institutions supported both the research and writing of this book. My home institution, Michigan State University, provided me with a Research Initiative Grant for summer travel to archives at the preliminary stages of the project, a Humanities and the Arts Research Program grant for a semester of final research and writing, and a sabbatical leave to complete the book. For all of the institutional support including funding undergraduate research assistants, I am deeply grateful. I would also like to express my appreciation to the Wabash Center for Teaching and Learning in Theology and Religion for its financial support of this project through a 2002 summer research grant.

Most of the texts that I consulted at the beginning stages of this project are housed in Special Collections in the Main Library at Michigan State University. I spent two summers going through the materials in the lovely reading room and returned many more times in following years. I owe a great debt to Peter Berg, the Head of Special Collections, and all of the librarians and assistants who were extremely helpful and supportive with my multiple requests and questions. I offer my thanks to the library staff who arranged for me to present my research at an early stage through the MSU Library Colloquia series. That experience convinced me that my project was worthwhile. It has been so encouraging to have enthusiastic support from the librarians who are such careful caretakers of the texts and manuscripts in the collection.

I have presented my work at many conferences and as an invited lecturer at colleges and universities over the years and I have always profited from the thoughtful questions and comments from the other panelists, respondents, and the audiences. I offer my thanks to all of those who have extended invitations to me. Those opportunities over the years invigorated my thinking about this topic and encouraged me to continue. I circulated my work among scholars and friends at different points in the process. I thank the following people for giving generously their time and creative energies in their thoughtful feedback and gentle nudging: Anna Celenza, Maria C. Sanchez, Alice Dreger, Philip Goff, R. Marie Griffith, Georgia Frank, Randall Balmer, Martha Finch, Betty DeBerg, Nathan Rein, Kathryn Lofton, Malcolm Magee, Patrick Rivers, Sara Moslener, Evyatar Marienberg, Amy Frykholm, Peter Williams, David Morgan, Benjamin Pollock, Jyotsna Singh, David Stowe, Erica Windler, James Bielo, Ed Blum, Brian C. Wilson, John Schmalzbauer, Rebecca Davis, and, at the very last minute, Hilary Wyss and Erin Lang Masercola. Many more people have contributed to this book by providing scholarly encouragement through casual conversations or a well-timed email. Thank you, all.

I am very lucky to have excellent colleagues in my department. They have supported my scholarship and made coming to work a joy. I am also appreciative of the graduate and undergraduate students who have worked with me over the years enhancing my teaching experience and assisting me with research. I especially want to thank my undergraduate research assistants who helped me with this project: Kristy Slominski, Allison Andre, Zachary Johnson, and Allegra Smith.

I am grateful to Theo Calderara and the editorial staff at Oxford University Press for all the attention and care they gave to this project. I have benefitted from the sound editorial advice and intervention at all stages of production. Many thanks, also, to the anonymous readers who provided astute observations and helpful suggestions that greatly improved the book.

Many more people helped me to write this book. I thank the members of the NTTR book club for keeping me sane, all of our sitters over the years for keeping my children safe, and my extended family for knowing when to ask about this book and when to leave it alone. After long, full lives my parents died during the writing of this book and, though I miss them everyday, I have been sustained by the love of my fiercely loyal siblings, who are always ready to listen and offer advice. My life-long friends Catherine McLean and Maria Hey Dahl, continue to inspire me with their kindness and humor. Finally, I wish to express my deepest gratitude to my son's teacher, Mrs. Renee Olance, who creates a rich and safe learning environment for him so I am free from worry while he is in school. This is a rare gift that can only be given by an outstanding teacher. Without it I wouldn't have been able to complete this book.

There are no words to describe the support given to me by Chris Frilingos over the years while I researched and wrote this book. He read many versions of the text, found materials for me, and listened to me discuss evangelicals and sexuality far more than anyone should be required. I thank him for his patience and for reminding me time and again that this book would eventually be done. He and our children, Emma and Joe, have shown me the extraordinary joy possible in living ordinary days together. This book is dedicated to them with love and gratitude.

SAVING SEX

INTRODUCTION

Pastor Ed Young wants to incite a sexual revolution. Or at least sell a few books. In January 2012 Young and his wife Lisa conducted a "bed-in" on the roof of Fellowship Church in Grapevine, Texas. For twenty-four hours, as part of a launch for their new book, *Sexperiment: 7 Days to Lasting Intimacy with Your Spouse*, the couple sat in bed and live-streamed interviews about the need for married evangelicals to have more frequent sex.[1] Since 2008 Pastor Young has been issuing challenges to the married congregants of his megachurch: have sex every day for seven days in a row. He garnered a lot of mainstream media attention by claiming that his sexual ministry to married heterosexuals is radical. For too long, Young explained to daytime talk show hosts, evangelical churches had been silent about marital sexuality, leaving believers with the mistaken impression that sex could not be both biblical and pleasurable. His rallying cry became: "It's time to bring God back in the bed and put the bed back in the church."

Anyone who has observed American evangelical culture over the past few decades knows that, despite Young's claims, evangelicals cannot stop talking about sex. From salacious scandals of high-profile pastors, to campaigns to galvanize voters against same-sex marriage, to abstinence-only funding in public schools, evangelicals in the United States are deeply and publicly concerned about sex and sexuality. Pastor Young's specific interest in spicing up evangelical marital sex is hardly radical. Since the 1970s, evangelicals have been writing and reading marital guides that connect Scripture with sensual pleasures. Bolstered by social scientists and popular therapeutic language, many American evangelicals have come to believe that good marital sex is not just ordained by God, but is healthy and leads to strong self-esteem, financial prosperity, and heightened spiritual awareness. Evangelical sex writers refer to biblical verses, provide information about sexual techniques, and answer frequently asked questions about the boundaries for godly sexual acts. And like pastor Young, the most successful authors aim to convince readers that their approach is authoritative, countercultural, and that they alone are in the position to dispel all the myths and misinformation given by the church about sexuality and salvation.

Today almost one-third of Americans consider themselves to be "born-again" Christians, a diverse racial, ethnic, social, and theological group. The most visible spokespeople and bestselling authors on sexuality, however, are white, male, married evangelicals connected either to megachurches or to national organizations such as Dr. James Dobson's Focus on the Family. There are, of course, notable exceptions, some of whom are featured in this book. But the popular stereotype of an American evangelical comes to life in evangelical sex writing. It is visible in children's storybooks about purity and sexuality, in teen literature, marital advice manuals, and books that address late-life issues. In part, it is this mistaken popular view—of a monolithic American evangelicalism—that explains the infighting among very similar authors over who has the authoritative voice on the topic of biblical sex. As long as the faithful continue to buy the books, it seems likely that the market for biblical sex guides will thrive, with each new author claiming an innovative approach to help believers achieve a higher level of sexual satisfaction.

With regard to sexuality, like so many other things in evangelical culture, there is a gap between the ideal and the real. Evangelical ideals about sexuality and salvation can be found in books, magazines, pamphlets, websites, blogs, church bulletins, podcasts, and DVDs. The overwhelming majority of these texts support a conservative theological and social worldview that values chastity prior to heterosexual marriage and the establishment of a biblically ordered family with the father as leader and the mother as a complementary helpmate. In this sex literature, "natural" and scripturally sanctioned sexuality is directly related to strict gender norms often described as "old-fashioned" or "biblical" values. Readers are told that following God's model of purity prior to marriage and sexual pleasure within Christian marriage demonstrates one's faith. Sexual pleasure within marriage is both the sign of and the reward for godliness. And both purity (outside marriage) and pleasure (within it) are ways that evangelicals can witness to others.

That idea that sexuality has public consequences puzzles many non-evangelicals. For example, outsiders are perplexed by evangelical claims that same-sex marriage threatens heterosexual marriages.[2] But in the evangelical worldview sexual sins impact everyone. Evangelical sex writers claim that a person's sexual misdeed has individual, communal, and eternal consequences. Those who fall into sexual sin and impurity, according to most of these texts, jeopardize their own salvation, the salvation of their future children, and those souls waiting to be brought to Christ. Sexual sins—masturbation, premarital sex, adultery, and same-sex acts, and more—imperil the salvation of the individual, the building of the kingdom of Christ, and the salvation of the world.

In other words, for American evangelicals, sexuality and salvation are closely linked. That is not to say that evangelicals are "anti-sex." Contrary to popular stereotypes that characterize conservative Christians as sexually repressed, evangelicals did not turn away from the sexual liberation movement begun in the 1960s, they simply made it their own, publishing sex manuals, running sex workshops, and holding counseling sessions to instruct husbands and wives on the best techniques for a sexually satisfied marriage. Evangelical sex manuals published over the past sixty years present a uniquely Protestant approach to the joy of sex. The most authoritative text on sexuality, the authors of these manuals affirm, is the Bible. Scripture contains everything a believer needs to know about sex. Evangelical sex writers claim that theirs is the only authentic Christian approach unsullied by distorted visions of sexuality that arose from misinterpretation of Scripture or false Christian traditions (meaning Catholicism) that have erroneously emphasized celibacy or denigrated the body. Their manuals are devoted to providing—in excruciating detail—instructions about the proper use of sexual bodies. But these authors are simultaneously committed to larger theological and social agendas. They define themselves against other approaches to sex, both Christian and secular, and argue that long-term sexual satisfaction is only possible when the Bible is in the bedroom.

American evangelicals do not simply retreat from secular sexual culture—they engage with it. In some cases they employ familiar secular concepts and language to promote religious goals. For example, in chastity (also called purity) literature aimed at young people, many authors reclaim the language of female empowerment and liberation popularized by the feminist movement to support female submission to God, fathers, and husbands. Purity literature teaches young girls and women to view themselves as "lily white" princesses who will wait until God sends them Prince Charming. This, they learn to expect, will be their fairytale life. Girls can find true empowerment by having the courage to stand up to a sexualized secular culture through their commitment to purity and their belief that Prince Charming will arrive to save and protect them. Female virginity is characterized as brave, empowering, and liberating. The purity books and websites encourage young women to sustain a chaste lifestyle through rituals like attending purity balls or chastity rallies, going to modesty fashion shows, praying for future spouses, compiling courting lists, avoiding degrading movies, TV shows, or books, and even having "dates" with Jesus. The evangelical language of empowerment and the encouragement of youth to attend rallies and fashion shows sounds like an affirmation of secular views and activities. But this language and these practices are employed in the pursuit of religious goals. Sometimes this cooptation of secular discourse is used in subversive ways, such as the mantra that "submission is liberation." Other times, like with rallies and fashion shows, it is just a tool to get a message out to believers. Either way, American evangelical discussions of sex are tangled up in larger cultural conversations about sexual desires and practices. The language used and the activities suggested can take the form of accommodation or resistance. Nowhere is this more evident than in the acceptance or rejection of scientific and social scientific sex research by evangelical writers.

When it comes to sex, American evangelicals have a conflicted relationship with science. On the one hand, evangelical sex manual authors borrow freely from studies that support their theological claims. For example, it is not unusual to find references to Masters and Johnson's studies of sexuality in books published in the 1970s. On the other hand, early sex manual authors rejected the findings of the Kinsey Report that, among other things, argued for natural human sexual variation. Contemporary evangelical sex writers tend to place stock in biological scientific studies of hormones, ovulation, infectious diseases, and sometimes genetics. Among some charismatic evangelicals some argue that science proves the truths of the Bible, claiming that sexually transmitted diseases are actually sexually transmitted demons that can be passed genetically. In this case, the science of disease transmission and genetics is mustered in support of the biblical worldview.

More recently, some evangelicals have questioned the validity of scientific research on contraception, particularly as it relates to the concept of "safe sex" among youth. For example, evangelicals who promote abstinence-only education in the public schools have questioned public health studies that endorse condom use to prevent disease and pregnancy. Rather than "safe sex," they promote "saved sex," AKA abstinence. Some evangelicals question the legitimacy of any form of contraception within marriage. The so-called "pro-natalist" faction argues that contraception is unbiblical and unsafe. While many evangelical pastors support the use of contraception to encourage sexual pleasure in marriage, among the pro-natalists wives are told that they must always be sexually available to their husbands and that reproduction, not pleasure, should remain the focus of sexual intercourse. Pro-natalists who reject what they call the "fake" science of female reproduction and contraception raise large families, uphold strict gender roles, and believe that they alone are practicing true biblical sex. Although this group is somewhat outside the mainstream, pro-natalists claim that they have the orthodox interpretation of biblical sex and that their sexual practices are directly connected to personal salvation, and the building of God's kingdom on earth.

For American evangelicals the sexual body plays an important role in personal salvation. That is why in recent years American evangelicals have taken the lead in public and private discourse to describe and define the limits, possibilities, and purpose of human sexuality. Evangelical popular texts promote the idea that the sexual body is an arena for testifying to faith. Through "sanctified" sexual intercourse and purity rituals, evangelicals are encouraged to express their beliefs on the body. Godly sex, performed by the pure bodies of born-again believers, is an act that signifies salvation and can further the kingdom of God.

Scholars of Christianity in earlier eras have long recognized the importance of sexuality for demonstrating sin or salvation.[3] The study of Protestantism, however, has typically been viewed through the lenses of doctrine and texts uncritically reflecting the Protestant desire to shed Catholic "superstitions" about and obsessions with the body. But, religious belief and practice is always embodied. Protestants, today and historically, grapple with vexing questions regarding the role of the sexual body for salvation.[4] Lacking a celibate clergy or a tradition of asceticism, Protestant leaders and believers found creative ways to use the sexual body as a vehicle for affirming and practicing faith. I focus on sexuality as a site for the production and representation of evangelical belief, arguing that rituals link the physical health and practices of the sexual body with the state of the soul.[5]

The academic study of American evangelicalism has gained momentum since the 1980s. What began primarily as a subfield within Church History, dominated by intellectual historians, has expanded into multiple disciplinary fields that use a variety of methods. Within this growing field of knowledge, there are two primary scholarly camps regarding the question of how evangelicals engage with American culture. On one side, scholars emphasize evangelicals' embattled relationship with a perceived "secular" American culture. This stressful relationship, some scholars conclude, leads evangelicals to separate themselves from the sinfulness of the world and create pious enclaves, apart from a corrupt American society. On the other side, some scholars highlight the deep identification with a lost "godly" American culture that calls evangelicals to participate fully in the world and to bring America back to Christ. In this case, evangelicals do not retreat from secular culture, but seek to claim that "true" American cultural values are consistent with evangelical beliefs and practices.

These are broad scholarly categories. It is perhaps more accurate to state that evangelicals identify with different sides of this debate at different moments, and this is especially true when the topic is sex.[6] For example, in purity literature, evangelicals typically define themselves against a permissive and degrading American sexual culture. But evangelical marital sex manuals often claim that their advice is informed by the best scientific, secular literature. When it comes to the sexual body, evangelicals promote their beliefs and practices through both engagement with and retreat from American culture.

* * *

Before I proceed further, a word about terminology is in order. I use the term "evangelical" as an umbrella term for Protestants who affirm the necessity of a spiritual rebirth, a "born again" experience during which one accepts personal sinfulness and acknowledges that Christ's atonement is essential for salvation. For some this moment is a dramatic conversion experience that separates the believer's spiritual life between before the event and after the event. For others, it is a longer process of growing in faith to an acceptance of the spiritual truths of sin, redemption, and salvation. And while evangelicals exhibit diverse styles of worship, they are grouped together by their emphasis on personal conversion, the authority of Scripture, their belief in the imminent return of Christ, and their desire to spread the gospel. Evangelicals as a group tend to be concerned with expressing their theological beliefs through daily practices such as prayer, Bible reading, and what is generally called their "walk with Christ." There are liberal and progressive evangelicals, though they are the minority. Some evangelicals view the accumulation of wealth as a "blessing," others do not. Although many evangelicals purport to stand at a critical distance from "worldly" secular culture they do not refrain from adopting the tools of culture to make their message heard. While I use the term "evangelical" to characterize the authors of the texts I examine, it is sometimes difficult to identify their denominational affiliations and it is impossible to know those of readers. Most authors simply define themselves as "Bible-believing" Christians and their work as "biblically centered." Throughout this book I intersperse the term evangelical with "Bible-believing," "born-again," and sometimes "Christian."

One thing you will not find in this book is much discussion of homosexuality. It might seem a curious omission, given evangelicals' seeming obsession with the subject.[7] Clearly this is an important and fluid topic that merits close scholarly attention, and it has indeed received rich and thoughtful analysis in a number of books.[8] But evangelicals are equally obsessed with the proper practice of heterosexuality, and that has been virtually ignored by scholars, which is why I have chosen to focus on it in this book. For evangelical sex writers focused on advice regarding marital pleasure, homosexuality is simply beyond the pale. But being heterosexual is never enough. Boundaries must be policed, and authors make extraordinary efforts to alert readers to possible pitfalls. Desires are examined, acts are regulated, and bodies provide testimonial sites. How you dress, how you talk, when you have sex, whether you conceive, how many times you conceive—these practices take on theological meaning and are continually interpreted in the context of Scripture, the individual's life, the family, the community, and the world. The amount of evangelical literature and media dedicated to practicing heterosexuality attests to an insatiable appetite among the heterosexual faithful.[9] Sex sells, and the market for evangelical sex advice appears to be limitless.

Also absent from this book are the voices of everyday believers. There is undoubtedly value in hearing from the "people in the pews." Even a quick glance at the sales figures for the books discussed here demonstrates that sex advice books have struck a chord with a wide swath of the evangelical community. The popular books, websites, blogs, magazines, and other forms of media reflect the most commonly held ideals of sexuality by leading authoritative evangelical pastors and writers. These writings that prescribe ideal sexual practices deserve serious and sustained attention. In addition, while private conversations take place about sexuality in churches and homes all the time, the public discourse—the one that matters to evangelicals and non-evangelicals alike—takes place largely through media like those examined here. It is the accessible, prescriptive literature that is the subject of this book.

Some readers might feel that I have not been fair to the breadth of American evangelicalism. That is unavoidably true. My aim is to examine some of the ways that American evangelicals engage with conversations about sexuality. I have restricted this study to a few of the most visible spokespeople and some of the representative topics and schisms among evangelicals when it comes to sex. This is not an exhaustive survey of every book on sex written by an evangelical. In the end, I have left out many more texts than I have included. This is also not a survey of American evangelicals or the history of the evangelical movement. *Saving Sex* focuses on one topic that sheds light on broader themes of cultural resistance, engagement, and accommodation among American evangelicals. By examining their rules and regulations about sexuality, we learn much about their desires and hopes for salvation.

American evangelicals participate in the cultural conversations about sexuality in diverse ways that reflect the theological, social, and racial diversity of the movement. Rather than denying the sexual body, evangelical sex writers present distinct visions of how sexual acts and rituals can aid individual and world salvation. *Saving Sex* brings to light the many ways evangelicals use the tools of American culture to respond to, resist, and sometimes transform it. Evangelicals are able to do this effectively because they participate in the public conversations about sex in ways that are easily accessible and relevant while at the same time presenting a message that represents a distinct worldview: that heterosexual sex is holy and natural, is sanctioned by God, and should be practiced only in marriage. All of the other details are subject to debate.

CHAPTER ONE

SEX AND THE SINGLE EVANGELICAL

INTRODUCTION

In May 2008, at the Broadmoor Hotel in Colorado Springs, Colorado, a group of conservative evangelicals gathered for a gala event to honor their unmarried daughters. The hosts, Randy and Lisa Wilson, organized the Generations of Light Purity Ball, a glamorous occasion with floral centerpieces, a string quartet, dining, dancing, and beautiful decorations throughout the hall. The men were dressed in tuxedos with boutonnieres; the young women wore lavish A-line ball gowns embellished with sequins, beads, and pearls. Many of the young women had sparkling tiaras on their heads or had braided flowers into their hair. The sweetheart necklines, tulle skirts, pearl earrings, diamond necklaces, three-quarter length white satin gloves, and well-applied makeup, created the impression that every young woman at the ball was a princess in a fairy tale.

Throughout the evening the young women danced with their fathers, listened to testimonials about the power of purity, and, as one young woman summarized, reaffirmed their powerful choice to "say no for the greater yes." Younger girls dressed in all white performed a dance in front of a large, rough wooden cross, first placing white roses at its base and then spinning around the cross with their arms extended into the air, their skirts floating around their small bodies.

This annual event, the Wilsons believe, affirms young women's choices to refrain from any sexual contact prior to marriage. A godly father who escorts his daughter to a purity ball demonstrates to the young woman that she is valuable and deserves respect. Purity, they contend, is a sacred choice that puts young women at odds with an American culture that simultaneously degrades female sexuality and limits the father's role in the lives of his daughters. But participation in purity balls is contested even within evangelical circles. The Wilsons are aware that detractors claim that the purity balls are exploitative, commodifying female virginity as in the ancient practice of the "bride price."[1] Lisa Wilson explains in the documentary "Virgin Daughters" that forging a close relationship between fathers and daughters accomplishes a different goal: "It's about a bigger picture of expressing dignity and worth and launching our daughters into healthy relationships with men because they respect themselves and they have been taught by their fathers that this is the standard they should expect to be treated with incredible dignity." The celebration of female virginity at purity balls is directly linked to a strong and close relationship between fathers and daughters. For the daughter, the promise of waiting is the expectation of a gallant and godly husband, approved of by her father, who will provide her with a fairy-tale marriage.[2]

Purity balls stand out as a dramatic form of pledging virginity within American evangelicalism. The emphasis placed on the father's role in protecting his daughter's chaste body until marriage, and the daughter's commitment to her father as well as God, raises important questions about female autonomy and the value being placed on young girls' virginity. It also raises troubling questions about a young woman's ability to make informed sexual choices.

Since the late 1990s, father-daughter purity balls have been gaining media attention as a growing phenomenon among conservative evangelicals. According to the 2008 documentary "The Virgin Daughters," one in six girls in America takes a purity pledge.[3] The media attention focuses on the wedding-like atmosphere and the ceremonial moment during all purity balls when young women pledge their virginity to their fathers in return for their fathers' promise of protection. Unlike in the traditional father-daughter wedding dance at purity balls, the father is also *the date*.

Father-daughter purity balls are an extreme ritualized expression of themes that arise in evangelical purity literature. The gowns, tuxedos, flowers, tiaras, music, decorations, food, dancing, and the exchange of a ring, can leave even a sympathetic observer with the feeling that there is something unseemly about the intimacy encouraged between fathers and daughters. This is not your run of the mill daddy-daughter Valentine's Day dance. Unlike those increasingly popular community dances geared at elementary-school-aged children, purity balls are aimed at girls over the age of ten and into their early twenties. They also depart from daddy-daughter dances by the inclusion of a chastity pledge that the young woman makes to both her father and God. The climax of the evening is the ceremonial moment when daughters place white roses under a cross to symbolize, publicly and silently, their virginity pledge. The fathers encircle their daughters and read aloud their "covenant" to protect their daughters' bodies until marriage. Fathers also are asked to promise to be a model of purity for their daughters. "I, (daughter's name)'s father, choose before God to cover my daughter as her authority and protection in the area of purity. I will be pure in my own life as a man, husband and father. I will be a man of integrity and accountablity [sic] as I lead, guide and pray over my daughter and my family as the high priest in my home. This covering will be used by God to influence generations to come."[4] They then sign a document containing this promise and their daughters co-sign as witnesses. The pledge and contract are to remain intact until the daughter takes another vow, to another man, on her wedding day. According to New Life Pregnancy Centers, who sponsor many purity balls across the country, the aim is to support a meaningful relationship between fathers and daughters and to "help instill the principles and strength that your daughter will need to protect her heart and body until she commits to a man on her wedding day." Attending a purity ball, the sponsors claim, ensures that daughters will learn how a young woman should be treated and demonstrate to daughters that they are valued by their fathers. In fact, the organizers believe that the fathers are the only men the young women should "date" prior to courtship. Thus, the fathers are called to protect their daughters and are assured that participating in a purity ball will "make an investment that will last a lifetime!" Randy Wilson explains "because we cherish our daughters as regal princesses—for 1 Peter 3:4

says they are 'precious in the sight of God'—we want to treat them as royalty."[5]

In the context of purity balls, female sexuality is viewed both as sacred and dangerous, not simply because of unwanted pregnancy, disease, or emotional distress, but because sexual desire could compromise a young woman's value as a virgin prior to marriage. Scholar Breanne Fahs explains "purity balls enter women into a system of commerce in which their sexuality becomes an object to be traded between men."[6] The expectation among many of the fathers and daughters at purity balls is that the young women will never fall into sexual sin because she will be protected by her father and by her church community. Similarly, she will not make a poor choice of a spouse (and first sexual partner) because she will not be solely responsible for that decision. In her 2007 *Glamour* magazine article on purity balls Jennifer Baumgardner quoted a father who explained that he was not worried about his daughter maintaining purity because she would never be in a situation that would allow for sexual contact. "She is not even going to come close to those situations. She believes, and I do too, that her husband will come through our family connections or through me before her heart even gets involved."[7] This is a gentle way of stating that the fathers have the authority to pick a husband for their daughters with or without their initial consent.

Purity balls are just the tip of the iceberg. There is an industry in purity books, websites, blogs, podcasts, magazines, events, conferences, and more. On the other end of the purity spectrum from the balls are Christian rock concerts and chastity rallies such as True Love Waits and Silver Ring Thing. In these events, purity-pledged evangelical youth call their commitment to purity "radical" and "countercultural."[8] Although the people on both ends of the purity spectrum would disagree about language, rituals, and community, they agree that sex prior to marriage is unbiblical and dangerous. They also agree, mostly, that purity is larger than abstinence. It is a lifestyle that requires scrutinizing all one's innermost thoughts and feelings and working tirelessly to guard oneself from any evidence of improper sexual desires or actions.

In purity literature and rituals, young evangelical women are taught that they are powerful and valuable when they suppress their sexual desires and submit fully to the authority of their fathers. Young women are instructed that their sexual desires are dangerous to themselves—and to young men. Modest dress and behavior help young women remain pure and deter vulnerable young men from sexual sin. Therefore, they must participate in rituals of constant daily self-inspection to cleanse their minds of impure thoughts that might lead to sinful actions. Furthermore, young women are informed that the key to ultimate emotional, social, psychological, spiritual, marital, and sexual happiness rests with a strong relationship with and dependence on her father and God. This, they learn, is true liberation. According to purity literature, young women who depart from this path are not only living a sinful life of impurity but are endangering the health and happiness of their future spouses and children.

THE FAIRY-TALE LIFE

A purity lifestyle begins at an early age. There are a number of children's books, specifically geared toward girls, that employ a fairy-tale narrative. A princess seeks Prince Charming to teach the value and ultimate pay-off of remaining "pure" until a deserving and noble man arrives.[9] While many of these books are written for children, the knight in shining armor motif is also used for books aimed at teens and beyond. The message on the surface is simply that a princess will likely meet unworthy men before she meets her Prince Charming. While the unworthy men have many worldly possessions and charms, her true love will not hold the world's honors but will be honest, faithful, and pure. Rather than fighting a dragon, Prince Charming will prove his worth by saving all forms of intimacy for his future spouse.[10]

Jennie Bishop's *The Princess and the Kiss: A Story of God's Purity* is an excellent example. In this story aimed at preschoolers, at birth a princess is given a gift from God—her first kiss. It is guarded by her parents until she reaches maturity. When she is grown, her parents present her with her first kiss in a glowing orb that they inform her was given to her by God because he loves her. The princess is entrusted to guard the kiss or give it away as she sees fit. "'But use wisdom, my daughter,' warned the king, 'and save your kiss for the man you will marry. Never part with it for the sake of a stranger.'"[11]

For the remainder of the story the princess interviews Prince Peacock, Prince Romance, and Prince Treasurechest. They offer her strength, excitement, and wealth, but none is worthy of her kiss. Although the princess despairs, the queen assures her that God would either bring her a husband or she will keep the kiss and treasure it forever. Eventually a poor farmer arrives at the castle. He admires the princess and admits that he has no worldly goods to offer but he is able to give her his precious first kiss. They are married in a church and soon have a child who, in turn, receives his first kiss from God.

The princess purity books typically paint a picture of a long ago kingdom ruled by a just king and queen who protect their daughters from the world. In Bishop's book the daughter is entrusted to guard her first kiss and to use her judgment to discern who is a worthy suitor. This is strictly a book about maintaining purity prior to marriage. The reason for refraining from even a kiss is that the first kiss is a gift from God. But the reward for this behavior is marriage to a worthy man. Some princess-themed books focus on the relationship between father and daughter. For example, Katheryn O'Brien's, *I'd be Your Princess*, and to a lesser extent, Cindy Morgan's, *Dance Me, Daddy*, celebrate developing a close relationship between father and daughter, king and princess, to teach godly behavior.[12] Other princess-themed purity books stress that every girl is a princess when she realizes that the "true" king is God. In Sheila Walsh's, *Gigi, God's Little Princess*, the main character does not live in a castle, but learns that she is a princess as a child of God, the true king.[13] These books introduce themes that will be elaborated in purity books geared at teens. In Bishop's book, purity, which is given by God, encompasses all aspects of physical contact, especially the first kiss. Girls who guard their purity will either find a true Prince Charming and live happily ever after or will have the purity as a gift from God to prize for the rest of their lives. The theme, found in Walsh's book, that each girl's true parent and king is God will be elaborated in teen purity literature to emphasize that each person's body ultimately belongs to God.

The purity books geared toward girls who are 5–10 years of age continue the princess theme but develop it to include parents as crucial participants in the child's endeavor to remain pure. Unlike the early years and the teen years, which tend to focus on the father's role, in these middle years the mother–daughter relationship is highlighted.[14] This is likely a result of the assumption that mothers are in charge of childrearing and, at this age, the majority of a young girl's time is spent with her mother. A good example of this is Jackie Kendall's *Lady in Waiting for Little Girls*,[15] which is written for mothers and daughters to read together. Its goal is to help mothers mentor their daughters to develop their devotion to God in the manner of a princess waiting for her prince. The princess-themed purity books for this age group also expand on the idea presented in Walsh's story that all girls are princesses because they are part of God's royal family. In these books, the acceptance of and relationship with Christ is introduced. For example, Kelly Chapman's, *Princess with a Purpose*, informs readers: "you became a real princess the moment you prayed and asked Jesus to live in your heart. And since He is the King of Kings and you are His daughter, that makes you His princess."[16] For this age group there are a plethora of devotional guides and workbooks (penned by many of the same authors) to develop the princess–God relationship.[17] Notably, princess-themed bibles are popular for this age group. *My Princess Bible*, written by Andy Holmes in rhyming format, provides portraits of nineteen biblical women who displayed princess virtues.[18] *Princess Bible: Pink* has a bejeweled, bright, pink, sparkly cover that shows a crown and is a complete Bible in the International Children's Bible translation. The front cover advertises "the positively perfect gift for princesses of all ages."[19] There are many more princess-themed Bibles and workbooks.

The princess theme continues in abstinence literature geared toward the tween and teenage years, roughly 10–18 years of age. Not surprisingly, for this age group, the amount and variety of media concerning purity is tremendous: CDs, DVDs, websites, Facebook pages, blogs, conferences, festivals, music, novels, activity books, journals, magazines, podcasts, and more. Not all focuses exclusively on the princess theme. The concepts of being treated like a princess or acting like a princess, however, are common. Also popular are gift books that follow the fairy-tale narrative to promote purity without directly mentioning chastity or a first kiss. Lisa Samson's, *Apples of Gold: A Parable of Purity* tells the story of two poor sisters who live on a faraway island governed by St. Juste. The girls—Liza, who is ugly but wise, and Kate, who is beautiful but foolish—are offered a challenge by the Governor of the land. He asks them to promise to keep two red apples perfect for his son Claude, who will return home the following week. The girls are told that whoever keeps the apple intact will be rewarded with service in the son's household. Liza keeps her apple safely in a basket to protect it from ruin. Kate allows others to look at her apple, touch her apple, and eventually bite her apple. The apple becomes soiled and rotten. In the end, both girls must present their apples to the Governor and his son. Liza wins and is rewarded not with service to the son but with marriage. Throughout the story Liza worries that because she is not comely she will never find a husband. She learns that her ability to be obedient and guard something valuable demonstrates her true beauty and worth.

It doesn't take a Bible scholar to notice the references to the biblical story of Adam, Eve, and the apple. In Genesis, Eve is portrayed as the one responsible for divine disobedience by desiring the one thing that the creator father has forbidden her to take. It is Eve's treachery that initiates "The Fall." When she ate the apple and offered it to her innocent husband, they both gained forbidden knowledge, became mortal, and felt shame for their naked bodies. As a punishment for disobedience, Eve and her female descendants would forever desire sexual congress with their husbands but, as a result of the sexual act, feel terrible pain during childbirth. The biblical allusions to female sexual rottenness and public shame for desire in *Apples of Gold* would not be lost on young evangelicals who know their Scripture.

In the afterword to *Apples of Gold* the author writes directly to the reader and to the reader's female guardian or mother. She explains that the story illustrates that God set the purity standard out of love for humanity to help us avoid suffering. We should also love without judgment those (like Kate) who cannot reach this standard. "God wants us to stay pure because God knows this is the path of least pain. We must certainly still love those who have failed to maintain their sexual purity and meet them with grace and encouragement to begin again. God's mercies are new every morning."[20] Painful childbirth, of course, is the result of Eve's disobedience. Therefore, women who become sexually active—even within marriage—will never be truly free from physical pain. Purity allows young women to control their emotional pain and limit their shame before marriage. Although Kate, like her apple (and perhaps Eve), is ruined because of her disobedience, she deserves the chance to try to again.

Mothers are then asked to serve as positive or negative role models for their daughters. If they maintained purity prior to marriage they are encouraged to talk with their daughters about the importance of entering marriage as virgins. If they did not remain chaste they are urged to apologize to their daughters for sinning against them because they were not able to give that "gift" to their daughters. "If you cannot give the gift of your own personal commitment to purity because your past decisions weren't as wise as they should have been, might I suggest that an apology is in order? When we sin against our bodies and ourselves, we sin against our children too." Similar to evangelical sex manuals that emphasize generational curses (more on this later), Samson contends that purity runs through family lines. "Purity seems to be a generational blessing, and the commitment to it is something God honors. Encourage your daughter or granddaughter or niece or dear friend to be the first in a line of blessing. Admit your guilt to her, tell her you're sorry, and pledge your own commitment to her."[21] While the mother-daughter relationship is important in Samson's book, a mother's status and authority is called into question if she is perceived to be a sexual sinner. In that case, the mother owes her daughter an apology for her past sins. In this book, the father's sexual status is not subject to scrutiny, he is not held responsible for soiling the generational "blessing" of purity—and he does not owe anyone an apology.

Perhaps one of the best-known princess-themed purity books aimed at teens is Sarah Mally's *Before You Meet Prince Charming: A Guide to Radiant Purity*. Mally's book creates a bridge between the princess fairy-tale themes in the books for younger readers and the purity books and magazines for older teens that mirror secular teen literature on dating, relationships, beauty, and body image. Mally identifies herself as a home-schooled young woman who has pursued a purity lifestyle and founded "Bright Lights" a national organization that encourages purity among 10–13 year-old girls. When she wrote *Before You Meet Prince Charming*, she was in her mid-twenties and single. The book alternates between a fairy tale about a princess waiting for a noble prince and sober lessons about the meaning, purpose, and practice of purity. Purity, in Mally's view, extends to all aspects of a young woman's life and is grounded in her relationship with and firm commitment to God. The princess in *Before You Meet Prince Charming* is waiting for the right man but her ability to remain pure is based on her convictions. "It is your heart—your own internal commitments before the Lord—that will make the difference. Only those who have formed their own personal convictions will have the strength required to remain pure and the discernment needed to escape temptation."[22] A true princess relies on her inner strength to maintain purity.

Throughout the book Mally emphasizes that a young woman should not endeavor to find a princely husband; that is God's job. She is responsible for using her single years with purpose and for cherishing her purity. "I don't know about you, but if I get married someday, I want to be able to look back on my single years and see that I used them wisely, enjoyed each day, and made the most of every opportunity. My prayer is that I would be a trustworthy steward of the gift of singleness that God has given me." In Mally's view, the only thing a young woman should do to attract a worthy husband is to dedicate her life fully to God and remain chaste. Every day is a new opportunity to perform these two tasks. It is through God's will and her father's blessing that she will be united with a spouse. Any form of female initiative toward marriage, according to Mally, is potentially dangerous. "If it is God's will for us to be married, then He will not leave us single for even one day longer than He knows is best, right, and perfect. But whenever we jump ahead of His timing we find ourselves in an extremely dangerous position." This leads Mally to reject any form of interaction with males who are not relatives outside of church work and family gatherings. Mally insists that this approach frees her to devote her unmarried life to missionary work and strengthening her relationship with Jesus. "The years of your youth are some of the most valuable ones of your life. If you can catch a vision for how much potential these years have for the Lord, you will begin to feel that your life is a race—a race against time to accomplish as much as you possibly can for the kingdom of God."[23]

Mally relies on her father (and sometimes older brothers) to judge the worthiness of a potential spouse. This, she believes, helps her avoid making a poor choice based on emotions. One of the key pieces of advice that Mally gives to her readers is parental involvement in any relationship forged with males. "Whenever I talk to young ladies about this topic, I like to encourage them to make a commitment to direct any young men who express interest in them to their dads first. If you make this commitment now and tell your father, it can have many benefits." Mally, like other teen chastity writers who focus their attention on girls, suggests that both the girl and her parents independently make a list of requirements for marriage. The list should include necessary qualifications (the boy should be Christian) and desirable qualifications (the boy should have a pleasing face). After comparing the parents' and girl's list, the family should agree upon the necessary credentials for marriage. Mally believes that if the family is satisfied with a girl's list, her father's choice of a suitor will avoid disappointment, wasted time, and perhaps heartbreak. "If you have thought through your qualifications in advance and written a list, it will be a safeguard to keep you from being captivated or ensnared by someone who comes along but who may not have the spiritual strength to which you are committed."[24]

Mally depicts her rejection of dating as a specific form of female empowerment.[25] This is not the type of empowerment that secular women tend to seek. Mally's empowerment is not about controlling her body or finding strength and power in the workforce. Empowerment is not even about choosing a husband with whom to share her life. Empowerment is complete surrender to the will of her father and God. "I don't have to date, flirt or be searching for a husband. The Lord is more than able to arrange my marriage without my help." Dating, according to Mally, is pointless. It is not intended to lead to marriage and it often ends in heartbreak. According to Mally, since there are no examples of dating in the Bible, it is not a godly practice. Of course, there are no examples of texting or driving in the Bible, but those practices are not deemed ungodly. Young women, she believes, tend to degrade themselves by focusing on their physical appearance when trying to attract a young man to date. Ultimately, Mally finds no reason to support cultivating a romantic relationship for any purpose other than marriage. In fact, she casts her rejection of dating as a type of radical empowerment against the forces of secular culture. She comforts her readers with the shared understanding that many people will criticize and challenge her approach to waiting for God to bring a spouse and involving her parents in all aspects of this process. Standing firm and remaining pure is a particular type of witnessing. "Don't expect others to understand the commitments to which the Lord has led you....Strive to love and accept others who misunderstand you, but never be afraid to face criticism for standing alone." This courage is directly related to being a true princess of the true king. "A true princess realizes this danger (from outside forces) and understands her own need to be protected. This is not evidence of weakness or fear, but rather it is evidence of true courage. It requires courage to do things God's way, to wait for His timing, and to trust that He will bring you and your life partner together according to His perfect plan."[26] Mally's form of purity is liberating, empowering, and allows a true princess to display her courage.

One of the best ways to prepare for marriage, according to Mally, is for girls to focus their attention on their fathers. "Ephesians 5 commands husbands to love their wives, and wives to respect their husbands. As women desire to be loved, men desire to be respected. In order to be prepared to respect and submit to a future husband, it is crucial that we learn to honor our fathers. Ask the Lord to strengthen your relationship with your dad and to give you ideas about how you can honor him in your daily life."[27] It is noteworthy that Mally says little about her relationship with her mother. In Mally's view, and that of many other purity writers, a strong relationship with one's father is a significant safeguard against the perils of single girlhood. Mally, unlike other writers, suggests that girls practice for their future role as wife and mother in their relationship with their fathers. This approach is consonant with young women being their father's "dates" at purity balls. Ultimately, Mally explains, young women will move from the protection of their father's home to the protection of their husband's. Mally even rejects attending Bible colleges that, from her place on the evangelical spectrum, appear "too worldly" if they enroll women. The boundaries of an unmarried young woman's safe world are the walls of her father's home.

Mally's primary audience is girls who are too young to be married or in some cases young women who are waiting for their God-chosen spouse to arrive. After the lists have been made and the young women are involved in church work, the wait for a husband becomes a true test of spiritual commitment. The focus on earthly marriage, according to Mally, can sometimes lead young women away from God. While Mally insists that it is both natural and scripturally sound for a woman to desire marriage, she must not work too hard for it, and she must realize that it is not the most important goal. In other words, purity requires repressing sexual desires and specific future hopes. Although her book details all the ways that young women should prepare themselves for marriage by living a life of purity, there is a higher purpose. "As a young lady, you probably believe that God is calling you to be a wife and mother. This is a very noble calling. In fact, there is no assignment more important than raising a new generation to serve the Lord. Yet, marriage cannot be your ultimate goal in life. You must have a life purpose that is bigger than marriage. If you don't, you won't be fully prepared for marriage."[28] Specifically, you will not be prepared to navigate the rough terrain of a marriage that may not seem like a fairy tale.

Women who long for a husband must understand that marriage does not bring true fulfillment in life. Mally acknowledges that sometimes a husband brings heartache and despair. Only a relationship with the true bridegroom—Jesus—will satisfy all their needs and desires. Marriage, after all, is not perfect, and Jesus is available right now. "Marriage on earth is only a picture of the spiritual relationship that the Lord wants to have with every one of us. Anything we desire in marriage, we have completely in the Lord. We long for someone who loves us, understands us, listens to us, provides for us, protects us, cares for us—is crazy about us! God gives these desires. Don't you think the One who instills the desires knows how to fulfill them? In every one of these ways, the Lord is far more able to meet our needs than anyone on earth ever could." Unlike the careful safeguarding of emotional feelings and expressions of desire while waiting for an earthly husband, Mally encourages young women to pour out their emotions to Jesus. Young women should eagerly fall in love with Jesus by spending time alone in prayer with Him and reading his love letters (the Bible). She should set apart time to be alone with Him, frequently proclaim her love for Him, tell others how great he is, and keep journals of time spent together. All in all, young women should set aside time to be with her eternal beloved because "we will never experience the joy of falling in love with Jesus unless we make an effort to spend time alone with Him."[29] All of the emotion and conviction that is forbidden for young women to expend seeking earthly marriage is funneled into a direct, loving, spiritual communion with God.

Mally is concerned with developing beauty—"radiance" as she prefers the term—a quality that is different from mere physical attractiveness. Radiant beauty, she explains, is the outward reflection of inward purity. By following her prescriptions for living a pure life, girls and young women can expect to develop a luminous countenance that is visible to those with eyes to see true beauty. True purity is evident all over the body. To attain it, young women must be pure in all respects, not just their bodies but also their minds and hearts. "Being reserved for one includes not only physical purity but emotional purity as well. This requires guarding our hearts, our minds, our thoughts, our words, our emotions, and our eyes. It means saving that close, intimate friendship for one man only, avoiding premature emotional attachments, and staying free from the intimate bonds that can form so easily, but that are then painful to dissolve."[30] Purity requires vigilance. A total commitment to purity, in Mally's view, is a response to what God commands (1 Corinthians 6:18–20) and in the end is a promise to the heavenly bridegroom not the earthly one. When young women follow Mally's purity path the real beauty of a true princess shines through as she waits for her eternal prince.

The idea that inner purity shines outwardly is a common one, and not only in princess literature. Indeed, many of Mally's ideas—making qualification lists for suitors, including parents in decisions about spouses, rejecting dating for courting, the emphasis on the girl's relationship with her father, waiting for God to bring a spouse, and considering purity beyond physical chastity—appear in the majority of literature aimed at evangelical teen girls and beyond. Leslie Ludy, author, speaker, and co-founder (with her husband) of Ellerslie Leadership Training, refers to princess longings as natural and powerful, but connects them directly to claiming a radically pure life that is "set-apart" from the secular world. In Ludy's books and on her website she challenges young Christian women to become radiant through purity and to achieve the fairy-tale life by allowing men to follow the model of masculine leadership outlined in the Bible.[31] Wanting to be a princess, according to Ludy, is not only natural it is scriptural. "We dream of capturing the heart of a noble prince with our stunning beauty, like the princesses in our childhood fairytales. But our longing to be loved and wooed by a heroic groom didn't originate with Cinderella—it's actually a Biblical concept."[32] In order to fulfill these scripturally sound desires young women need to first develop a romantic relationship with God. "Our feminine longing for a fairytale was actually put within us by our Maker because He desires to fulfill it—first through our romance with Him and then through an earthly love story with a true warrior-poet, if His plan for us is marriage."[33] Like Mally, Ludy insists that this eternal romance leads to true beauty and ever-lasting fulfillment. "Instead of finding fulfillment through chasing after short-term flings with guys, I learned to find the deepest desires of my heart met in a romance with my heavenly Prince. Instead of desperately seeking to become attractive to the opposite sex, I desired to be beautiful in *His* eyes."[34] This, Ludy claims, is the ultimate romantic relationship that transforms a young woman into a radiant princess.

Ludy believes that young women who follow her program will transform into radiant beauties reminiscent of princesses in fairy tales. "The secret to becoming the radiant, beautiful, alluring, lily-white princess of childhood dreams is *forgetting all about self* and becoming completely consumed with only one thing—*Jesus Christ*." True loveliness shines through when a young woman devotes herself to Christ as the prince of her soul. This outward sign of inner glory sets her apart from other women. To achieve and maintain this state one must adhere to strict daily practices, living with what Ludy terms "sacred decorum." These acts encompass all aspects of a young woman's life and behavior. According to Ludy, a set-apart young woman who is pursuing a relationship with Christ eschews the beauty standards of the world. Through her dress, actions, thoughts, and behaviors she only seeks the approval of Christ, neither the approval of worldly men nor the secular fashion industry. Specifically, women who practice "sacred decorum" do not draw attention to their bodies as sites of physical beauty; their radiance comes from the purity of their souls as reflected in their daily actions. Ludy explains: "There is a sacred decorum of set-apart femininity, a pattern for daily living that marks a young woman as a true daughter of the King. When it comes to our clothes, words, actions, thoughts, pastimes, and pursuits, we must be, as Amy Carmichael puts it, 'dead to the world and its applause, to all customs, fashions and laws of those who hate the humbling cross'."[35]

Modest dressing is a particularly important issue for Ludy and other purity writers.[36] Modesty fashion shows, websites, and books are popular among LDS, Catholic, Muslim, and orthodox Jewish young women, and evangelicals sometimes follow their lead. For example, Ludy recommends Wendy Shalit's book *A Return to Modesty*, which argues that dressing practices in Orthodox Judaism and Islam help overcome misogyny and give women control of their bodies.[37] Most of the high-traffic modesty clothing websites and popular fashion shows emphasize that modesty can be also be high style. Bloggers often reference the traditional style of Grace Kelly, Audrey Hepburn, and now

Kate Middleton (in her wedding dress) as examples of modest high fashion. Ludy assures young women that although many Christian girls are influenced by impure beauty standards of the fashion industry, which encourage girls to dress to attract male attention, set-apart girls, clothe their bodies to please their heavenly prince. In the 2011 May/June issue of Ludy's online magazine, Annie Wesche discusses the challenges of stylish modest dressing in an article called "Beautiful Provision: When God Claims a Closet."[38] She writes that, through prayer and waiting, she found fashionable clothes at J. Crew and shoes at D.S.W. that were both modest and inexpensive. Following the article is a Q&A penned by Ludy that asks the question: "What kind of swimwear is appropriate for a set-apart young woman?"[39] Ludy recommends swim shorts and loose sports tops, anything that covers areas of your body that should only be seen by your future spouse. Dress, like all other aspects of a set-apart girl's life, reflects her commitment to purity and rejection of the world's standards of beauty. But it doesn't require her to be a fashion tragedy. "Becoming a set-apart woman—a 'lily among thorns'—doesn't mean we become physically unattractive. But it *does* mean that we live differently than the thorns around us, especially when it comes to guys. A set-apart woman does not seek to win male favor through enhancing her sex appeal or drawing all eyes to her body."[40] Male favor and attention should be earned by looking at a young woman's soul, not her body.

Perhaps more than other purity writers, Ludy focuses on the intimate relationship with the eternal heavenly prince as the primary relationship for young evangelical women. Like others, Ludy also encourages young women to keep their future earthly husbands at the forefront of their minds at all times. On the one hand, Ludy believes young women should keep their bodies pure because they are God's temples, and they should also refrain from any physical (or emotional) defilement to protect the divine marriage covenant. On the other hand, chastity is also essential for a strong earthly marriage. "Giving away your physical purity is not just a matter of 'crossing the line' but of sharing any part of your sexuality with someone outside the marriage covenant."[41] A young woman should only give her emotional intimacy after an engagement and, of course, physical intimacy should occur only after the marriage ceremony. If this path of purity is followed, if a young woman waits for God to bring a perfect spouse, and if she allows the man to take the lead in courting, then, Ludy assures her readers, their future husbands will treasure and protect them like princesses. Young women are responsible for guarding themselves emotionally and physically from forbidden feelings and actions. If they succeed, they will move from the protection of their father's household to the safety of their husband's home. Maintaining purity and receiving protection are the building blocks of God's fairy tale.

Young women are praised and valued for maintaining purity, not for making individual choices or stepping outside of the role set for them by their fathers and God. For people within the purity movement, female virginity prior to marriage is critically important because it allows men to fulfill their biblical gender roles as fathers and husbands. Without virgin brides, there is no need for noble princes and there are no fairy tales. In stories in which men are the actors and women are waiting to be saved, only virgins are worth fighting for. This is God's plan for marriage. "God's pattern restores the long lost art of masculine nobility and feminine dignity—returning us to the days of gallant lords and fair maidens. Following God's design is what sets the stage for those seemingly impossible dreams to actually come true. If finding our deepest romantic longings fulfilled is what comes of following God's design, then I think we need more of His amazing 'old fashioned' ways."[42] The Bible, according to Ludy, is the ultimate princess narrative.

THE PURITY RITUALS

The purity industry focuses on the things a young woman should do while waiting for her future spouse. While waiting young women might take a purity pledge, wear a purity ring, dress modestly, make qualification lists for a future spouse, attend seminars on Christian feminine charm to maximize physical beauty and traditional female social graces, attend purity balls, and eventually court.[43] Not all young evangelical women participate in, or believe in, all of these activities. For example, some purity writers reject all forms of dating in favor of courtship (more on courtship later), while others allow for dating if the young man has the potential to be a spouse.[44] But all of these writers affirm that purity is more comprehensive than abstinence and success requires young women to "guard" their hearts, minds, bodies, and spirits. Young men also must strive to maintain purity. It is assumed, however, that because of their hormones and their nature, young men are easily led astray by young women. An immodest young woman can be a danger to herself and to a young man's virtue. Young women, therefore, are responsible for their own purity and for helping young men remain pure. Purity rituals aid them in this endeavor.

Since July 1994, many young people have affirmed their desire to remain chaste prior to marriage by making a "True Love Waits" pledge on covenant cards. To make the vow, teens sign their names to the following: "Believing that true love waits, I make the commitment to God, myself, my family, my friends, my future mate, and my future children to a lifetime of purity including sexual abstinence from this day until the day I enter into a biblical marriage relationship."[45] Pledgers typically wear a True Love Waits ring as a sign of their pledge and continual commitment to purity. In the early days, teenagers committed at national events or through local church groups. Today, this group, sponsored by Lifeway Christian Resources, an arm of the Southern Baptist Convention, claims to have an international reach through its website, a blog, and online discussion groups.[46] Lifeway asserts that True Love Waits uses "positive peer pressure" to encourage teens to help each other refrain from premarital sex.[47] Other faith-based groups follow a similar model, encouraging evangelical youth to celebrate and support chastity through rallies, events, and concerts. All of these venues include the buying and selling of items such as t-shirts, rings, and bumper stickers that display a youth's vow of abstinence.[48]

Attending a True Love Waits rally or wearing a purity ring signals a commitment made by young women to pursue a purity lifestyle. Young people who attend a True Love Waits rally, a Silver Ring Thing event, or a chastity club at school, pledge in ritualized ways to honor

God and their future husband by remaining chaste prior to marriage.[49] Recent research has shown that virginity promises are generally ineffective and in some cases can expose pledgers to higher risks of sexually transmitted infections.[50] Analysis of the federal government's National Longitudinal Study on Adolescent Health has shown that 82 percent of pledgers between 1995 and 2001 broke their promise.[51] According to sociologist Mark Regnerus, 80 percent of evangelical teens reported to him through interviews that they believed sex should be saved for marriage, but this same group tended to lose their virginity at a younger age than mainline Protestants or Catholics who don't take the pledge. And they are more likely to have more sexual partners prior to marriage.[52] Regnerus also demonstrates that chastity pledges work best when the people involved view themselves as a minority group that is taking a stand against the status quo. If the group is part of a majority in a school or social situation, the participants are more likely to break their promises. This may explain the recent trend of evangelical writers stressing that abstinence is countercultural.

The emphasis on a purity *lifestyle* has emerged partly in response to the popular perception that evangelical teens define virginity as refraining only from heterosexual vaginal intercourse but not other forms of sexual activity. According to the writers of purity literature, sexual abstinence is one aspect of purity that has far-ranging consequences.[53] But purity is more than that. It is a total system of maintenance and surveillance of sexual desires based on daily rituals. Purity is depicted as a lifestyle that—in direct opposition to secular life—honors the body, mind, heart, soul, and God. It is not just about keeping "technical virginity," by abstaining from intercourse. It requires following a code of conduct that is directed toward a future life with a spouse and children and an eternal life in heaven. In essence, the pure body becomes the arena for honoring God.

"The Purity Code is not just about sex," writes Jim Burns in *The Purity Code*. "It is about living in a way that can bring you the most freedom and set your future up for joy. People who live by the Purity Code carry the least amount of spiritual and emotional baggage (bad memories, regrets, etc.) into relationships and their eventual marriage."[54] Besides refraining from premarital sexual contact, purity involves healthy food choices, exercise, shielding eyes from degrading images and ears from unsavory words or sounds, and keeping thoughts pure. A person who pursues a purity lifestyle refrains from vulgar and intimate speech while always directing their mind and heart toward God. As Leslie Ludy explains, "God's sacred intent for us goes far beyond just saving sex until marriage, wearing one-piece swimsuits instead of skimpy string bikinis, or idolizing Christian bands instead of secular ones....His sacred intent for you and me is nothing short of absolute abandonment of Jesus Christ, entire separation from the pollution of the world, and ardent worship of our King with every breath we take."[55] Refraining from sexual activity is one part of a complete system of dedicating your body and mind to God. These are daily practices that encompass all moments of the day and all aspects of a person's life.

The advice given to young men and women regarding maintaining purity differs because of the presumed distinctions between the sexual desires of males and females. As Heather Hendershot has demonstrated in her examination of Focus on the Family magazines *Brio* (for girls) and *Breakaway* (for boys), boys are told to expend physical energy to overcome sexual thoughts while girls are told to find meaningful activities to keep their minds off of romantic desires.[56] Boys are encouraged to participate in sports and body building. Girls, on the other hand, are encouraged to control their bodies through proper dress, diet, and decorum because they are not perceived to struggle with sexual desires to the same extent as boys—but they could be responsible for leading boys astray.[57]

Practicing purity requires an enormous amount of self-surveillance. It is precisely in these daily life practices that the authors of purity literature have found their publishing niche. There are scores of books, magazines, and blogs that provide endless suggestions for maintaining purity to help young women face their unique challenges.[58] Purity is not simply following external rules it is also paying attention to internal thoughts and desires. Young born-again women must continually stay alert to any thought that might lead to sin. If a thought or feeling surfaces that is impure or might lead to an impure action, girls are instructed to confess their struggles to a parent, friend, or to Jesus. They are not asked to simply refrain from a sinful action, but to confess all forms of potentially sinful thoughts and desires.

Purity writers offer a variety of techniques for young women to self-monitor, both when they are alone and when they are in the company of young men. Most of the authors assume that, if they are not chaperoned, it will be the young woman's responsibility to stop sexual advances. They believe that men are visually stimulated and are unable to control their sexual desires, while women are emotionally stimulated and not as interested in sexual activity. A repeated phrase in the purity literature is that men have intimacy for sex and women have sex for intimacy.[59] In *Technical Virgin*, Hayley DiMarco writes to all young women "who crave male attention but just don't know where to draw the line." She distinguishes herself from many purity writers because of her willingness to accept that young women will date and will have some physical contact with young men. Young women, she cautions, are responsible for any sexual sin that might occur. "It's not enough to agree that sex is wrong," she explains, "you have to agree that guys are visual creatures and that you have a huge responsibility in protecting them from your body." Not only will sexual encounters defile young women but, according to DiMarco, they will also be responsible for leading young men into sin. "Notice God blames the woman (in Prov. 23:27) for her evil ways, not the man. He just warns the man about her. If you are allowing a guy to use you for sexual satisfaction, then you are leading him down a path of destruction and God is blaming you." Sexual sin, according to DiMarco's reading of human nature and Scripture, is always the woman's fault. Like other writers DiMarco argues that purity is not simply about virginity and that if a young woman is uncertain about appropriate physical behavior she should simply pretend that a camera is filming your every move and at the end of the day your parents will watch.[60] In other words, if self-surveillance doesn't work, imagine an actual surveillance camera.

Visualizing future consequences is one of the most common techniques proffered by purity writers for curbing sexual behavior. Parental punishment is not the only concern. Over and over again, young women are enjoined to imagine and pray for their future spouses. Part of guarding the mind, soul, and body is practicing rituals of envisioning the delight or disappointment a young woman will bring to her future husband. Leslie Ludy warns, "You may not know his name, but every decision you make right now—big or small—in relating to the opposite sex will affect the purity and beauty of your future marriage."[61] This topic is taken up by all of the most prominent purity writers who gear their books to young evangelical women. Imagining a future husband is not daydreaming; it is serious thinking that provides focus for daily actions. Elisabeth Eliot asks her female readers, "Is there a man anywhere who would not prefer to have a virgin for a wife? A woman who would not prefer that the man she marries has never slept with anyone else?"[62] Secret #2 on Dannah Gresh's list of *Seven Secrets to Sexual Purity* encourages young women to dream about their future husbands. She suggests making a list of qualifications for the spouse, to practice picturing a godly husband and above all "to start the habit of praying for your future husband. Pray that God would protect him in the physical battles that he faces, but especially in the spiritual battles."[63] Although a young woman does not know who her future husband will be, he is out in the world and, according to Gresh and others, she should devote some of her time to praying for him while waiting for his arrival in her life.

Another common technique suggested to young women for maintaining purity is "guarding" the heart by acknowledging the danger of flirting. Most purity writers go to great lengths to explain to young women why flirting is unkind to young men and may lead to trouble. Flirting is also unwise and unnatural because it makes young women the instigator in relationships. Elisabeth Eliott urges young women to "Ask God for that gentle and quiet spirit that is a thing very precious in His sight. There is no need to flirt.... You will be glad you did not do the hunting."[64] Dannah Gresh pleads with young women to monitor what they say, how they dress, and to refrain from sharing their innermost thoughts and feelings with any man until engagement. Shannon Ethridge and Stephen Arterburn suggest, "If you are looking for a safe relationship to pour your attentions and affections into, you don't have to look any further than your relationship with Jesus Christ. He can delight your heart and soul and satisfy every fiber of your being much more than any boy on the planet."[65] Flirting confuses gender roles and leads to misunderstandings.

Besides outlining the dangers of flirting, Etheridge and Arterburn argue that young women must reject the myth of secular romance. "There's no such thing as love at first sight, only attention at first sight. Love isn't an exhilarating feeling, it's a serious commitment that you make after getting to know a person through an extended investment of time and energy."[66] Romance is vexing for purity writers because it contradicts the long careful process of waiting, praying, and fully examining the potential spouse through check lists and adult supervision. Romance, in their view, involves an immediate emotional response, not a reasoned testing and checking of a person's qualifications against a list. That is why many purity writers ask young women to avoid secular romance novels and romantic films.[67] These books and movies, they argue, create unreal hopes and unscriptural desires in young women. Before reading, viewing, or talking about romance a young woman should always think carefully about the consequences and whether it will lead to a godly marriage or simply create unrealistic expectations that will be an obstacle for happiness with her future Christian spouse.

On the other hand, many of the young women reading purity literature have been raised on the idea of waiting for their noble prince to arrive. While the literature aimed at older teens moves away from the fairy-tale narrative it continues to emphasize Jesus as the true prince. The challenge that Mally and Ludy propose to young women to develop a relationship with Christ as the true bridegroom, in some literature evolves into deeply intimate language to depict the power of that romantic bond. "He will reveal Himself to us as our magnificent Lover, draw us into a deeper emotional connection with Him, and stir up a longing for His lavish love to fill our hearts to overflowing. Once we experience Jesus in this way, all other people and relationships soon pale in comparison."[68] Romance with Jesus is true love, desires for an earthly romance miss the mark. In the ultimate princess narrative, Jesus is the prince.

FATHERS AND DAUGHTERS

In purity literature, a young woman's father is a crucial participant in the drama of protecting her purity and, in some cases (such as purity balls), serving as a proxy for her future spouse. Many writers suggest activities focused on fathers as a way to practice for biblical marriage. Mally suggests that while young women wait for their earthly prince they practice for marriage by doing things to please their fathers. Gresh agrees that young women should spend time with their fathers because in her words, "your father can fill that special guy-shaped hole in your heart."[69] Most of the writers believe that developing a strong father–daughter relationship will aid in the pursuit of purity because the young woman will focus on gaining her father's attention and respect rather than seeking attention from young men her age. Young women are encouraged to go on "dates" with their fathers, spend time learning about what they like, and talking with their Dads about their emotional and spiritual lives. Mothers are curiously absent.[70]

All of the purity books have a dedicated section on the importance of parental involvement. While some writers include both parents in the discussions of a future spouse, the majority of writers tend to emphasize the father's role in approving a husband.[71] In cases where a parent is absent or a non-Christian, the young woman is encouraged to seek out a wise older couple, another family member, or pastor to help her decide on a future husband. In all cases, the young woman who has devoted herself to maintaining purity through ritualized practices of guarding her heart, mind, and body, is enjoined to submit to the guidance of her father (or father substitute) when choosing a spouse. According to this literature, this decision is far too important for her to make on her own or to rely on her mother's guidance.

Purity writers provide nearly unlimited advice to young women once a potential spouse arrives. The crucial next steps are evaluating the merits of a suitor and the rules for spending time in his company. Many authors reject "dating" and encourage "courtship." Courtship, according to Josh Harris, its most well-known advocate, entails a commitment to get to know someone emotionally and spiritually only after deciding that marriage is the goal of the relationship.[72] A decision to "court" should begin with conversations with each party's parents and should include the guidance of parents or other "wise elders" throughout the process. In Harris's rendering, there should be no physical contact prior to the wedding, and this is best accomplished by inviting a chaperone to accompany the couple when they are together. Other writers believe it is appropriate to hold hands after an engagement is announced but not to kiss. Similarly, courtship advocates caution against professing love prior to an engagement. A couple becomes officially engaged after the young man asks the permission of the young woman's father and only then asks the young woman. While the couple that is courting understands that they are in the process of moving toward an engagement, the decision to marry remains with the man acting with the woman's father's blessing. Young women are told that it is best to allow a young man to make this decision because any action on her part will threaten his masculinity. As Ludy explains, a man who has wooed a woman according to "God's perfect pattern" is less likely to take her for granted and more likely "to preserve and nurture the heart of the princess whom he worked so hard to win."[73] She may, of course, choose not to accept his marriage proposal, but she certainly may not offer a proposal of her own.

SEX AND THE SINGLE EVANGELICAL

What happens if the godly prince never arrives? Where does a dedicated single young woman fit into the promise of purity as the years go by and marriage seems an unlikely prospect? Purity literature focuses overwhelmingly on the naturalness of heterosexual marriage and the significant role it plays in God's created order. Authors emphasize the joy of marital sex (without guilt, without disease) as a pay-off for years of maintaining purity. Many writers urge young women to make certain that they have no regrets or shame to spoil their perfect wedding night. A young woman who is sexually active prior to marriage, Dannah Gresh claims, will be burdened by memories of former lovers on her wedding night and will be robbed of a special moment that should be reserved only for husband and wife.[74] Gresh is not alone in outlining all of the physical and psychological dangers that young women are exposed to—STIs, unwanted pregnancies, depression, shame, poor self-esteem—if they are sexually active prior to marriage.[75] But, Gresh promises young women something more than freedom from sexually transmitted infections. "If you wait, then it will be a blast. If you wait, then you will make babies with great celebration. If you wait, then you will be one. If you wait…then you will be blessed."[76] This promise, if a young woman maintains purity prior to marriage then she will find a princely husband and have a perfect marriage that is a "blast," seems particularly cruel for women who never find a spouse, or for those who end up in unhappy marriages.[77]

When the single evangelical woman moves into her late twenties and early thirties, the promise of godly marriage may no longer seem realistic. As Sara Mally entered that age group she, like other writers, continued to emphasize the importance of her relationship with God and her work for the church. The effort to maintain purity is for a future spouse who might come along, but it is also to honor her relationship with God. This is a practice that she urges on other women in her situation. "But do not think that you have to leave home in order to meet someone. I believe that the very best place for a single young lady to be is at home, under her father's authority and direction. The world's system that encourages a time of 'independence' for young ladies is a dangerous and unbiblical idea."[78] Until her prince arrives, Mally intends to remain under the protection of her father.

Leslie Ludy, the author who urges young women to be "set apart," offers a different option for single evangelical women. In her writing and speaking she features heroic single women (either unmarried or widowed) from Christian history to demonstrate that a woman's purity and value is ultimately in her relationship with Christ, not with her earthly husband. Ludy admires Elisabeth Elliot, who has written extensively on purity. Elliott waited years for a husband and then tragically lost him during missionary work. She offers herself as an example of a woman who fully surrendered to God's plan for her life. She finds no point in mourning the loss of the dream of marriage. "If you are single today, the portion assigned to you for today is singleness. It is God's gift. Singleness ought not to be viewed as a problem, nor marriage as a right. God in His wisdom and love grants either as a gift." Furthermore, a woman who is single and would like to marry should not take matters into her own hands. That, she believes, should be left up to God and up to the man who by nature is the "hunter" and must decide through prayer when to act.[79] According to Elliot, it would be unnatural and unbiblical for a woman to pursue the man, so a woman must wait. Singleness, therefore, is neither a problem to be solved nor evidence that the pursuit of purity does not always have a fairy-tale ending. According to Elliot, singleness, like marriage, is a gift from God.

Most purity writers, however, believe that remaining single is an exception to the rule of Christian marriage. While Elliot uses her own life as a model of singleness and refers to countless single men and women in Christian history who have performed heroic feats, Kris Vallotton finds singleness to be a unique calling, the great exception to God's plan.[80] "To stay single your entire life," Vallotton argues, "will necessitate a special endowment from Heaven because it takes a man and a woman to be a complete person. How do you know if you have received the gift of singleness from God? That's simple....Paul said that the single life is preferable, but that 'it is better to marry than to burn with passion.' (1 Cor. 7:9). You are not supposed to be single for your entire life if you burn with passion for sex."[81] According to Vallotton, healthy, born-again young people yearn for sex (although boys and girls yearn for different reasons). He agrees with Elliot that women and men think differently, act differently, and have different roles in courtship and marriage. Rather than use Elliot's metaphor of "hunter," Vallotton prefers "cultivator." Women, on the other hand, are "incubators," or in Vallotton's words "womb-men." Women and men, by nature and Scripture, are meant to be together, combining the roles of cultivator and incubator. That is God's plan for humanity. There is little room in this literature for young women to remain single, but the reality that a princely spouse has not been sent by God for some pure women must be explained.

Other young women, who have not remained pure, but wish to adopt a purity lifestyle while single, can rewrite the fairy-tale narrative. Lakita Garth explains in *The Naked Truth* that she was not raised in a godly household and, as a result, participated in risky behavior, including premarital sex, as an adolescent.[82] After having a born-again experience, she adopted "secondary virginity," which she describes as a commitment to wait to have sex from the moment of testimony until marriage. In her book she urges others to practice "saved sex" rather than safe sex. Kris Vallotton also encourages single women who have engaged in premarital sex to become secondary virgins. He claims that God will sometimes provide the miracle of hymen restoration on the wedding day as a sign of forgiveness. Many other writers urge secondary virginity as a means to seek forgiveness for sexual sins and to begin again on the road to sexual purity. This is not the ideal narrative, but it is one available for young women who have strayed.

CONCLUSION

Five years after "The Virgin Daughters" aired, another director returned to chronicle the Wilson family's final turn hosting the Colorado Springs purity ball. In the 2012 documentary "Virgin Tales" viewers learn that in the intervening years one sister has married a soldier who is deployed to Afghanistan, an older married sister has had her first child, and one brother has graduated from Patrick Henry College and married a fellow student. The documentary focuses on the eldest unmarried daughter, who gamely prepares for the final ball and discusses her thoughts on remaining unmarried. Throughout the documentary she muses about "the day I will get married and meet my incredible man, it just gives me hope and encourages me to continue on in this walk of purity." She is confident about her future. "I've just always known that I want to be a wife and a mother. I would hate to go off and spend thousands of dollars for an education I wouldn't use." When the film ends, her prince has still not arrived. She has remained in her parents' home and begun leading an etiquette course for young women. She keeps busy helping her mother and attending evangelical conferences. Although she is convinced that her plan for purity will result in a happy marriage like her siblings', there is sadness in her voice as she talks about waiting for a husband. When asked what she would do if she remained single, with a sigh and a fragile smile she responds, "Well, I guess I will need a lot more grace."[83]

The contrast between the two films is striking. The second film is melancholy because it is the last ball, but there are also some troubling scenes filmed with the Wilson children. One daughter comes completely undone when her husband is sent to Afghanistan. She explains to her parents via Skype that she has no idea how to fill her days without her spouse. The daughter with a toddler comes for the ball but appears tired and distant. The recently married son gives an awkward interview in which he discloses that his wife was a better student in college and they both emphasize the difficulties of their first year of marriage. There is nervous laughter but not much joy in their conversation. Their marriage hardly seems like a fairy tale. Finally, the unmarried older daughter waits with diminishing hope for her married life to begin. The only Wilson children who seem happy are the younger son and daughter, who are not yet old enough for marriage but act out being a pretty princess and a gallant prince. It is possible that the filmmaker unfairly highlighted the ambivalence in the second documentary to expose the pressure points in the purity movement. It is difficult to know. By the end of the film, however, the viewer is left to wonder less about the merits of the effort to remain chaste and more about the promise of a fairy-tale marriage as the reward for purity.

Evangelical young women who pledge to live the purity lifestyle are caught in a bind of constantly talking and thinking about the one thing they cannot do. Young women are taught to scrutinize their behavior and to examine their thoughts and intentions to scrub away any possibility of sexual activity, lest they lose their virginity and, with it, their beauty and value. To make the situation more challenging, young women learn that they are responsible not just for themselves but also for the sexual desires and potential actions of young men, who by nature cannot help themselves. In other words, sexual sin is their responsibility and sexual defilement is their eternal shame.

Purity authors go to great lengths to present young chaste women as empowered, countercultural heroines who are taking a brave stand against a world that degrades their sexuality and humiliates their faith. The secular world, they explain, presents a distorted vision of female beauty and power that is merely a con game to persuade young women to live unbiblical lives. What the purity literature offers is a response to what is perceived by some evangelicals to be the breakdown of traditional American values. The fairy-tale narrative offered to daughters is available to those young women who remain chaste and under the protection of fathers who are leaders in the family. Unlike the "lies" told by secular culture, the true worth of a young woman is not her accomplishments but her virginity, which is a sign of her faithfulness to God and her father. Following these biblical rules is a sign of strength and commitment.

The insistence that taking a stand for virginity is both brave and empowering is a sign of evangelicals' anxiety about promoting biblical roles for women in secular America. As more American women enter college and the workforce, their roles as mothers and wives are transforming. Women put off childbearing and increasingly are choosing to have children without husbands. Many women in traditional nuclear families work outside the home, and some have husbands who assume the role of primary caregiver for the children. Conservative evangelicals who believe women should not work outside the home or remain single are faced with a challenge. How do you present an appealing role for women that stands apart from secular culture yet still provides women with a sense of self-worth that fits their cultural expectations? It seems that at least when it comes to youth, it is not enough to say that young women should remain virgins because the Bible tells you so. What was once called "chastity" evolved into the "purity movement," a radical lifestyle that separates the strong from the weak. Remaining a virgin until marriage stopped being old-fashioned and submissive and became strong and even rebellious. Declaring themselves "pure" enables evangelical young women to be empowered, strong, valued, and beautiful. In fact, it appears to provide all of the advantages of women's liberation without the drudgery of going to work or having to make tough choices for themselves. Young women can even claim that they are making reproductive choices by choosing to refrain from sex. Viewed in this way, it is easy to see the appeal.

Evangelical purity literature provides young born-again women an important role to play in God's plan for humanity. Rather than being disempowered pawns in a patriarchal exchange of sexual property among men, as outsiders might believe, they are taught that they are empowered by their countercultural choice. Indeed, in their worldview it is in the secular world that women must sell their bodies to succeed. In the purity world, their bodies are ultimately not their own to sell. Although the secular world pretends to offer women freedom through personal agency, reproductive choices, and career options, the purity writers argue that real freedom is the release of responsibility from worrying about jobs or finding a husband. True liberation is leaving those decisions up to God and your father. A fulfilled life comes when a young woman learns to abide by scriptural rules about sexuality and gender roles that are as true today as they were in biblical times. The purity movement just gives the rules an update.

What happens when God finally sends you a husband? The pay-off for "waiting" is the promise of a shame-free wedding night and great, sanctified biblical sex. But chaste newlyweds who have spent years avoiding sex will presumably need some instructions for their nuptials and the years beyond. The evangelical media industry is here to help.

CHAPTER TWO

SEX, MARRIAGE, AND SALVATION

INTRODUCTION

In the evangelical publishing industry, just like in the secular one, sex sells. Far from being the anti-sex crusaders they are often portrayed as, evangelicals can choose from a wide array of sex advice books and other media. In their 2012 book *Real Marriage*, a #1 *New York Times* bestseller, Pastor Mark Driscoll and his wife Grace gave their blessing to anal sex, oral sex, and masturbation within biblical marriages. And while they undoubtedly aimed to shock—and surely succeeded in some quarters—there is nothing new about the Driscolls. Since the 1970s, evangelical husband and wife teams have co-authored sex manuals as alternatives to secular sex guides, seeking to convince evangelicals that sanctified sex is superior to secular sex.

Tim and Beverly LaHaye's 1976 evangelical sex manual, *The Act of Marriage: The Beauty of Sexual Love*, is one of the most popular such books, remaining in print for decades. At the beginning of the book, the authors relate the following story about a young married woman who sought Tim LaHaye's pastoral advice: "One loving wife asked what she could do for her husband whose business had just collapsed. Since she had already prayed with him and they had committed their economic future to God, I suggested that she make aggressive love to him, that she dress provocatively and use her feminine charm to seduce him." Men's fragile egos, weakened by financial and emotional setbacks, the LaHayes explain, can quickly be strengthened by vigorous sex with their wives. Although the young wife worried that her husband would become suspicious of the seduction tactics because he had "always been the aggressor in that department," LaHaye urged her to try, clarifying for the readers that he knew that "her dynamic, choleric husband" was "not complicated enough to get suspicious." Her sexual wiles worked like a charm. Enraptured in sensual ecstasy, her husband perceived no ulterior motive and within five minutes after their steamy encounter, he shared a new business idea with his wife. Today, LaHaye notes, the husband enjoys a successful career.[1]

This sounds like the kind of thing you would be more likely to find in the pages of *Cosmopolitan* than in a Christian marriage manual. But evangelicals did not turn away from the sexual revolution, they simply made it their own, publishing sex manuals, running sex workshops, and holding counseling sessions to instruct husbands and wives on the best techniques for a sexually satisfied marriage. The sex manuals run the gamut from suggesting loving language to put your spouse in the mood to providing information about STDs: "sexually transmitted demons." Sexual techniques, positions, and specific acts are discussed in detail to provide guidelines for the married faithful. The sex manuals also offer guidance about male and female characteristics as well as gender roles as they relate to sex and marriage. These books are most often found in Christian bookstores, but a few also are shelved in Barnes and Noble. As the publishing industry continues to churn out books of sexual advice, and Americans continue to argue in public debates about the limits and purpose of sex, evangelicals have joined the conversation and provided an answer. Sex is natural, biblically sanctioned, and—if practiced in the proper arena of heterosexual marriage—sex can be a sign of salvation.

Evangelical sex manuals present a uniquely Protestant approach to sex. The most authoritative text on sexuality, the authors of these books claim, is the Bible. Scripture contains everything a believer needs to know about sex. The finer points—sexual positions, use of sex toys, types of intimacy—simply require some interpretation, and these authors are happy to oblige. The books also embrace the Protestant tradition of privileging words over images. Although the authors discuss bodily functions and bodily fluids, they are careful to remove representations of the body from their texts. When there are illustrations, they are clinical, fragmented diagrams disconnected from human bodies.

43

Evangelical sex manual authors defend their advice as the authentic Christian approach unsullied by distorted visions of sexuality that arose from misinterpretation of Scripture or false Christian traditions (namely, Catholicism) that have erroneously emphasized celibacy or denigrated the body. The manuals are devoted to providing—in excruciating detail—instructions about sexual bodies, but the authors are simultaneously committed to larger theological and social concerns. They seek to promote the primacy of Scripture (*Sola Scriptura*) and to argue that long-term sexual satisfaction is only possible when the Bible is also in the bedroom.

A BRIEF HISTORY OF SEX MANUALS IN THE UNITED STATES, 1950s TO THE PRESENT

The American sex manual industry exploded in the early 1970s. In the previous decade the FDA approved the use of the Pill (1960), the Supreme Court affirmed the legal right for citizens to obtain birth control (1965), and Masters and Johnson published *Human Sexual Response* (1966). The "Sexual Revolution" was underway. And that revolution had its own Bible: Alex Comfort's 1972 *The Joy of Sex: A Gourmet Guide to Lovemaking*, a runaway bestseller that encouraged men and women to liberate their minds and explore their bodies. The book provided illustrations and detailed explanations of sexual positions and techniques without assuming that the couple employing them would be married.[2]

The Joy of Sex was a departure from the typical secular sex manual. Popular texts written by physicians in the early twentieth-century—Thomas Van De Velde's 1930 English edition of *Ideal Marriage: Its Physiology and Technique* (1926) and Marie Stopes's *Married Love: A New Contribution to the Solution of Sexual Difficulties* (1931)—emphasized the importance of mutual sexual satisfaction in marriage while placing the responsibility for sexual pleasure squarely on the husband's shoulders.[3] Van De Velde and Stopes present the husband as the leader and educator in the sexual relationship, even though he at times was unprepared for this important office. The wife apparently entered the marriage oblivious to both her body and her emotions. "The wife must be taught," writes Van De Velde, "not only how to behave in coitus, but, above all, how and what to feel in this unique act!"[4] Husbands are urged to "awaken" their wives' dormant sexuality through any activity that brings on orgasm. The most reliable techniques are constant "wooing" and clitoral stimulation. Women are portrayed as stimulated to sexual peaks first through their minds and hearts. Men are guided entirely by their bodies. Both Van De Velde and Stopes cautioned that a sexually unfulfilled wife would likely develop health problems including nervousness, fatigue, and insomnia. Women in these books do have a measure of responsibility for their own sexual satisfaction: they must decide to enjoy sex; they should never remain mentally passive during sexual encounters.

By contrast, the secular sex manuals that were published after 1945 tended to emphasize male sexual pleasure and placed the responsibility for a successful sexual encounter (and ultimately marriage) on the woman's ability to find pleasure in sexual intercourse either without orgasm or by facilitating her own orgasm.[5] Women who appeared incapable of sexual climax were described as emotionally and psychologically deficient; frigidity, prudishness, and neurosis were the words used to describe the nonorgasmic wife. Men were no longer criticized for faulty technique (as they had been in previous decades); women were blamed for lack of sexual responsiveness and far less was written about the importance of clitoral stimulation. Edward Podolsky, author of *Sex Technique for Husband and Wife*, represents this consensus: "The clitoris, while important, is not nearly as important as most of us have been taught or lead to believe."[6] The wife in these manuals is responsible for ensuring her husband's sexual success by bringing him to climax and responding to him in ways that reassure him that he is a sexually potent man. A happy marriage, according to the authors, did not rest on mutual sexual satisfaction but on women learning to enjoy sexual intercourse despite her psychological and emotional inability to achieve orgasm. "Normal" or "typical" men are described as easily sexually stimulated and also easily emotionally wounded by a wife who will neither satisfy his urgent sexual desires nor affirm his masculinity by achieving orgasm under his ministrations.

By the 1970s, secular sex manuals were responding to the sexual revolution, no longer assuming that sex would only take place within marriage. *The Joy of Sex* is the best early example of this type of literature, although other titles, including David R. Reuben's *Everything You Always Wanted to Know About Sex*—(*But Were Afraid to Ask!)* also enjoyed a wide readership. "Typical" men and women in these manuals were described as heterosexuals who wished to experiment with different types of sexual activity. The majority of these manuals, however, were ostensibly written for married couples eager to spice up their sex lives.

Alex Comfort, an English biochemist and gerontologist who moved to Santa Barbara in the early 1970s, became a world-renowned sexologist at the age of 54 with the publication of his watershed book. In *The Joy of Sex* Comfort took to task medical professionals who defined "normal" sexual behavior as somehow different from the sexual acts people performed for erotic pleasure. Throughout his book, Comfort mocks the clinical approach to the mechanics of sex that pervaded other books. Calling his work a "manifesto," Comfort eschewed medical professionals' prescriptions in favor of the individual's sexual discovery through personal experimentation. The bedroom, he argued, was the best laboratory.

The Joy of Sex is organized like a cookbook, with appetizers, entrees, and desserts to emphasize individual sexual tastes. Sexual desire, Comfort explains, is as varied as cravings for sweet or salty delicacies and can be as complicated as a five-course French meal or as simple as a sandwich. Humor, appetite, and individual desire are the essential ingredients. Comfort urged his readers to try new and exotic sensory tastes, textures, aromas, and flavors. The joy comes from sampling from the smorgasbord and discovering new pleasures along the way. Unlike previous sexual manuals, which focused on orgasm, Comfort encouraged lovers to seek other forms of bodily delight and to reject the notion that there is one ultimate goal in sexual activity.

Most striking today, as when it was first published, are the vivid illustrations that accompany the text. The book jacket is a demure white with plain black printing, except that the word Joy is in red, meant to evoke the cover of *The Joy of Cooking*. Upon opening the book and thumbing through a few pages, you find a hirsute and slightly flabby man and woman casually engaged in oral sex.[7] This is a far cry from the anatomical diagrams that typically illustrated sex manuals—clinical cross-sections of disembodied penises and vaginas. Comfort's drawings are erotic illustrations of a heterosexual couple practicing various sexual poses. The pictures provide examples of particular sexual techniques and positions, but more importantly they cement the message that sex should be creative and pleasurable in all its varied forms. The hairy lovers sprawl across pages of the book, graphically displaying the story of their sexual adventures.[8] Comfort also included erotic Japanese woodblock prints to stir his readers' sexual imaginations and to demonstrate that sexual variety has been accepted and enjoyed at different moments and places in human history.

Alex Comfort—like those who would imitate his style in the future—made a point of presenting his book as a radical break from the prudery and repression of the past. Readers could escape the iron grip of Victorian values and join him in a quest for problem-free, liberated sexual bliss. This approach gives Comfort what philosopher Michel Foucault termed the "speaker's benefit."[9] Simply by having the temerity to talk openly about what he claims is a taboo topic (sex), Comfort lends himself authority and the power of transgression. This strategy would be repeated in both secular and evangelical sex manuals for years to come. The main difference is that the authors of evangelical sex manuals claim they are freeing readers from the sexual repression of Catholicism or the prudery of other Protestants or "old women."

EVANGELICALS AND THE SEXUAL REVOLUTION

Evangelical sex and marriage manuals followed the general trend, becoming bestsellers in the 1970s. By 1976, with the growth in evangelical denominations, parachurch organizations, and nondenominational religious groups, evangelical books on family and marriage sold at an unprecedented rate. Marabel Morgan's *The Total Woman* had sold 500,000 copies by 1975, James Dobson's (the founder of Focus on the Family) *What Wives Wished their Husbands Knew about Sex* sold 105,000 copies the same year, and Tim and Beverly LaHaye's *The Act of Marriage* had sold 178,000 copies by 1976, 500,000 by 1979, and, by 1993, over 1.5 million copies.[10] Although many of these books were first published in the 1970s and 1980s, they continue to be reprinted and they cast a long shadow on new publications. By the 1980s there was a whole industry of Christian psychologists and marriage counselors who specialized in sex education. And it wasn't just books. There were audio and video tapes, lectures, seminars, and workshops (most famously Marabel Morgan's Total Woman workshops). While it is hard to gauge the impact of evangelical sex manuals, it is clear that today the market continues to bear more and more products that are aimed at evangelicals interested in improving their sex lives.

Evangelical manuals that discuss sexuality and sexual technique range in scope and targeted audience. I use the term "sex manuals" for a large variety of publications; however, it might be more precise to refer to these texts as "sex and marriage" manuals. They contain sexually explicit information that the authors believe is only appropriate for adult readers who are married or engaged. There have been changes over the past fifty years, and there certainly are some differences among the manuals, but in general it is fair to say that evangelical sex manuals support conservative Christian values of heterosexual marriage and family through a literalist interpretation of Scripture.

Some writers are shockingly literal in their exegesis. Tim and Beverly LaHaye, for example, quote an interpretation of the Song of Solomon 2:6 as a guide for the literal mechanics of clitoral stimulation. "His left arm is under my head, and his right arm embraces me."[11] Typically the evangelical sex manuals begin by proclaiming what are scripturally sound desires and then linking those desires closely to what the authors contend are "natural" sexual acts. If sex acts are mandated in the Bible, they are required in marriage. For example, in his 2003 book *Sheet Music*, evangelical psychologist Kevin Leman explains that 1

Corinthians 7:3–5 affirms the natural sexual desires of men and women and dictates that these needs are met in marriage. "The husband should fulfill his marital duty to his wife, and likewise the wife to her husband. The wife's body does not belong to her alone but also to her husband. In the same way, the husband's body does not belong to him alone but also to his wife." According to Leman, "if you call yourself a Christian, and if you're committed to being obedient to what the Bible teaches, then you'll have to learn to fulfill sexual obligations within marriage."[12] In nearly all cases evangelical sex writers insist that their approach to sex is the authoritative (and often "liberated") biblical way to have sex.

Most early twentieth-century Protestant authors who wrote about sex discussed it in moral and spiritual terms, leaving sexual "dysfunction" and technique to trained medical experts. Between the 1920s and the 1960s evangelical marriage manuals that included information about sex tended to focus on the goodness of sex as part of God's creation and the perils of sexual activity outside of a Christian marriage. That all changed with the publication of the first popular evangelical sex manual, Herbert J. Miles's *Sexual Happiness in Marriage: A Positive Approach to the Details You Should Know to Achieve a Healthy and Satisfying Sexual Partnership* (1967). Miles's book was exceptional for two reasons. First, he argued forcefully for an understanding of sexual union in which sex always creates a "one-flesh" relationship between the two people involved. This union between husband and wife, he explained, was the basis of a Christian marriage. Marriage without sexual union was both fragile and contrary to God's will. Miles's stress on the unitive function of sex as equal in importance to its procreative function for building a Christian marriage was well-received by evangelicals who, in growing numbers, began accepting birth control as a proper form of family planning. This emphasis continues to characterize evangelical sex manuals today. The second exceptional aspect of Miles's book is his focus on the importance of female orgasm during sexual intercourse. By drawing attention to female orgasm, Miles bridges the divisions between the pre– and post–World War II secular sex manuals. On the one hand, he insists (as do early twentieth-century secular sex manuals) that women should achieve orgasm. But he also agrees with the male and female dispositional stereotypes that became popular in the later secular sex manuals. Women, he writes, must "think" their way to orgasm, and men can have their egos easily wounded if they feel sexually inadequate. The good news that Miles preaches is that sex is only Christian sex if both spouses are sexually satisfied.

Following Miles's model, most contemporary manuals offer practical sexual advice about the logistics of consummating a marriage—precise explanations of tried and true sexual techniques for engaged men and women to study prior to their wedding night, since they are presumed to be virgins when they say, "I do," at the altar. Tim LaHaye, the co-author of the bestselling post-apocalyptic *Left Behind* series, began his career writing a sex manual. In *The Act of Marriage*, Tim and Beverly LaHaye urge prospective brides and grooms to read the chapters entitled "Sex Education" and "The Art of Lovemaking" alone as many times as necessary before the wedding and together during the honeymoon. The two chapters discuss the finer points of human physiology in a clinical way that seems likely to drain the couple of any passion they feel, but evangelical sex writers stress that knowledge of human anatomy is the starting place for good sex. The LaHayes remind their readers, "God has never put a premium on ignorance, and that includes the matter of sex education."[13] In fact, the LaHayes and others go to great lengths to erase any mystery and spontaneity in the first sexual encounter. The LaHayes script the entire event in excruciating detail. For example, during foreplay on the wedding night, "as the husband is tenderly caressing the clitoris or vaginal area with his hand, the couple will probably be lying on the bed with the wife on her back. If she will spread her legs, keeping her feet flat on the bed, and pull them up toward her body, it will be helpful for them both. The husband finds this voluntary act of cooperation very exciting and it makes her most sensitive areas accessible to his caressing fingers."[14]

There is a reason for this step-by-step instruction. The authors claim that their motivation for writing these sex manuals is for husbands and wives to avoid some of the sexual frustration suffered by uninformed Christians who blindly approach the marital bed. But they provide more than the mechanics of orgasm; they want to define what constitutes a "normal" response to sexual stimulation. This is most obvious in bold statements that are refuted in secular sex manuals. Regarding female orgasm, for example, the LaHayes write "a woman never ejaculates or expels fluid as does a man; instead he is the instigator and she the receiver, not only of the male organ, but also of the sperm." This statement is at odds with contemporary secular sex manuals, which discuss female ejaculation and the famous "G-Spot." A few lines later the LaHayes add that "a man's ejaculation is almost ensured without benefit of prior experience; a woman's is an art that must be learned by two loving, considerate, and cooperating partners." One wonders what an orgasmic bride and a flaccid groom would do with such advice? Statements that couple physiological differences with assumed typical sexual responses recur throughout these manuals. The particulars of body positions and emotions give the reader the unsettling feeling that the LaHayes are not just orchestrating the first sexual experience but watching the entire event. Evangelical parents and well-wishers cannot intrude on the sanctity of a new marriage, but the authoritative voice of the evangelical sex manual can insinuate itself at this most private of times and into the most intimate areas, defining the parameters of orthodox Christian sex.[15]

Evangelical sex manuals devoted specifically to Christian heterosexual intercourse within marriage are typically written by husband and wife teams.[16] In keeping with the larger evangelical theme of male leadership and female submission, the authorial voice throughout the text is generally male, although in some cases the female co-author pens her own section, such as in Ed and Gaye Wheat's *Intended for Pleasure: Sex Technique and Sexual Fulfillment in Christian Marriage*'s chapter, "The 'Perfect' Wife." Both partners are responsible for their spouse's sexual fulfillment, but men are addressed more frequently in these books and given more information about female anatomy and psychology. The authors contend that "normal" men are easily sexually aroused, so their wives need fewer instructions.[17]

Despite the variety of evangelical sex manuals and the growing numbers of authors, the content, layout, sources, and "facts" provided in them are surprisingly uniform. There are, however, arguments among the more prominent writers on the topics of masturbation, oral sex, and "marital aids" (otherwise known as sex toys). Most writers, like the LaHayes, advocate "mutual masturbation," especially for newlyweds, to increase the possibility of orgasm, but caution that solo masturbation or reliance on "artificial" manipulators such as vibrators might lead to lack of interest in intercourse with your spouse, which is the ultimate, sacred goal. Clifford and Joyce Penner, authors of *The Gift of Sex,* approve of oral sex if both parties are willing. The LaHayes, as well as Ed Wheat and Gloria Oakes Perkins, authors of *Love Life for Every Married Couple,* cannot find scriptural evidence to forbid oral sex but worry that it might transmit disease and distance partners who are not face-to-face during intimacy. Kevin Leman vehemently disagrees about the risk of spreading disease and encourages couples to try oral sex. "It certainly isn't a matter of hygiene. To put it bluntly, when a woman kisses a man's freshly washed penis, the woman's mouth has far more germs than the man's penis. If you're truly concerned about hygiene, forget mouth-to-mouth kissing and go straight to oral sex!"[18] Despite these minor squabbles, the authors of evangelical sex manuals agree on the value and beauty of sexual intimacy between husbands and wives. Sex is neither forbidden nor shameful. When evangelicals turn their attention to God in the bedroom, the potential carnal joys are endless. Similarly, the joining together that can only occur through sexual intercourse between husband and wife brings a couple closer to God's plan for creation.

The message of this multi-million dollar publishing industry is clear: evangelical Christians have the best sex. And the reason is simple. According to the authors, evangelicals understand that God created men and women to sexually enjoy each other's bodies within the sanctity of marriage, and the most effective way to do that is to clearly understand the "natural" differences between male and female sexual desires. Rather than labeling men selfish, sex-craved cads, James Dobson uses scientific language to explain that when "true" Christians realize that sex differences are rooted in biology and manifested in social and emotional characteristics, they are better able to understand and please the "natural" desires of their spouses. "There is also considerable evidence," Dobson writes, "to indicate that the hypothalamic region, located just above the pituitary gland in the mid-brain, is 'wired' very uniquely for each of the sexes. Thus, the hypothalamus (known as the seat of the emotions) provides women with a different psychological frame of reference than that of men."[19] Ultimately, of course, God is behind these truths: "God designed man to be the aggressor, provider, and leader of his family. Somehow that is tied to his sex drive."[20]

The authors go to great lengths to explain the "natural" characteristics that differentiate men and women. Men, for example, are described routinely as stimulated by sight ("visually lustful") while women are more responsive to kind words. While these differences may prove challenging to newlyweds, the authors of evangelical sex manuals insist that they are both good, because they are given by God, and indisputable, because they have been proven by Scripture, observation, and in some cases formal and informal surveys. A wise spouse, the writers tell us, learns to work with these natural, God-given characteristics and understands that they are directly related to sexual desires.

The key to sexual happiness in an evangelical marriage, therefore, is to understand each other's "natural" sexual desires and to help your spouse attain sexual satisfaction. All marriages should be sexually satisfying to both partners, and sexual pleasure within marriage is an end in itself. The majority of secular sex manuals agree with this basic premise. Indeed, evangelical sex manuals often mimic secular ones. In some instances, evangelical writers rely on the same scientific surveys or claim accreditation by participating in secular sex therapy workshops.[21] What distinguishes the evangelical sex manuals from their secular counterparts is the insistence on defining "natural" sexual desires and placing those desires in a larger theological framework that teaches individuals the meaning of masculinity and femininity. Put bluntly, God created men and women with natural sexual desires, which are rooted in biology, and which determine how men and women should behave toward each other in the household, church, and society. All of these truths are written in the Bible.

Christian bookstores maintain shelves of publications related to sexuality and evangelical marriages, but despite the multitude of authors and the variety of approaches, they are almost all the same. If you walked into a Christian bookstore somewhere in America and randomly chose a sex manual off the shelf, nine times out of ten it will have a section on the wedding night, it will contain few illustrations, much of the discussion will be about how the different sexual needs of men and women is explained by the biological distinctions God created between males and females, and it will contain precise instructions about how to achieve orgasm.[22]

THE WEDDING NIGHT

Herbert Miles's *Sexual Happiness in Marriage* is typical of many evangelical sex guides in its focus on the first sexual encounter between a husband and wife. To assure success, Miles provides a detailed map of the evening. He begins by urging the newly married couple to travel only forty or fifty miles after their wedding, then find a motel, lock the door, draw the shades, and open their Bibles. After reading preselected Scripture, the couple should kneel by the bed and pray.[23] Miles suggests that the newlyweds undress each other slowly and examine each other's naked bodies, which he believes is normal practice for the first sexual encounter and in complete harmony with Genesis 2:25: "Adam and his wife were both naked, and they felt no shame." Of course, Miles notes, the young wife has spent many years practicing modesty, so this might be difficult for her, and if she is too shy, it is acceptable to leave the undressing until the third or fourth night. In most cases, Miles explains, the husband will not share his wife's modesty and undress without difficulty. "Normal" men are eager to be naked in front of their new wives.

Miles presents a step-by-step guide to the physical mechanics of a couple's first sexual experience along with commentary on how normal men and women will probably feel and behave. Since there are many things that could go wrong, "it is well for us to think through, in detail, the procedure of first intercourse." After procuring contraceptives, Miles recommends that the couple engage in a "love-play" period extending as long as it takes to sexually stimulate the wife (typically

15–20 minutes). Miles describes a few body positions that are aimed at sexually pleasing the virginal woman. Although the wife's arousal might decrease as the husband initiates intercourse, with "ample lubrication" and with the husband using "an iron will to keep his self control," and not prematurely ejaculate, the couple may consummate their marriage. Miles understands that this process may be physically and emotionally difficult for young women. Therefore, he urges women to "concentrate on the clitoris, the vagina, and the rhythm of the penis moving back and forth" and on ideas such as "I've looked forward to this for a long time" and "God has wonderfully planned this to be part of my life." At this critical moment she should not worry about her husband's sexual satisfaction because, as Miles explains, "He will take care of himself."[24]

Numerous Christian manuals copy this formula; some also suggest that the woman have a full physical exam prior to her wedding night and have her hymen cut if the doctor determines that her first sexual encounter might be a painful. "All prospective brides should visit their doctor several weeks before the wedding, discussing with *him* the advisability of breaking the hymen in the privacy of *his* office" (emphasis added).[25] In essence the young woman is encouraged to lose the sign of her virginity on the doctor's table. Ken Leman gives women the "assignment" to visit their doctors to have their genitals inspected for first intercourse. "If you are a virgin, your doctor will need to consider your hymen and perhaps your vaginal muscles." Besides exercises, a doctor can prescribe "vaginal dilators" and other methods to "gently stretch yourself" prior to the honeymoon. "I know this may sound embarrassing," he concedes, "but trust me on this one: It's far better to go through this embarrassment with your doctor than to disappoint yourself and your husband on your honeymoon because sex means nothing but pain to you."[26] The authors worry that if the first intercourse is painful, women might resist future sexual overtures. Cutting the hymen ahead of time or using dilators to stretch vaginal muscles is not romantic, but it might prevent sexual dissatisfaction that can lead to an unhappy marriage. There is no allowance for refraining from intercourse in marriage even if it is painful to the woman.

The remainder of Miles's wedding night discussion is devoted primarily to "sexual interstimulation," a practice suggested if the couple is not ready for intercourse on the first night. Miles recommends that the wife manually stimulate the husband first and provides a brief paragraph noting only that the wife should use her hands and fingers. There are no descriptions of how one manages this presumably because Miles contends that "Usually, there will be little or no problem involved in the wife stimulating her husband to an orgasm." Normal men, according to Miles, are easily stimulated, and women appear to be quick learners. After gently stimulating him, "She will simply observe what happens."[27] Men, however, need detailed instructions on how to sexually arouse women, from hand and body positioning, to timing and descriptions of the multiple emotive and physiological responses that might indicate sexual pleasure. Women are by nature more complicated, and men need more directions. This fundamental distinction is repeated in the majority of evangelical sex manuals. A cursory glance at the amount of space devoted to Kegel exercises to strengthen vaginal walls compared to male sexual concerns such as impotency and premature ejaculation amply demonstrate the authors' belief that women's minds and bodies are responsible for the majority of sexual problems. If the couple follows their advice and the honeymoon goes well, Miles and others promise, it will set the standard for a lifetime of glorious sexual intercourse.

The fine-tuning of the first sexual encounter stands in stark relief to the growing assumption in secular sex manuals that newlyweds have had some sexual experiences prior to the wedding night.[28] But in early twentieth-century secular manuals both spouses were presumed virgins at marriage, and such manuals bear striking similarities to today's evangelical guides. Edward Podolsky's *Sex Technique for Husband and Wife* focused on the wedding night, arguing that one of the most common causes of lifelong frigidity in women is pain endured during the first intercourse. Young husbands, Podolsky warned, must proceed with care because "every normal woman wants to be possessed. She expects her husband to take her."[29] A brutish first encounter or a hesitant, nonperforming husband could ruin the sexual relationship from the start. This sexual truism, lost in later secular sex manuals, is revived in the evangelical literature.

SOLA SCRIPTURA AND THE FEAR OF IMAGES

One of the most striking differences between evangelical sex manuals and secular sex manuals is the lack of illustrations. Evangelical sex manuals in most cases only use a few anatomical illustrations and rely solely on textual descriptions of sexual positions. Rarely does one find drawn representations of men and women engaging in sexual intercourse. Instead, the texts use detailed depictions of disembodied genitalia to instruct the readers in male and female anatomy. Herbert Miles's *Sexual Happiness in Marriage* provides three anatomical illustrations. Two are of the internal reproductive organs of a male and a female, and one depicts female reproductive organs. Male external reproductive organs are not represented. Ed and Gaye Wheat's *Intended for Pleasure: Sex Technique and Sexual Fulfillment in Christian Marriage* adapts eleven illustrations from *Female Pelvic and Obstetrical Anatomy and Male Genitalia*. The only image that represents people engaged in sexual activity is a modest drawing of a couple positioned to control premature ejaculation. This is accompanied by two illustrations of a female hand (nails manicured) holding a crudely drawn penis in a manner suited to control ejaculation. These three drawings are noteworthy because the male and female bodies are drawn without sexual characteristics. In the drawing of the reclining couple, the reader can differentiate the naked female from the male by her long hair and curved shoulders. The male is represented as flat chested, with short hair and a pointed chin. Neither figure has sexual organs or facial features. The only distinguishing detail in the two other illustrations is a female hand (identifiable because of manicured long nails) holding a penis. The organ is outlined, but there is enough detail to show that it is not a male hand.[30]

Why are the images so few and so vague? The answer lies in three terms that are problematic for evangelicals: pornography, homosexuality, and masturbation. Each of these activities is forbidden, but, in a sense, illustrations can be pornographic and encourage masturbation. The line between instructional use and visual pleasure is not entirely clear. It is worth noting that the only sexual position illustrated is meant to stall premature ejaculation, demonstrating that male sexual pleasure is important enough to merit an illustration that might be construed as pornographic. To avoid this, the characters are drawn without sexual organs or bodily features that might arouse visual pleasure. The two diagrams of the hand holding the penis to control another male sexual problem are drawn to indicate clearly a female hand, therefore neither suggesting a homosexual nor a masturbatory act. The text and illustrations can direct the reader toward approved sexual acts but cannot prevent the reader from using the diagrams to learn how to perform sexual acts that these writers consider selfish at best and deviant at worst. Because evangelical sex manuals include few images, those they do provide are of particular importance. In this case, male sexual pleasure is illustrated in such a way that it might encourage a reader to take the problem into his own hands.

Tim and Beverly LaHaye's *The Act of Marriage* includes ten illustrations, all of them clinical, detached from the human body, looking as though they could also appear in a medical textbook. Two of the drawings depict the male and female reproductive organs. The remaining eight, found in the chapter entitled "The Key to Feminine Response," show differing levels of vaginal muscle tone. Figure 8 in the LaHayes' book shows an artist's conception of good vaginal muscle development (on the left) and poor vaginal muscle development (on the right). Two more illustrations depict a doctor's finger probing the pubococcygeus muscle, highlighting the theme of the female body as sexually problematic. It is remarkable that there are so few visual representations in a text devoted to increasing sexual pleasure by perfecting technical skills. One clue to the reason behind this might be the emphasis the LaHayes place on the male's propensity for "visual lust." Detailed descriptions of sexual techniques provide instructions, but pictures might allow for sinful fantasies, or the replacement of the marital sexual act with sexual thoughts (and perhaps acts) ignited by the illustrations.

This, however, does not explain why there are so many illustrations of vaginal muscles, including two depictions of a finger inserted into a vagina. The companion chapter, "The Impotent Man," contains no illustrations at all. Although the LaHayes take great pains to expunge all but the most necessary illustrations, foregoing any depictions of sexual positions or couples engaged in sexual intercourse, nine out of ten of their illustrations are of vaginas, placing the female genitalia on display and making the central feature of sexuality to ponder from all angles and to see penetrated, not be a loving husband's penis, but by a medical professional's finger.[31]

Female authors rarely include illustrations in their publications. The illustrations in the male-authored or co-authored manuals are provided as clinical or authoritative images from medical or sexual authorities. The female writers adopt no such official tone in their works, nor do they seek to provide medical advice. Depictions of sexual organs or sexual positions, therefore, do not fall under their purview.

It is noteworthy that the sex manual that has the most explicit illustrations advocates the pleasures of massage, masturbation, oral stimulation, and forms of sexuality that are dismissed in many other manuals. In his 1993 book *A Celebration of Sex*, Dr. Douglas E. Rosenau explains that seeking varied forms of sexual pleasure is not contrary to Christian values: "The sin is not experiencing pleasure but in calling pleasure sinful and not allowing us to enjoy God's many gifts, including genital sensuality."[32] Rosenau argues that the Bible is silent on masturbation. Christian denunciations of it are the result of misinterpretations of Scripture, such as reading Onan's refusal, through withdrawal during intercourse, to impregnate his sister-in-law (Genesis 38:9) as an indictment of masturbation. In the past, Rosenau contends, masturbation was discouraged because church authorities viewed it as a form of birth control within marriage or as a symptom of uncontrolled lust. Here again we see the radical break from false notions of the distant past—specifically a Catholic past—giving Rosenau the "speaker's benefit" of truth and authoritative transgression. Evangelical sex manual authors are always operating on the two levels of theological and sexual salvation. Masturbation—or, he prefers to call it, "genital pleasuring"—is an acceptable form of sexual activity as long as the couple follows "God's Guidelines." Those guidelines include refraining from such activity if it excludes your partner, routinizes sex, sets an erotic standard that the mate cannot duplicate, promotes fantasies, or turns into an addiction.

Rosenau, like other evangelical sex writers, pays particular attention to the female orgasm. Readers are given a three-part workshop broken down into thirty-minute sessions to examine and address this issue. After thinking and writing exercises, Rosenau leads women through lessons on "Exploring your Body," which teach women how to pleasure themselves. Besides the simple mechanics, Rosenau suggests helpful fantasies: "Now proceed to more explicit sexual fantasy and pleasure your clitoris as you use your imagination and enjoy making love with your husband." The final part of the workshop, "Becoming Orgasmic with Your Mate," allows women to integrate their new attitudes and heightened body knowledge into sexual relations with their husbands. Clearly Rosenau is walking a thin line between teaching women to masturbate (and providing helpful fantasies!) and solving the problem of sexual frustration experienced by some spouses during heterosexual intercourse. That is why Rosenau must not only allow fantasies but also suggest the correct type of fantasies. Through his reading of the Bible, Rosenau finds that most forms of sexual pleasure are scripturally sound. Rosenau reminds his readers that Scripture is silent regarding not only masturbation, but also oral sex, so it is the couple's responsibility "to sort and pray through various behaviors as you choose what to include in your repertoire of lovemaking." Anal sex is questionable because of the risk of infection, but it is not outside the realm of possibility under certain godly circumstances.[33]

SEXUAL BODIES AND SALVATION

The expectations of "typical" male sexual responses reflect broader understandings of natural male behavior. Manhood in these manuals is primarily a matter of aggression that is linked to a man's social and

60

religious role as provider and family leader. Because men are naturally aggressive, they also have strong sex drives. This, according to the discourse of the evangelical sex manuals, is "normal" male behavior and is the sign of a man who is able to perform all of his marital duties. A strong sex drive is not only normal for a man but is also tied to his ego, his sense of self. Therefore a man's "natural" drive to satisfy his sexual needs must be constantly met and greeted with approval in order for him to maintain a healthy ego and perform his obligations to his family. A married man whose sexual needs are not met will have low self-esteem and will be lazy. As LaHaye's advice to the woman whose husband's business collapsed at the beginning of this chapter proves, "A sexually satisfied husband is a motivated man."[34]

Men's primary role as aggressors, providers, and leaders are linked to their secondary features of being uncomplicated, unemotional, non-communicative, and visually aroused. The primary characteristics are viewed as positive attributes tied directly to men's sexual needs and desires, while the secondary features are obstacles to be worked around or used judiciously in a wife's efforts to sexually please her husband. LaHaye's suggestion that a wife switch roles and be the sexual aggressor was offered with confidence because he knew that the husband was too uncomplicated to realize that the wife had orchestrated a role swap. In this scenario, LaHaye teaches his female inquirer to fulfill her husband's "natural" sexual needs by acting out a dominance scenario to assist him in his primary role as provider for the family. The wife is aided in her efforts by her husband's "natural" lack of curiosity.

For the men depicted in these manuals, sex is a natural force that they can just barely keep under control. In *How to Be Happy Though Married*, Tim LaHaye writes, "The sex drive in a man is almost volcanic in its latent ability to erupt at the slightest provocation."[35] This can lead to premature ejaculation, a situation that a strong man with a focused mind should work to avoid. Ed and Gaye Wheat devote a subsection of a chapter to overcoming this problem. "Some men mistakenly feel that a quick release is a sign of masculinity. Thus they never realize the need to learn to control the timing of their ejaculation so that they can experience the joy and oneness that comes with consistently bringing the wife to orgasm during intercourse." This statement seems a bit implausible. Given the stress in other sections on the importance of a man's ability to be strong and control his body, why would readers think a "quick release is a sign of masculinity"? In a chapter entitled "For the Impotent Husband," the Wheats explain that the inability to sustain an erection can be attributed to a man's fear of failure. The problem is easily remedied: just trust in Christ. "God has given us resources far greater than the spirit of fear, and resting in that knowledge will provide the Christian husband with a stability and relaxation that can go far in solving almost every impotency problem."[36] In *What's the Difference? Manhood and Womanhood Defined According to the Bible,* John Piper explains, "mature masculinity expresses its leadership in romantic sexual relations by communicating an aura of strong and tender pursuit."[37] Unlike women, according to Piper, mature, healthy men are driven to seek sex. Dr. James Dobson concludes that "men are not very discriminating in regard to the person living within an exciting body....He is attracted by her body itself."[38] While sex for women is emotional, for "normal" men it is simply physical. Only Douglas Rosenau concedes that not all healthy men fall into one category. In *A Celebration of Sex*, he modifies the repeated generalizations about male sexuality: "Overall, men seem to be more focused on genitals and explicit sensual activity, and women tend to be more holistic with an enjoyment of sensuality and personality behind the body. But men and women should not be stereotyped. Some men appreciate gentle, romantic ambience more than their wives do. Some women may be very visually stimulated by genitals and enjoy immediate, direct sexual stimulation."[39] This is a case of an exception proving the rule. Sex for men in the majority of these books is a driving force that leads healthy men to want intercourse with any woman who visually stimulates them. It is only through maturity, fortitude, and prayer that they can control their unyielding desires. Marriage allows men to channel their natural sexual energy toward one appropriate woman.

Perhaps the most effective missionary for the joy of sex within evangelical marriage was not Herbert Miles, Tim LaHaye, or Ed Wheat, but Marabel Morgan, author of *The Total Woman* (1973) and the brains behind the Total Woman Workshops, which taught evangelical women how to please their husbands in all aspects of daily life but most especially in the bedroom. Morgan's book is a product of its time, responding to the sexual revolution and the feminist movement by claiming female sexual power while maintaining sex-defined roles in the household. Morgan urges married women to reprogram their minds to eliminate negative views of sexuality and to learn to be the object of their husband's greatest sexual fantasies. Morgan suggests, for example, that wives dress up in costumes and play roles: "You can be lots of different women to him. Costumes provide a variety without him ever leaving home....You may be a smoldering sexpot or an all American fresh beauty. Be a pixie or a pirate—a cowgirl or a show girl." She also encourages women to set sexual scenes in different rooms in the house, to use props (such as a trampoline), to initiate sex, and above all to learn to respond positively to their husbands' sexual overtures. Men, she explains, are less complicated than women, and while women want to be loved, men simply want to be admired. It is relatively simple, according to Morgan's formula, to keep your husband happy. The easiest and most effective way is to openly praise his virility and sexual performance. For women to feel loved, they must make themselves beautiful to their husbands by fully submitting to him: "It is only when a woman surrenders her life to her husband, reveres and worships him, and is willing to serve him, that she becomes *really* beautiful to him." Morgan's primary interest is in building strong marriages by exploiting the husband's "natural" sexual longings and reaping the wife's material desires.[40]

It is easy to criticize Morgan's balance between wifely submission and nasty girl sex queen as the Christian homemaker's recipe for a successful marriage. And many people objected loudly. In a review (entitled "Fundies and their Fetishes") of Morgan's *Total Joy,* scholar Martin Marty quipped that since the typical reader "expects an imminent and literal Second Coming,... I want to be around to see the enraptured raptured from their trampolines, he as a dime-a-dance ticket taker and she in raincoat and gorilla-head mask."[41] Some evangelicals rejected her approach as childish, manipulative, and demeaning to both men and women, while feminists and journalists wondered whether Morgan was being submissive or subversive in her zeal to perfect her life and get what she believed she deserved.[42]

The Total Woman was the product of Morgan's effort to train a network of female leaders to run Total Woman workshops across the country. The classes, offered in church basements at a modest price (four eight-hour classes for $75), taught women to reject the notion that sex is sinful. For, as Morgan claimed in an infamous statement, "sex is as clean and pure as eating cottage cheese." The workshops encouraged women to think about the naturalness of sex as well as the physical and spiritual benefits of mutual orgasm. While all sexual pleasure between husband and wife is good, in Morgan's workshops and books the goal for a Christian marriage is orgasm. According to Peter Gardella, Masters and Johnson's claim that women were capable of having fifty orgasms per hour and *The Hite Report's* (1976) statistics that only 30 percent of women orgasmed during sex, set the cultural stage for Morgan and other evangelicals to put the female orgasm at the center of true physical and spiritual sex.[43]

Morgan also provides assignments for her readers to help them along the way. Assignment "Sex 201" reads: "Be prepared mentally and physically for intercourse every night this week. Be sure your attitude matches your costume." The way to keep a husband, Morgan explains, is to be his sexual fantasy; in Morgan's pragmatic view, a sexually unfulfilled husband is in "a dangerous state. A married man shouldn't be wandering around with an unfulfilled libido." Wives who faithfully follow Morgan's plan will find that their sexuality empowers them in ways that far exceed the sexual empowerment of "liberated" women and the political empowerment of the feminist movement. Evangelical female sexual empowerment can be gauged materially, though not through a paycheck. Morgan related that after she had sex with her husband on the dining room table, he agreed to buy her new curtains. A testimonial from a former workshop student explains that before she took the Total Woman workshops her husband ignored her. A week after following Morgan's plan, he gave her "two rosebushes and a can opener!"[44]

Morgan told her readers to initiate sex, but that did not mean that she advocated female authority in marriage. Morgan rejected equality in marriage as contrary to the Bible and explained that submission to male authority is required for the well-being of the entire family. Although Morgan published years before the purity movement took speed, many of the themes found in her books resurface in the chastity literature: most notably, the idea that female sexuality is a commodity that is subject to economic exchange. In Morgan's view, women reap direct economic benefits, in the form of can openers and curtains, from providing sexual satisfaction to their husbands. In the purity literature, women are valued for refraining from sexual contact prior to marriage and as a pay-off they can expect to be honored and protected in marriage. Sex, in *The Total Woman*, is heterosexual intercourse that leads to male sexual pleasure through orgasm. Sexual intercourse is essential for channeling a healthy man's "normal" passions and frequent sex will guarantee a successful marriage. Women can train themselves to enjoy sex, but more importantly, they will delight in the material rewards of a sexually sated husband. It might be tempting to dismiss Morgan's approach as outdated or simply a product of the time when she first published her books, but that would be a mistake. The claims she makes about male and female sexuality and husbands' and wives' gender roles continue to surface in contemporary evangelical sex manuals. We will see echoes of Morgan's sex advice in biblical womanhood literature and Titus 2 ministries (examined in chapter 4).

CONCLUSION

When Mark and Grace Driscoll published their *Real Marriage*, the response from evangelicals was varied: there was shock, praise, and ambivalence.[45] For evangelicals familiar with the Mars Hill pastor and neo-Calvinist celebrity, the sexual advice in the book was hardly surprising. For many years Driscoll has been preaching the gospel of masculine authority and female submission in marriage, a form of "complementarianism" that upholds strict gender roles. His preaching style is notorious for his vulgar language (he is known as the "cussing pastor"), his attacks on "types" of Christians with whom he disagrees, and his explicit talk about sexuality. Driscoll's target audience is young, urban men whom he seeks to reach with his message of the masculinity of Jesus and the need for strong, godly men to lead families and the church.[46] For those who attend one of the Mars Hill churches or listen to his podcasts, Driscoll's approval of oral sex, anal sex, and masturbation within heterosexual marriage is common knowledge.[47]

Even those outside of Driscoll's demographic concede that many evangelical authors of marital sex manuals allow sexual variety within marriage if both partners consent. Some evangelicals responded to the commotion over his book with bemusement because, they argued, it hardly merited being labeled "scandalous" in light of the type of advice available in the booming market of evangelical sex advice literature. One writer who published a review in a prominent evangelical journal claimed that there is nothing new about the content or approach of *Real Marriage*.[48] Other evangelicals objected strongly to the idea of promoting sexual acts that appeared too close to same-sex acts and self-pleasuring. But the real trouble with *Real Marriage* was Mark's shaming characterizations of Grace as sexually sinful and his insistence that wives must remain sexually available to their husbands at all times. This attitude, which disturbed many evangelicals, who felt it bordered on sexual servitude and degradation, reflected what detractors believe was Mark Driscoll's primary goal: to promote male sexual pleasure.[49] Perhaps, but this complaint, when considered in the context of all evangelical sex manuals published today, appears more of a problem of degree than of kind.

Real Marriage, though abhorrent to some evangelicals, fits within the boundaries of common views about gender roles, Scripture, biology, and sexual acts found in evangelical sex advice literature. The book is primarily about a biblical approach to marriage, but in it the Driscolls devote a considerable amount of space to the effects of sexuality on marriage. Unlike the majority of sex manuals discussed, the book does not provide detailed information about sexual positions and techniques. But there is a chapter called "Can We_____" on permitted and forbidden sexual acts within biblical marriage.

The chapter begins with a disclaimer warning that people who "are older, from a highly conservative religious background, live far away from a major city, do not spend much time on the internet, or do not have cable television" will be shocked by the contents of the chapter and should get "the medics ready on speed dial." The Driscolls make clear that parents, grandparents, teachers, missionaries, clergy, and others need to realize that "the questions today are different, and if people don't get answers from pastors and parents, they will find them in dark, depraved places."[50] Like so many sex advice authors before them, the Driscolls claim the "speaker's benefit" to provide the most up-to-date, relevant sexual information. Although upsetting to out of touch or misinformed readers, it is essential knowledge for the success of biblical marriages and the cause of Christ. Claiming this sort of authority, along with notoriety, also helps sell books.

The question-and-answer section is divided into three parts: Is it lawful? Is it helpful? Is it enslaving? The topics include masturbation, oral sex, anal sex, menstrual sex, role-playing, sex toys, birth control, cosmetic surgery, cyber sex, sexual medication, and marital sexual assault. With the exception of sexual assault, all of the sexual topics are biblically lawful, according to the Driscolls, if practiced within heterosexual marriage. Most of the sexual acts (excluding cyber sex and cosmetic surgery) are discussed in other evangelical sex manuals, although not all are considered biblically sound. The Driscolls are careful to state that there are circumstances when these sexual acts may not be helpful for a marriage and might become addictive or "enslaving." For example, "many Christian couples have decided that while anal sex is permissible, it is not beneficial, as they deem the risks too great. Some, however, have chosen to at least try it, for the variety." In all cases a married couple must know their sexual desires and pay attention to their own sense of right and wrong. "We are explaining what a married couple may do, not what they must do. The Bible often gives more freedom than our consciences can accept, and we then choose not to use all our freedoms." Rather than viewing the Bible as a set of austere sexual restrictions, the Driscolls present an interpretation of Scripture that might be too sexually permissive for many believers. In sum, when marital partners mutually consent to sexual practices, it is likely to be biblical and therefore permissible.[51]

If the Driscolls hoped to create controversy in the evangelical world, their sex book, for a short time, accomplished that goal. On any given day, Mark Driscoll's style is certain to elicit strong responses of praise or condemnation regardless of his topic. The strong response to *Real Marriage* demonstrates something obvious but often overlooked: American evangelicals do not hold a definitive view about sexual practices within marriage. There is no one authoritative voice. That explains why born-again Christians have simultaneously lauded *Real Marriage* as biblically sound advice and dismissed it as pornographic and sexually degrading. Yet while the Driscolls' tone and style might not be palatable to all evangelicals, their approach to biblical sex is consistent with some contemporary evangelical sex manuals. It is neither as radical nor as unique as they and their detractors claim. The lesson of the Driscoll's success is there is always room for one more evangelical sex manual on the market.

The main message of evangelical sex manuals is that frequent and mutually satisfying sexual encounters are crucial for a strong marriage. Sex is sanctioned by God, should be practiced in marriage, and is one of the wonders of creation. In most cases, the writers downplay reproduction and focus on mutual sexual pleasure as the fulfillment of God's plan for humanity. Evangelical sex manual authors employ the "speaker's benefit" to claim authority in the same way Alex Comfort decried false "Victorian" attitudes toward sex. The difference is the theological agenda of distancing evangelicals from, on the one hand, the Catholic Church's "false" scriptural interpretation that, the authors argue, erroneously connected sexuality and sin and, on the other, "old wives' tales" perpetuated by superstitious old women who hated men and sex. The evangelical manuals can awaken readers' sexuality, correct inaccurate sexual information, and help readers to see another aspect of the true meaning of Scripture that ultimately leads to salvation.

To combat the inaccurate pairing of sexuality with sin, authors of evangelical sex manuals stress that heterosexual desire is natural and good because it is given by God. The best sex manual, the authors argue, is the Bible, which, if properly interpreted, shows that sex is not a sinful but a godly act.[52] And yet, the faithful still need to purchase sex manuals to help them interpret what the Bible says. Regardless of the author, born-again readers learn that God's plan is for people to have frequent sex within marriage. It is part of God's plan for creation and for advancing the kingdom. True Christians, who interpret the Bible correctly, have frequent and mutually satisfying marital sex.

One question remains: If evangelicals really are having the best sex, as the authors claim, why do born-again Christians continue to buy sex manuals? Looking at a bookstore shelf, we can safely assume that for many book buyers sex is *not* natural and instruction manuals are helpful. It would be easy to argue that sex manuals are just one more cog in the evangelical wheel to imitate and appropriate secular culture for its own theological ends. That evangelical sex manuals is simply niche marketing. But there is more to it than that. The manuals define the limits of "natural" sexual behavior and scripturally sound desires. More importantly, they represent a crucial aspect of evangelical faith and practice. The popularity of evangelical sex manuals demonstrates that one can (and should) express one's faith not only through spoken testimony but also through bodily acts.

The authors of these books are not just vying with each other to grab a corner of the evangelical sex advice market for themselves. They are also writing *against* secular culture. Secular sex manuals present many forms of sexuality, often without assumptions of fixed or "natural" sexualities or marital relationships. They tend to promote the freedom to explore an individual's sexuality without the guidelines of a sacred text or a set of rules that might limit self-discovery. In response, evangelical sex writers go to great lengths to demonstrate all of the sexual freedoms within heterosexual, biblical marriage. The Driscolls exemplify this approach well when they argue that the Bible often provides more freedoms than a couple will accept in good conscience. The Bible doesn't hold people back, these authors argue, it celebrates sexual exploration and discovery. The distinction in evangelical sex manuals is the insistence that such sexual exploration and discovery must occur within a heterosexual marriage. Monogamy and heterosexuality are both good and "normal" because they are sanctioned in Scripture. For a heterosexual marriage to be sexually satisfying, each spouse must understand the gender roles that are the product of their natural biological characteristics. These characteristics are revealed in the Bible and provide a blueprint for how men and women should behave in marriage.

The effort to place "normal" gender behavior in the context of biblical heterosexuality points to larger anxieties within American evangelicalism. As more American women continue to enter the workforce and hold jobs that previously were reserved for men, evangelicals have offered an alternative that maintains that traditional gender roles lead to marital happiness, sexual pleasure, and economic security. They argue that maintaining biblical gender roles allows men to lead the family, succeed economically, and have better sex. Amidst an increasing shift in American popular opinion about causes of sexual desire, and, specifically the growing approval of gay marriage, evangelicals find themselves having to work even harder to promote the idea that heterosexuality is natural for all people in all places. The authors of these books argue that heterosexuality is not only "normal" and scriptural; it is also sexually adventuresome and can fulfill anyone's sexual desires. As the Driscolls show, acts that are forbidden when performed by a same-sex couple are permitted within heterosexual marriage.

Evangelical sex manuals allow the faithful to participate in an American culture that they often describe as "over-sexualized" while still affirming biblical principles. Readers of these manuals learn that, within marriage, they can fulfill all their sexual desires—even those that don't seem orthodox—and still be assured of their salvation. In fact, by being sexually satisfied in marriage, believers witness to the truth of the Bible. If married couples maintain their gender roles, the sensual possibilities are limitless. The trouble arises when sexual activity occurs outside of these biblical parameters. That is the subject of the next chapter.

CHAPTER THREE

DEMONS, STDs, AND GOD'S HEALING SPERM

INTRODUCTION

Everything went to hell for the Reverend Ted Haggard in fall 2006. Haggard, the senior pastor of the 14,000-member New Life Church in Colorado Springs, was fired from his post after a former prostitute, Mike Jones, accused him of paying for sex on a monthly basis for three years. He also claimed that Haggard used methamphetamines during the liaisons. Haggard, who had fought vigorously for a ban on same-sex marriage in the most recent state elections, at first denied the accusations. But, three months after the story broke, Haggard resigned as president of the National Association of Evangelicals, a group that reportedly represents thirty million born-again Christians. In a public letter to New Life members, he wrote, "The fact is I am guilty of sexual immorality. And I take responsibility for the entire problem. I am a deceiver and a liar....There's a part of my life that is so repulsive and dark that I have been warring against it for all of my adult life."[1]

Religion, sex, drugs, dishonesty: the Ted Haggard scandal had it all. After three weeks of intensive therapy, Haggard declared himself "completely heterosexual" and confirmed that Jones was the only man with whom he had sexual contact. His supporters sympathized with his struggles and admired his long-suffering wife. His opponents delighted in pointing out his hypocrisy and mocked his bold claim to be totally transformed in a matter of three short weeks.[2] Yet, for Haggard and his congregants, there was nothing unusual about it. To those outside the charismatic wing of evangelicalism, warring against a "dark side" provided an apt metaphor for Haggard's psychological turmoil and seedy behavior. For Haggard and his constituents, there was nothing metaphorical about it. The demons of sexual deviance were all too real, dark and repulsive forces he had been battling his entire life. Haggard was ill, and he needed to be restored to spiritual health. In other words, he needed to be "delivered."[3]

In the spirit-filled world of charismatic evangelicalism, sexually transmitted diseases bring science and religion together. The sexual body is a site of spiritual battle, and some evangelicals rely on popular science, especially genetics, for material evidence of that. One extraordinary text, *Holy Sex: God's Purpose and Plan for Our Sexuality*, co-written by Terry Wier and Mark Carruth, contends that sexually transmitted diseases are, in fact, demons lodged in genetic material that can be transferred through body fluids and bloodlines.[4] These claims are extreme and would be rejected by most readers of mainstream evangelical sex manuals. Nevertheless, while *Holy Sex* may be a marginal text, it is not an irrelevant one. It reflects deep-seated anxieties about sexual bodies, spiritual concerns, and disease. Idiosyncratic though it may seem, *Holy Sex* taps into wider concerns among evangelicals about the spiritual vulnerability of the physical body. It also makes the case that scientific knowledge ultimately affirms biblical sexual practices.

SEXUALITY AND SPIRITUAL WARFARE

"Spiritual warfare" has garnered increased attention in the mainstream media in recent years. Perhaps no one has been more prominent in this movement than evangelical pastor Lou Engle, founder of "The Call" and member of the International House of Prayer (IHOP) headquartered in Kansas City, Missouri. Engle is part of what is now termed third-wave Pentecostalism or the New Apostolic Movement. During "The Call" Engle holds 12-hour prayer and fasting rallies throughout the country to cleanse the nation of spiritual demons and to protest abortion and homosexuality. He is perhaps best known for his efforts in Uganda to fight a spiritual war against homosexuality.

This is not, of course, the first time in Christian history that demons have been connected with human sexuality.[5] Diseased and sexually disordered bodies have remained closely connected to both sin and evil throughout the history of Protestantism. Puritans and other early modern Christians, for example, viewed the body as porous and the female sexual body as particularly vulnerable to demonic penetration.[6] Indeed, well into the late twentieth century, many conservative Christians believed that AIDS was God's punishment for sexual sins. Advances in scientific knowledge did not necessarily overturn this perception; in fact, they tended to reinforce it. One needs to look no further than the debate regarding a biological basis of sexual orientation and the search for a "gay gene." For the majority of evangelicals, who vigorously argued that homosexuality is a lifestyle choice, finding a biological basis for homosexuality would undermine their view that heterosexuality is normative and part of God's design.

But for other evangelicals, like the authors of *Holy Sex*, the argument that there is a biological basis for sexual orientation not only explains why people make sinful choices but also provides material evidence that there is something deeply (i.e., genetically) disordered about people who participate in transgressive sex.[7] People cannot help but make sinful choices because there is evil inside of them. In this view, science has not dispelled views regarding sinful sexual bodies and demonic influence, it has confirmed them. Science has provided a new vocabulary and the material evidence to identify evil—it resides in "damaged" chromosomes or in the deep recesses of our brains—that is, in the most fundamental and intimate aspects of our biology. Unlike the spirit-filled bodies that reflect purity through a glowing countenance, demonically infected bodies exhibit warts, pus, and lesions.

The mapping of the human genome has allowed for further research into the causes and cures for genetic disorders and disease, but it also raises troubling ethical and theological questions.[8] One could argue that who you are and how you behave is determined not by your own will but by your genes. Following this logic, the hidden truth of an individual's identity is fixed at the moment of conception and is discernible under a microscope. If a genetic sexual "abnormality" can be explained—but not changed—by science, perhaps religious intervention is in order. Not surprisingly, *Holy Sex* suggests that for some there is a short leap from being genetically "damaged" to being genetically "demonized." The course of treatment in such cases begins with confession and ends with deliverance from demons, as with Ted Haggard.

In order to understand *Holy Sex* within the context of American evangelicalism and in relationship to larger cultural questions about identity and science, we must dig deeper into evangelical sex manuals and deliverance writings, which explain how to save people who are inhabited by demons. Both types of literature tackle the problem of the relationship between spirit and flesh. *Holy Sex* purports to be a book about Christianity and sexuality; it shares some common themes, approaches, and assumptions with mainstream evangelical sex manuals. The focus of *Holy Sex*, however, is not on the joys of marital sex, but on the dangers of transgressive sexuality. *Holy Sex* resembles deliverance writings. Readers learn that the human body (including its genes) provides an arena for the battle between good and evil, which the authors describe and define in sexual terms. The human body can either be filled with the Holy Spirit or defiled by demonic residents. What distinguishes *Holy Sex* from other deliverance writings is its reliance on the research and language of popular science to support its claims. But when it comes to sex and the supernatural, this is just one side of the coin. Sex can put you in contact with demons, but it can also help you commune with the divine.

EVANGELICAL SEX MANUALS: FROM SEXUAL TECHNIQUE TO SPIRITUALIZING SEX

In the past decade, a new group of writers has sought to expand the scope of evangelical sex writing. Authors such as Tim Allen Gardner, *Sacred Sex: A Spiritual Celebration of Oneness in Marriage*, C. J. Mahaney, *Sex, Romance, and the Glory of God*, and Gary and Betsy Ricucci, *Love that Lasts: When Marriage Meets Grace* insist that evangelicals must discover the spiritual component of sex.[9] These authors credit those pioneers who taught born-again Christians to enjoy sexual intercourse within marriage, but worry that too much emphasis has been placed on the physical side of marital love. This is a clear distinction from earlier evangelical sex manuals, which competed with secular manuals in the sexual technique and methods market.[10] Rather than concentrating on proper techniques for sexual satisfaction, this new crop of writers urges spouses to consider the mystical possibilities of marital sex. As Tim Gardner explains in *Sacred Sex*, "Sex really is holy. It's a sacred place shared in the intimacy of marriage. And it's an act of worship, a sacrament of marriage that invites and welcomes the very presence of God. That's the meaning and benefit of holy sex."[11] The purpose of sexuality within marriage becomes, in this view, not only happiness or procreation but also an intimate connection with the divine. Spiritual marital sex always involves three parties—husband, wife, and Holy Spirit—who are joined in a sacred relationship.[12] As Tim Gardner makes plain, "The number-one purpose of sex is neither procreation nor recreation, but *unification*. . . . In other words, the 'Big O' of sex is not orgasm; it's oneness."[13] Just like the Trinity, in holy sex the mysterious occurs: three become one.

One question, however, goes unanswered. If marital intercourse opens participants to the spirit world and grants unity with the divine, what happens during sexual encounters not sanctioned by God? This is where *Holy Sex* comes in. The authors take up the problem of the demonic side of sexuality. In it the authors contend that the human sexual body is the entry point for both the divine and the demonic.

DELIVERANCE LITERATURE: DEMONS AND THE PHYSICAL BODY

Holy Sex discusses "God's original design for the ultimate expression of your sexuality" but does not contain the usual emphasis on sexual positions, techniques, and marital advice. Instead, the book details the spiritual consequences of illicit sexual activity in terms that go far beyond those discussed in mainstream evangelical sex manuals. It is, moreover, written in the context of deliverance literature, yet in *Holy Sex* there is a shift in the construction of demons and their relationship to the body. In early deliverance writings of the 1970s and 1980s, the authors imagine demons as personified vices that are organized in military ranks to assault weakened wills. *Holy Sex* fits in this tradition, but offers a new understanding of demons as insidious, microscopic agents that are transferred through bodily fluids.

Numerous deliverance books, such as Donald Basham's *Deliver Us from Evil*, Frank and Ida Mae Hammond's *Pigs in the Parlor*, Francis MacNutt's *Healing*, Kenneth McAll's *Healing the Family Tree*, Alex W. Konya's *Demons: A Biblically Based Perspective*, and Derek Prince's *They Shall Expel Demons*, outline the spiritual warfare raging between demonic forces and ordinary humans.[14] According to these authors, demonic influence, obsessions, and possession are proven occurrences, and deliverance ministers can provide help for people possessed by demonic spirits. Some writers claim that it is impossible for a true Christian to be harassed by demons; others argue that the faithful are particular targets and great prizes for Satan when they fall. All agree that an invisible war is being waged between the forces of evil and those of good, and humans are caught in the struggle. Merrill F. Unger writes:

> It was my privilege to participate with several other believers in a prayer session on behalf of a young born-again man who was severely troubled by demonic powers harassing him. Only as the demons were faced, forced to give their names, and challenged through the power of God's word and on the basis of Christ's shed blood did it turn out that the vile spirits of lust were the most vexing and, in this case, the most resistant.[15]

Typically in these writings, demons are named for a vice or destructive emotion, such as greed, blasphemy, hatred, abuse, pessimism, jealousy, or any other manner of evil that might enter a believer's body. According to the authors, the demons of lust and sexual perversion present particularly daunting challenges to both the afflicted and the deliverance minister, who may "catch" the problem by close proximity.

Demons of sexual abuse and "perversion" make frequent appearances in the literature.

Deliverance literature published in the United States increased dramatically in the 1970s. According to Michael Cuneo in *American Exorcism*, charismatic deliverance ministry began in earnest in the 1960s, hit a peak in the 1970s, and today remains credible to many Americans.[16] The movement grew alongside of Pentecostalism, which has a long history of connecting healing miracles with exorcism.[17] Protestant charismatics place an emphasis on baptism in the Holy Spirit and the transformative power of God working through them. Charismatics embrace the spiritual gifts of the New Testament such as speaking in tongues and the power to discern the world of spirits that circulate around them. During a deliverance, they often characterize healing the body of infirmities or of addictive behavior as ridding the body of "cancer demons" or "demons of gluttony."

The person generally credited with promoting charismatic deliverance in the United States is Don Brasham who worked as a deliverance minister and wrote a widely read book, *Deliver Us from Evil*. By the 1970s, a number of popular titles circulating among Protestant and Catholic charismatics outlined the basic theology that demons are real supernatural forces that seek to afflict us in our everyday lives. Spirit-baptized Christians were said to be able to discern demons and deliver people from them through prayer and healing. As the authors became better-known, many developed a reputation for being "professional" deliverance ministers. The deliverance authors freely reuse each other's dramatic stories as well as examples from their own pastoral experiences, testifying to the biblical truth of demon affliction—as true today, they claim, as it was in Jesus' time.

Deliverance ministries are hotly contested within evangelicalism. One evangelical writer who is deeply troubled by what he considers a sham writes, "The key to supernatural protection in the invisible war is not found in *exorcising* demons, but in *exercising* spiritual disciplines."[18] Although deliverance writers may represent a marginal group within evangelicalism, American popular interest in deliverance is widespread. Sparked by the 1973 Hollywood hit *The Exorcist* (though the film depicts Catholics, not evangelicals), deliverance gained legitimacy a decade later when psychotherapist and best-selling author of *The Road Less Traveled* M. Scott Peck became a born-again Christian and began chronicling exorcisms that he performed on patients.[19] Cuneo credits Peck's first exorcism book, *People of the Lie*, with "giving exorcism its first real jolt of middle-class respectability."[20] In a 2005 bestseller *Glimpses of the Devil: A Psychiatrist's Personal Accounts of Possession, Exorcism, and Redemption,* a book dedicated to his mentor, the infamous late exorcist and author Malachi Martin, Peck presents the dramatic cases of Jersey and Beccah, two women harassed by demons.[21] Peck insists that although Harvard Medical School trained him to find psychological reasons for ailments, he has come to believe firmly that some maladies are evil in origin and can only be cured by exorcism. In Peck's clinical (and colorful) narrative, the onus of the exorcism is always on the "patient" who must choose not to believe the lies of demons. Even children in impossibly abusive situations are ultimately responsible for their spiritual choices. For Peck, the mind is always the locus for demonic entrance and disturbance.

Many other deliverance writers turned their attention from the mind to the body. Peck's firm belief that mental illness can be the result of demonic influence is closely aligned with the faith healing tradition that calls on Jesus and the Holy Spirit to mend physical and mental "brokenness." Some believers practice healing that connects spiritual malevolence to clinical conditions such as epilepsy, Alzheimer's, and, in at least one case, Autism Spectrum Disorder.[22] Deliverance writer Derek Prince claims to have used his spiritual gifts to heal someone of a "genetic disorder," and another of food allergies, and to have delivered people from demons of epilepsy, blindness, deafness, muteness, and arthritis.[23] In his rendering, a body free of illness and free of quirks (such as lactose intolerance) is a truly spirit-filled body.

Prince is hardly the first deliverance writer to connect physical ailments with evil. Bodily representations of evil and the anthropomorphizing of demons stretches back to the most popular writers of the 1970s. Frank and Ida Mae Hammond's *Pigs in the Parlor: A Practical*

Guide to Deliverance, first published in 1973, remains perhaps one of the most influential deliverance texts among Protestants. The book is a no-nonsense manual for identifying demons, with a step-by-step approach to expunging them. The emphasis is on personal—not professional—deliverance. Throughout the book the authors deploy the common deliverance metaphor of soldiers waging war against spiritual enemies on the front lines. Demons are invaders, battle tactics must be followed, and spiritual weapons must be brandished, so that victory will be achieved when the kingdom of God is saved. The demons are organized in military ranks—soldiers and commanders, with princes and viceroys above them.[24] The title refers to the book's comparison of present-day demons to unclean animals (pigs) under Jewish purity laws. Just as pork defiles the body, so too do demons.[25] Christians who wish to live in purity must cleanse their bodies of unclean spirits to prepare a tidy home for the Holy Spirit. The authors go to great pains to demonstrate that believers need look no further than themselves for the power to overcome demons. Demons, according the Hammonds' reading of Matthew 12:43–45, seek a body "home" in which to reside.[26] And they note that demons speaking through a person during a deliverance often scream: "This is my house!"[27] These spiritual enemies have no right to inhabit a believer's body, which belongs to the Holy Spirit. All believers have the authority, given to the apostles by Jesus in Mark 16:17, to cast out demons.[28] "We today have the same authority and power for ministry that was given to the church initially," the Hammonds proclaim. "This power and the authority of Jesus' name are given that the believer might overcome demon power."[29] Demons, they argue, must be treated as evil trespassers with the wicked intent of building Satan's kingdom one body at a time.

For a demon to enter, a door must be opened. The primary portal for the demon's entrance is a vulnerable or weakened will. This can happen in a number of ways. Any willful sin, such as greed or envy, creates an opening for evil spirits. "When a man yields to temptation he sins in the flesh. Through such sin the door is opened for the invasion of the enemy. Then he has a compounded problem—the flesh and the devil. The solution is two-fold: crucify the flesh and cast out the demons."

Children in unhappy households are especially vulnerable to demon attacks because they are weak and often not spiritually protected by their parents. Additionally, people who are told that they will be just like their unstable parents—either physically, mentally, or emotionally—may become so terrified of this prediction that they unwittingly invite demons to torment them. Frank Hammond relates his own history with the "ruse of inheritance." Many members of his family had died from heart attacks, and a doctor warned him that he likely would develop heart problems. A few years later he suffered two heart attacks. Rather than fall into despair, he enlisted the help of his congregation to heal him of his demon of heart attacks. "That was five years ago," Hammond reports, "and I have never had another pain in my chest and no longer expect to have one. I do not accept the proffered inheritance of the devil but accept the healing and health of the Lord Jesus." Hammond writes that one can have the spiritual gift of discernment (such as experiencing physical pain in the presence of a demon) or one can detect a demon by common symptoms presented in the afflicted person. These physical and psychological symptoms include emotional problems, mental problems, speech problems, sex problems, addictions, physical infirmities, and religious error.[30]

A house (body) filled with the Holy Spirit must keep the doors closed to prevent future demonic intrusion. For the Hammonds, like so many other deliverance practitioners, this is a matter of maintaining a strong will. One of the primary means that the will is weakened is mental illness. Of the many demons that can afflict an individual, the demons of schizophrenia are, according to the Hammonds, the most often misdiagnosed by the medical profession. Ida Mae Hammond received a revelation from God on this subject. According to her account, God directed Ida Mae to draw her hands on a piece of paper and, in a striking resemblance to palmistry, guided her to write the name of specific demons on each finger and the palms of her hands. What Ida Mae discerned is that schizophrenia always begins with the demon of Rejection, and this demon can enter even in the womb. "Schizophrenia," she argues, "can be demonically inherited. Notice I said 'demonically.' By that I mean it is not in the blood system, not in the genes—it is in the demons!"[31]

Either the parent has rejected the child and created an opening for that particular demon, or the mother who has this demon and transfers it through close proximity to the child.[32]

What does *Pigs in the Parlor* have to do with sexuality and salvation? The book provides an important and instructive contrast with *Holy Sex*. The Hammonds contend that demons are not part of a genetic inheritance and demons are not transferred through bloodlines. Demons seek entrance through a weakened or vulnerable personality through the "ruse of inheritance," the fear of inheriting genetic traits, and close proximity to others who are afflicted. Women tend to be transmitters because pregnancy and childrearing bring them in close and constant contact with children whose wills are weak. Unlike the quasi-scientific conclusions offered in *Holy Sex*, the Hammonds vehemently deny that demons are transferred via genetic material.

The spiritual battles depicted in early 1970s deliverance literature made use of conventional warfare metaphors and focused on the will as the main entrance of the body. Thirty years later in *Holy Sex*, the spiritual battle is waged on the physical body itself. The primary avenues for demonic entrance are bodily openings and fluids. The demons are not metaphor; they are literal and assume material form. Other contemporary deliverance writers concur. Derek Prince affirms that there are nine orifices through which a demon might enter and exit the human body. Typically demons evacuate bodies through the mouth accompanied by physical signs such as choking, coughing, and occasionally vomiting. "When a demon is coming out, some people—usually women—may go on screaming without receiving any release. This indicates that the demon has stopped in the narrow section of the throat and is holding on there to avoid being expelled." Elsewhere Prince confirms that demons come through all sorts of bodily thresholds. For example, in one case, the demon of doubt entered a boy through his left ear, while the demon of masturbation frequently enters through pores in the fingers. In *Holy Sex*, however, the primary carrier of demons are bodily fluids, including blood, semen, and saliva. For readers keeping count, women have more bodily openings than men and, therefore, have more opportunities for receiving and expelling bodily fluids. Women are thus "naturally" more susceptible to sexual demons.[33]

Sexual activity, *Holy Sex*, is the principle arena for demonic action. That is not to say that sex is evil. On the contrary, contemporary deliverance authors affirm that God created humans as sexual beings and attest to the sanctity and holiness of intercourse within heterosexual Christian marriage. It is so important that one writer contends, "[w]ithholding of what is due the marriage partner is a perversion of sexuality, sometimes carried out in the mistaken belief that Scripture teaches that sex is for procreation alone."[34] Any sexual activity outside of heterosexual marriage, however, such as homosexuality or adultery, is illicit and creates an open doorway for demons to enter the body. A body that transgresses God's design for sexuality remains vulnerable to the forces of evil. The physical body, therefore, must be protected from demonic intrusion. Deliverance ministers write about prayer coverage, which both shields individuals from demons and supports angels who fight demons. Spiritual armor, put on through faith and prayer, is necessary to protect the body and soul. Most important, these writers emphasize the indwelling of the Holy Spirit to fill up the believer and not allow space for demons to enter the body. Bodies filled with the Holy Spirit are shielded from demonic intrusion because they refrain from unbiblical sex.

HOLY SEX

Holy Sex affirms the existence of sexual demons to illustrate that the born-again body is in grave danger. Even believers who refrain from sinful sexual acts are at risk of demonic contagion. The portals of demonic entrance can be microscopic and demons can be inherited from ancestors and passed down to descendants. Every cell, every chromosome, every ovum, and every sperm is potentially vulnerable to demonic presence that reveals itself through disease. Believers who think they are pure of body and spirit might actually be carriers and transmitters of invisible evil. The only way to protect against demonic sexual disease is to scrutinize each spouse's family trees, to confess your sexual sins and those of your ancestors, and to be sexually reborn in Christ. As the fall of Ted Haggard suggests, even the most ardent believer remains vulnerable to the attack of unseen malevolent forces. The fiercest spiritual battles are waged on sexual bodies, and in the end, everyone is at risk.

Holy Sex is a far cry from the mainstream evangelical sex manuals that engaged the American reading public since the early 1970s. Those books sent a uniform message: Christians can achieve sexual bliss through tried and true sexual techniques. *Holy Sex* warns that sensual fondling and sexual arousal will satisfy only carnal desires.

> Many marriage manuals would recommend at this point that the wife buy a new negligee and the couple learn some new lovemaking techniques. But this is only an effort to keep lust alive for a little while longer. . . . What the couple needs is to learn how to touch each other's spirits during sexual union. Even if they eventually become skilled enough to give each other the ultimate in physical stimulation, they still have not gone "all the way"—to a joining not only of bodies and souls, but also of spirits.

When married Christians "go all the way," unity with the divine is achieved. "Husbands, can you fathom loving God with your spirit as you make love to your wife and enjoying His presence in her, loving you back? Wives, can you receive Jesus as your spiritual Husband, loving you through the body, soul and spirit of the man you married?" Sexual union, the authors explain, joins couples physically, emotionally, and spiritually to each other and to God.[35]

Wier and Carruth, the authors, agree that bodies are created to express love through heterosexual intercourse. But their concern is with the body as a spiritual battlefield, not as a sexual playground. The authors explain that *Holy Sex* is based on the principle of "God's Law of Sexual Union," a biblical guideline to bring humanity in line with God's will for all of creation. To begin with, the authors contrast "God's Law of Sexual Union" with the sexual indulgences that are driven by demonic forces eager to build a "Kingdom of Sexual Perversion." Any sexual act outside of heterosexual marriage is not just contrary to God's will—it is demonic. The stakes are high. Not only does illicit sex endanger an individual's soul; it also counts as a loss in the cosmic struggle between good and evil. Once one has sexual intercourse, he or she is spiritually bound to the partner even if the lovers eventually marry others. Sex is not just a physical act; it is spiritual, emotional, risky, and potentially lasts forever. The eternal tie that binds is sexual intercourse, not marriage.

Demon-free born-again bodies exhibit godliness because the state of the soul is visible on the flesh. The health and purity of the human sexual body—one free of sexual diseases or sexually disordered behavior—reflects the condition of the soul. Like the authors of mainstream evangelical sex manuals, Wier and Carruth borrow heavily from contemporary popular science to prove their points. Unlike earlier manuals that looked to sex experts and sex surveys, these authors refer to public health literature to support their contention that dangerous transmissions travel through illicit sexual intercourse. The authors redefine what public health officials identify as diseases carried through bodily fluids. Wier and Carruth contend that sexual diseases are physical signs written on the body, even lodged sometimes in genes that indicate demonic encounters or affliction. Here religious beliefs are embodied through sexuality, and the spirit is revealed vividly on the flesh. Scientific research and language is used in the service of theological and sexual goals.

The truth of God's laws for sexual purity is born out in both the spiritual and physical realms. Empirical research, according to the authors, proves that orthodox sexuality is safe, natural, and will lead to the continuance of the "fittest" family lines. This is how the authors believe born-again Christians should view their role in furthering the kingdom of God. Not only by preaching to the unsaved but also through the continuance of the purity of godly bloodlines. The born-again physical body becomes a laboratory for the spiritual goal of populating the earth with believers. In fact, the direct relationship between the sexual and the spiritual begins on the microscopic level with the chemistry of sexual attraction. In *Holy Sex*, sexual attraction is a matter of hormones and natural chemicals such as testosterone, pheromones, oxytocin, and endorphins, which surge to produce quantifiable, physical manifestations of desire. All current scientific research, the authors explain, proves that God designed humans with a natural capacity to become physically attracted to their mates. In addition to biologists, the authors rely on psychologists who argue that the first sexual encounter—positive or negative—has a lasting effect, imprinting a model for future sexuality. Biological and social science support God's design for human heterosexual desire and the rules for sexual monogamy. Science simply confirms what evangelicals already know from Scripture.

But sex is not only a matter of biology and psychology. During sexual intercourse, Weir and Carruth explain, a Christian's spirit reaches out and joins with the spirit of one's spouse. If a spirit reaches out to an unclean spirit during sexual intercourse, an attachment to a demonic spirit is possible. Rather than extending the kingdom of God, spirit and body will be defiled. In that case, the unhappy person is now bound to demonic forces eager to build the "Kingdom of Sexual Perversion." In one sexual act a believer's body can be transformed into a tool for Satan, sometimes without the individual realizing the dire spiritual consequences.

DEMONS AND THE SEXUAL BODY

As the material body is transformed into a spiritual battleground, the authors of *Holy Sex* sexualize the language they use to describe the combat between good and evil. This is perhaps the single most striking difference from both the mainstream evangelical sex manuals and older deliverance literature. In the battle to keep the sexual body holy, the authors employ images of insemination and pregnancy to ground their spiritual concerns. The authors claim that God's Holy Spirit is like *holy sperm*. The believer must become *pregnant* with God's spirit. The language is significant because it demonstrates the biology and physicality of the spiritual battle. The Holy Spirit is sexualized and masculinized to impregnate the believer who is in turn feminized. The uncorrupted seminal fluid acts to form a prophylactic shield by creating a state of holy pregnancy.

Holy pregnancy is consistent with a particular interpretation of Scripture. Wier and Carruth point out that the Greek word *sperma* translated as "seed" in many biblical passages is also the Greek word for sperm.[36] The body, the authors contend, is not just a tidy house swept clean for the Holy Spirit (as the Hammonds imagine it); it is a fertile womb that will be filled with either good or evil seed. The porous human sexual body is imagined as female and serves as a gateway for spiritual forces. Yet, both men and women are open to holy insemination or to demonic invasion. Wier and Carruth explain that a sinful sexual union creates fragmented spiritual beings. Illicit sex breaks each person's spirit into pieces, making them vulnerable to demonic intrusion. This, according to the authors, is the true meaning of STDs: sexually transmitted demons. "It seems that sexual sin—more than any other type of sin except occult practices—opens a spiritual doorway, or breaches some type of God-ordained protective barrier, which allows demonic access to the bodies, souls, and even spirits of persons involved."[37] Although evangelicals tend to distrust condoms and ideas of "safe sex," the authors argue that we must rely on spiritual barriers to protect the body. Like condoms, this form of protection is not 100 percent effective. If a body is infected, the only way to exorcize the demons is to be born again in Christ.

Not surprisingly, in *Holy Sex* the notion of "born again" differs from that of mainstream evangelical literature. "Born Again," the authors explain, "is a sexual term." To receive God's cleansing spirit as well as his genetic characteristics, the petitioner must become open to God's healing sperm.

> God's Word is like His *spiritual sperm*. Knowing what we do today about genetics, we could even say that, like the genes carried in the head of a sperm, God's Word carries God's characteristics. So, for you to be "born again," God's Word, His sperm, must be implanted in your heart by the Holy Spirit. If your heart chooses to receive His Word, a new spirit will be birthed within you.[38]

Once spiritual conception occurs, demons will evacuate the body. Here the authors rely on scientific conceptions about the transfer of genetic material at insemination to define "born again." The implanting of God's sperm creates a holy pregnancy, which forms a barrier that shields the body from demons that would otherwise be transmitted through bodily fluids during illicit sexual activity. Sexuality, genetics, and theology are merged. Born again is a sexual term.

In *Holy Sex*, "sexually transmitted demons" are not simply a rhetorical parallel to STDs or an apt metaphor for disease transmission or contagion. The demons are literal beings, they travel through fluid such as blood and semen, they are lodged in genetic material, and their presence is revealed on the flesh by sores and warts and other visible signs. Even when there is no obvious physical sign, a demon might be present. In the same way that sexually transmitted diseases sometimes remain invisible without a microscope and can vary in symptoms, sexually transmitted demons are also invisible to the untrained eye and afflict victims to varying degrees. The authors note:

> Some promiscuous people seem to have quite a number of sexual experiences before becoming infected with a curable sexually transmitted disease. Other less fortunate ones become infected with an incurable STD, such as HIV, during their very first sexual encounter. I have seen a similar range of risk for contracting sexually transmitted demons.[39]

Just as STDs are real and those troubled seek a medical or pharmaceutical cure, demons are real and need to be expelled from the body by a trained deliverance professional. In both cases there is a diagnosis, a plan for procedure, and the prospect of a cure. The body, infected with diseases or demons, reveals the truth of sexual transgression.

The authors of *Holy Sex* seem to realize that their discussion of STDs will alienate some readers. Rather than supporting their views by making reference to other evangelical sex manuals, they instead cite deliverance literature. "So, while the information I am presenting here may be shocking or unbelievable to some, I believe it reflects the current consensus of those ministers who have learned how to deal with the demonically afflicted by using the special abilities or gifts given by the Holy Spirit." For those steeped in the deliverance literature, sexual demons are alive and well.[40]

SPIRIT AND FLESH: GENETICS

The relationship between spiritual warfare and bodily genetics is the most distinctive aspect of *Holy Sex*. It is, however, not unique to that book. The genetic transfer of holiness or evil builds on a growing belief in intergenerational demons among some deliverance writers and practitioners. A few deliverance writers claim that inherited demons are lodged in genes and argue that spiritual health is coded genetically in the same way as physical health. Others, in the tradition of the Hammonds, believe this is part of a "ruse" to scare believers into thinking that they are ill. Many deliverance writers see a direct connection between the immoral behavior of ancestors and the demonic harassment of descendants.[41] Despite these variations, Wier and Carruth's claim that demons are lodged in genetic material is the next step in the evolution of deliverance literature from a weak will to a porous body.

In *Holy Sex* the authors maintain that the best protection against physical and spiritual contamination "[f]or the sake of your children yet to be born" is "to look for a spouse who comes from a godly lineage, someone whose ancestors valued virginity and obeyed God's commandments for sexual purity. Otherwise, you increase your risk of marrying into a disease-ridden family and passing on those diseases to all your descendants."[42] Wier and Carruth draw from missionary and physician Kenneth McAll, who argues in *Healing the Family Tree* that individuals suffer psychological and emotional trauma by being spiritually bound to afflicted people. Based on his years of work with "demonically afflicted people," McAll cautions that "the bondage of the living to the dead, whether to ancestors, to those not related, to still-born, aborted, or miscarried babies, or to those who once inhabited a particular place now occupied by the living, can present considerable difficulties in diagnosis." The most effective strategy for discovering the name and particular problem of the harassing spirit is to draw up a family tree. Somewhere in the ancestral line, a demon is hiding.[43]

Besides genetically inherited demons or direct sexual encounters with demonically infested persons, demons may also enter one's body through handling or viewing any object that is "cursed," such as pornography. Pornographic materials put people at risk because, the authors of *Holy Sex* explain, "[D]emons commonly congregate around these objects and use them as tools to ensnare and control people." Pornography also is dangerous because it degrades sexuality, and it can produce bodily responses, such as orgasm, that physically weaken the body's defenses against demonic intrusion. "[O]rgasm lowers our natural defenses against spiritual invasion. Being in a state of intoxication, where your reasoning power cannot function, is often reported to facilitate demonic invasion." Here the authors echo earlier deliverance literature, which emphasized that a weakened will could be a threshold for the demonic. A weakened sexual body—physically and mentally—provides an entryway for demons.[44]

Born-again Christians who understand the dangers of illicit sex, infected bloodlines, and cursed objects, who keep their bodies and spirits pure, and who follow God's design for human sexuality will be part of God's kingdom. Their healthy bodies reflect their pure spirits, and the erotic joy they experience in sanctioned sexual intercourse unites them with the divine. Those who stray from biblical sexual mandates will become infected with demons and diseases and will pass this evil on to future generations through damaged genetic material. Those unlucky souls will need to undergo a sexual conversion to be reborn spiritually through God's healing sperm.

CONCLUSION

Many scholars have reflected on the close relationship between demons and sexuality in the history of Christianity, from Jesus' dramatic exorcisms in the New Testament, to contemporary apocalyptic fiction that equates sexual deviance with the reign of the Antichrist.[45] Within the context of contemporary deliverance literature, demons of lust, sexual perversion, and adultery seek entry points through the vulnerable sexual body and exhibit on the flesh through the physical signs associated with disease. In the context of mainstream evangelical sex manuals, there is something else to notice. The recent emphasis on STDs points to changing concerns among at least some evangelicals. While it is difficult to say exactly who is buying and reading these books, it seems clear that the authors are writing to an assumed audience different from the mainstream evangelical sex manual readers. The authors' aim is not to instruct Christians in sexual techniques to enhance heterosexual marriage but to demonstrate that marital sex is holy.

Although the premise of *Holy Sex* is the reality of the spiritual world, the book is neither anti-reason nor anti-science. On the contrary, the writers argue that their biblical view of sexuality is consistent with science. To prove the point the authors state, "You will see that everything that modern medical science is discovering about sexuality confirms this principle, and that scientific discoveries support every biblical commandment for proper sexual behavior."[46] Rather than ally with secular sex manuals as mainstream evangelical manuals do, *Holy Sex* positions itself in discussions of public health by suggesting that science and the Bible are in agreement about the transmission of diseases and the significant role of genetics in future generations of holy bodies. Science affirms the truth of the Bible. *Holy Sex* finds support for the spirit world, and specifically demonic activity, through scientific research on sexually transmitted diseases. The truth that demons operate on the human sexual body is outlined in Scripture, demonstrated through science, and visible on the flesh.

In *American Exorcism*, Michael Cuneo argues that the rise of deliverance ministries and literature is due in part to the influence of the American popular entertainment industry, noting that the release in the 1970s of *The Exorcist* and the publication of popular exorcism books coincided with a precipitous rise in American interest in demon deliverance. This fascination with exorcism, he contends, took hold in the post-1960s therapeutic culture that promised quick fixes to any problem and a renewed life free from past addictions, compulsions, abuse, or other demons.[47] Although the belief in demonic possession might, on the surface, appear to be an outdated superstition from the Middle Ages, it makes sense in the modern, rational world where trained professionals work to rid the body of impurities in an effort to effect spiritual transformation. In a therapeutic culture, the emphasis on individual growth through spiritual and physical healing can take many forms. Cleansing the body of toxic impurities and purging spiritual demons are part of a larger therapeutic enterprise of personal transformation. What could be more toxic than a demon?

Deliverance from sexual demons is not as countercultural as it might at first seem. The extreme assertions in *Holy Sex* represent an engagement with a larger cultural discourse regarding the role of genetics in predicting disease and creating identity. The more scientists learn about genetic coding, the more questions arise about the purpose and need for that type of information. How much of a person's behavior, personality, or illness is genetic? Why would some people inherit damaged genetic material while others would not? Is a person's genetic code God's design or is it the devil's work? *Holy Sex* provides concrete answers to those weighty questions. The sexual diseases that result from unbiblical sex are translated into evidence of demonic presence in genetic material. It is unclear whether demonic genes compel an individual toward "ungodly" sexual acts or create sexually diseased genes that are unknowingly transferred to a spouse or children. In either case, evil resides in the invisible but real, empirical world of genetics. The only way to repair demonized genes is through spiritual methods. In *Holy Sex*, science and religion, as well as sexuality and salvation, are intimately linked.

Evangelicals often make the case that in American popular culture the human body is degraded and sexualized at every turn. No one is immune to society's message that sex is only for pleasure and is available to all without rules and with little or no costs. In the evangelical imagination, secular culture teaches people that what you do with your body is ultimately meaningless. *Holy Sex* explains that the Christian sexual body is sacred and symbolic. It is a testimonial site. Religious prescriptions and beliefs are embodied through sexual behavior. The sexual body is an avenue for unity with either the demonic or the divine. The true state of the spirit is revealed through the health of the body, which manifests concrete signs of sexual misconduct, including the transgressions of past generations. The sanctioned activities of the Christian sexual body bring the reward of physical pleasure and create an avenue for communion with the divine. These pure and holy, disease-free, spirit-filled bodies—communing with the divine through biblically sanctioned marital intercourse—will reproduce future generations of believers. According to *Holy Sex*, a spiritual battle for the kingdom of God is being waged in the genetic codes of all people. In a type of spiritual eugenics, demonically damaged genetic family lines will die out as the strong genes of believers, the spiritually "fit," will survive. Spirit and flesh, fully engaged in "godly" sexual acts, will further the kingdom of God.

In this spiritual and physical battle, scientific research affirms sexual truths. It is also employed in the service of theological truths. In the next chapter I will consider a group of evangelicals who uncover the negative side of science, particularly the claims made by doctors and public health officials about female reproduction. Rather than concerning themselves with demons and genetics to further the kingdom of God, these evangelicals seek to repopulate the world for God the old-fashioned way.

CHAPTER FOUR

BE FRUITFUL AND MULTIPLY

In 2002 a young evangelical couple wrote a Christian marriage guide described as "a fresh vision of love, sex, and marriage." The authors claimed "within marriage, the free exchange of bodily fluids is a means of experiencing the grace of God." Sexual intercourse among the saved, in their view, should never involve contraception "but every time a husband and wife come together, they ought to do so in earnest, in an open embrace, withholding nothing from each other—including their fertility." Unlike other evangelical sex manuals, this 144-page book does not advise sexual intercourse for the sake of strengthening a marriage or for keeping a husband from straying far from his wife. On the contrary, "we believe that when a husband and wife have serious reasons to avoid pregnancy, it's better to abstain for a time than to diminish the meaning and mystery of sex." Marital sex is for reproduction. This approach, they argued, is both mystical and biblical. Marital intercourse allows women to realize their role in God's plan for humanity. A key biblical passage for the authors is 1 Timothy 2:12–15. It connects women (unlike men) to Eve's deception and sin. Women are neither permitted to teach nor have authority over men. They "will be saved through childbearing."[1] Salvation for Eve's daughters is achieved through conception.

Open Embrace: A Protestant Couple Rethinks Contraception, co-authored by the husband and wife team Sam and Bethany Torode became an immediate hit among the Protestant anti-contraception crowd.[2] The Torodes promote Natural Family Planning (NFP), tracking female fertility cycles and abstaining from sexual intercourse on high-fertility days, claiming it was the only biblical way to engage in marital sex. Distancing themselves from other evangelicals, the Torodes reject all forms of artificial birth control, especially the Pill, a method that they contend is in fact an abortifacient. Seven years later, after four children, an excommunication, and a divorce from her husband and co-author, Mrs. Torode (now Ms. Patchin) publicly disavowed her former position on biblical sexuality. "It's a theological attack on women," she said, "to always require that abstinence during the time of the wife's peak sexual desire (ovulation) for the entire duration of her fertile life, except for the handful of times when she conceives."[3] While she had been an important voice in the anti-contraception movement, she eventually conceded that condoms interfere with neither marital happiness nor God's plan for humanity.

Open Embrace and similar books provide fascinating examples of marginal evangelical groups that define their views of marital sex not just against "secular" cultural views but, more importantly, against mainstream evangelical views. Specifically, in *Open Embrace*, the Torodes distinguish their convictions about the purpose and practice of marital sex from those of popular evangelical sex manuals (such as the Wheats' and the LaHayes' books) by their rejection of artificial birth control, their insistence that intercourse unencumbered by reproduction is "selfish," and their belief that the history of the use of contraception in the United States is directly linked to the legalization of abortion. Throughout their slim book they contend that a married couple need not seek to conceive each time they have sex, but "by participating in marital relations, they should be indicating their willingness to accept whatever naturally follows; during the fertile times of a woman's cycle, this may include children." One of the purposes of marriage is to raise children, the authors explain. "Any so-called intimacy which is deliberately closed to new life is merely a collaboration in selfishness."[4]

Like mainstream evangelical sex manuals, *Open Embrace* affirms that sexual intercourse is scriptural, created by God, and a unique component of a healthy Christian marriage. But the authors do not focus on techniques for fulfilling sexual desire as a means of cementing a union between husband and wife. The Torodes find fault with these manuals because they are too wedded to secular culture and "some Christians end up elevating pleasure above the procreative and unitive aspect of sex." Referring specifically to the LaHayes and the Wheats, the Torodes challenge their readers to "check out the shelves of most Protestant bookstores—you'll find the books on sexual technique that rival the pages of *Cosmopolitan*." The advice and techniques proffered in these evangelical sex manuals, they argue, promote the values of secular culture rather than providing a biblical response to the culture. Sexual fulfillment, according to the Torodes, should be the happy, God-created result of conjugal sex. But pleasure should not be its main purpose.[5]

The pages of sex manuals for the faithful generally culminate in the promotion and use of artificial birth control for family planning. Writing against this trend the Torodes note that contraception is linked to the cultural pursuit of self-pleasure and "it's no surprise that many of the Christian sex guides, like their secular counterparts, sing praises to the Pill." The Torodes, like other evangelical authors, emphasize the "unitive function" of sex. But while for mainstream evangelicals that means creating a strong bond between spouses through the exclusive practice of physical pleasure, for the Torodes it means the potential of new creation through the union of egg and sperm. "Respect for the one-flesh mystery of marriage gives us serious qualms about the use of contraception." It concerns the Torodes enough that if there are serious reasons (perhaps health) to avoid pregnancy they believe "it's better to abstain for a time than to diminish the meaning and mystery of sex." The Pill, so often prescribed by evangelical sex writers, serves to replace the act of selfless love with mere physical pleasure. This, the Torodes believe, can harm a marriage. "But the pursuit of sexual pleasure apart from the inbuilt procreative aspect of sex can be a major obstacle to a healthy marriage characterized by self-giving love." That approach, the authors claim, will lead to an unhappy—and unbiblical—marriage.[6]

The larger message of *Open Embrace* is that evangelicals should resist the pull of "engaging with culture," especially regarding sexuality.

Biblical marital sex doesn't mean learning how to please your spouse, but remaining open to conception as a continual selfless act of love and sacrifice. This Christ-like act allows evangelicals to demonstrate their holiness through sexual intercourse. This is a view that puts the Torodes at odds with secular culture and mainstream evangelical culture. "Christians should have an entirely different view of life's purpose than the surrounding culture. Ours is a life of sacrifice, to be modeled after Christ's. Both husbands and wives are called to sacrifice their immediate sexual desires for the good of their union; to sacrifice financial success for the sake of welcoming new life; to sacrifice their vocational and personal priorities for the sake of being excellent parents. Our lives are to be poured out for others in love."[7] Significantly, while mainstream evangelical sex manuals argue that evangelicals have the best sex and that sexual pleasure in marriage is a witness to the culture, *Open Embrace* rejects that position and calls evangelicals to turn away from the standards of culture and toward a countercultural position that emphasizes sacrifice rather than pleasure.

Although the Torodes eventually divorced and disavowed their anti-contraception viewpoint, their book is still read among evangelicals who adopt a pro-natalist stance.[8] Pro-natalism, within the evangelical community, is a pro-birth position that promotes child-bearing and parenthood and rejects contraception and abortion. Pro-natalists are particularly focused on the natural—by which they mean biological—and scriptural role of mothers. Their view of motherhood and the larger biblical mandate for wives is closely linked to their views on contraception. Motherhood is a sacred vocation that is given by God through "open" marital intercourse. Nothing should interfere with that God-given role. "If God gives you children, be a mother with your whole mind, soul, and strength. If he has given you the talents to be an engineer, the same thing applies. But I am dubious that he would ever ask us to be fully both at one time."[9] *Open Embrace* acknowledges that women are bright, capable, and able to do all sorts of jobs (including typically male professions such as engineering); they simply should not do that when they have young children. Their biblical role is to be in the home raising their families. Pro-natalists use this argument to define themselves against culture and other evangelicals.

Open Embrace, and other books like it, circulate among conservative Protestant women in loosely affiliated groups that identify with the labels Titus 2 or "Biblical Womanhood."[10] There is no one specific denomination or umbrella group that coordinates groups within this movement. The individuals who blog, write books, run workshops and seminars promoting Biblical Womanhood, or who identify as Titus 2 women, may hold differing theological views and practices. Some tend toward Reform Protestantism others are more charismatic. Titus 2 writers are united around the belief in the inerrancy of Scripture and the effort to define the meaning of biblical womanhood—the view that men are the head of the household and obedience to a husband is ultimately obedience to God's will—in their everyday lives. There is a spectrum among Titus 2 ministries but the majority affirms that married women should fulfill their biblical role through homemaking skills, childrearing, and following their husbands' leadership. This goal typically is portrayed as a countercultural position that is challenging for young wives who have grown up in country that supports feminism. Typically in the Titus 2 movement, men are not characterized as brutes who force women to stay in the home and serve them. Women choose this role. It is the job of older women to teach younger women that true liberation comes from fulfilling their proper biblical roles.[11] Some— but not all—of these groups also oppose contraception. Whether they allow for family planning or not, biblical women position themselves against feminism, which they believe destroys godly families, ruins the lives of women with false promises, sanctions unbiblical sexuality, and promotes a pagan religion.

THE EXCELLENT WIFE

Biblical womanhood is defined by the most visible leaders of Titus 2 as an effort to reclaim women's proper scriptural role of "helpmeet." According to Nancy Leigh DeMoss, older women must teach younger women to serve their husbands and God before all others, and together they will change the world. In her words, it will be "a revolution" (unlike feminism) "that will take place on our knees."[12] Writers like DeMoss find biblical authority and definitions for female submission throughout Scripture.[13] For specifics, however, they focus on Titus 2:3–5. In this letter from the Apostle Paul to Titus, his colleague living in Crete, Paul provides rules for organizing new churches, including the proper roles for Christian men and women. The specific verses state: "Likewise, teach the older women to be reverent in the way they live, not to be slanderers or addicted to much wine, but to teach what is good. Then they can urge the younger women to love their husbands and children, to be self-controlled and pure, to be busy at home, to be kind, and to be subject to their husbands, so that no one will malign the word of God."[4] Besides detailing the qualities of a "good" woman (modest, loves her children, etc.), proponents of biblical womanhood emphasize wifely submission to support the word of God. A Christian wife's willing submission to her husband, they explain, is a unique, daily way of witnessing to Christ.

There are a range of views regarding the meaning and practice of wifely submission based on Titus 2:3–5. Some glorify the Christian homemaker and her ability to provide hospitality. Others instruct women to stay with physically and emotionally abusive husbands— abused women should look to Christ, the divine model for suffering. Still others present an expansive vision of biblical womanhood, explaining that women are created by God to excel at multi-tasking in all areas of life, not simply in homemaking. Monique Mack, the founder of Titus 2 Women's Network, praises a woman's God-given abilities but does not specifically state that women work only in the home.

Women, Wife, Mother, wherever you find yourself in the following pages, you are unique. God masterfully created you with enormous ability. As women we have the ability to effectively function in nearly any arena that we enter. As mothers we have a tremendous ability to multi-task in the greatest sense of the word. As wives, He called us "helper" and enabled us as such to bring a greater capacity to the human relational experience. We are uniquely fashioned to bring a level of fulfillment to those we are connected to. God has duly equipped and enabled us to be triumphant in multiple roles.[14]

Biblical womanhood is a fluid category that can include single, married, and widowed women who may or may not be mothers or homemakers.

Still, the majority of Titus 2 writers believe that women can best fulfill their biblical roles from within the home. Homemaking is a sacred calling. Here again there is a range of opinions regarding women's roles and authority within the household. Some Titus 2 writers affirm that women are in charge of the domestic sphere. A few writers believe that husbands should be in control of all matters in the family, including household management. In her 2009 book *Quiverfull,* Kathleen Joyce notes that "among some purists, it means submitting a list of daily activities to one's husband for approval and following his directions regarding work, going to church, clothing, head covering, and makeup choices, as well as what a wife does with the remainder of her time. Sexually, it means being available at all times for all activities (barring a very limited number of 'ungodly,' 'homosexual' acts)."[15] Despite these range of opinions, all Titus 2 women agree that God created them as distinct from men. Women have unique roles, talents, and obligations to their husbands, children, extended family, other women, as well as to the church. These roles and obligations are given by God and found in Scripture.

Biblical womanhood, according to Titus 2 proponents, offers women a role in Christian missions without leaving the home. Authors such as Martha Peace consider a Christian woman's cheerful submission to her husband's authority as a form of ministry to him and to others.[16] Peace looks to examples of celebrated Christian wives such as Edith Schaeffer, author and wife of Francis Schaeffer, who created a hospitable household and supported her husband even when he made poor decisions for the family.[17] This, according to Peace, was Edith Schaeffer's "accidental" contribution to her husband's ministry. Creating a beautiful home with dutiful children and a happy husband, Peace believes, presents a compelling witness to non-believers. Homemaking becomes a form of missionary work. Lonely and unsaved men need look no further than the honored Christian husband, admired by his wife and children, living in a peaceful, charming home, to find compelling non-theological reasons to accept Christ. Peace and many other writers make clear that this complementarian understanding of spousal roles does not define wives as lesser than husbands. Each simply has distinct roles and obligations within marriage. The husband's is to provide for and guide the family; the wife's to support the husband in all of his endeavors and nurture the children.

Many of the leaders of the Titus 2 movement turn to the life and writings of Edith Schaeffer for inspiration.[18] Edith and Francis Schaeffer were missionaries to Switzerland sent by the Independent Board for Presbyterian Foreign Missions. In 1955 they started L'Abri (meaning "shelter") in their home. Over time the community grew and by the 1970s L'Abri became known as a place for evangelical youth to stay for a few months. There, they engaged in heated discussions about philosophy, theology, art, music, culture, and literature. Francis Schaeffer presided at the center of the community, a charismatic preacher and teacher who desired to meld conservative Protestant doctrine with the history and intellectual concerns of Western culture.

Edith Schaeffer developed a reputation in evangelical circles as an extraordinary hostess who cheerfully cooked and cleaned for countless young adults who backpacked to her house and dropped in for a few months.[19] Schaeffer wrote over a dozen books but the most important for Titus 2 women is her 1971 *Hidden Art*, later retitled *The Hidden Art of Homemaking*.[20] *Hidden Art* provides artistic inspiration for home design using natural and readily available resources (such a pinecones or scraps of material). In her slim book Schaeffer makes a case for the power of beauty and art to enrich a family's life even in small and homespun ways. In her view, the home provided daily opportunities for a woman to express her creativity and love for her family.

Martha Peace is not the only conservative Protestant woman who valorized Edith Schaeffer. In the 1970s and 1980s her thrifty ideas and focus on the beauty of homemaking caught the attention of many Titus 2 women, who have gone on to enthusiastically recommend and cite her book over the years. In his 2011 memoir, her son Frank who left his family's faith writes: "An Edith Schaeffer cult (made up mostly of born-again middle-class white American women) grew up around Mom's books after she began to be published in the late 1960s. I've met countless women who say that they raised their children 'according to Edith Schaeffer.' Of course what they mean is that they raised their children according to the 'Edith Schaeffer' fantasies they encountered in her books."[21] Whether fantasy or reality, Edith Schaeffer's life and writings provide a model of the quintessential Titus 2 woman who is a husband's "helpmeet."

Martha Peace's portrait of a godly wife represents a fairly mainstream evangelical view on gender roles. The theological stance that men and women have distinct roles that "complement" each other in marriage was codified at the Southern Baptist Convention's annual meeting in 1998.[22] The preferred language for the wife's God-given role in Titus 2 literature is "helpmeet." Peace explains, "Basically, we have said that the wife's role is to glorify and submit to her husband. She was created to fulfill her role as 'helper' for her husband. It's easy to see Eve's role, but what about you? How, practically, can you carry out your God-given role?"[23] The key to success and happiness in Christian marriage is for each person to fulfill his or her specific role and respect the unique qualities and distinctions between husband and wife. Trouble begins when either spouse acts outside of their God-given gender role.

On the margins of the Titus 2 spectrum are authors like Debi Pearl. In *Created to Be his Help Meet*, Pearl suggests that even in abusive situations women are called by God to remain with their husbands.[24] She believes that this type of submission is a visible and important testimony to faith. According to Pearl, even the most loathsome husband should be respected and supported. Submission to an awful husband is godly because it is ultimately service to Christ. "If you look at your husband and can't find any reason to want to help him—and I know some of you are married to men like that—then look to Christ and know that it is He who made you to be a help meet. You serve Christ by serving your husband, whether your husband deserves it or not." Pearl urges women to look to all areas—including the tiny details of their lives—to find a reason that they may be the cause of their husband's discontent or failures. "Always remember that the day you stop smiling is the day you stop trying to make your marriage heavenly, and it is the first day leading to your divorce proceedings." Some husbands will act in despicable ways toward their wives. This, however, is not a reason for divorce. A wife should always find ways to improve herself in her husband's eyes and that effort will save her marriage. Marriage always requires sacrifice.[25]

It is tempting to cast Debi Pearl as a radical outlier. For example, the blogger Mary Kassian of "Girls Gone Wise," a blog dedicated to promoting biblical womanhood, characterized Debi Pearl as "fringe and extremist. She certainly is not representative of the modern complementarian movement."[26] But her position is not as far-flung as some proponents of biblical womanhood have argued. John Piper, one of the founders of the Biblical Council on Manhood and Womanhood, author, and Chancellor of Bethlehem College and Seminary, stated in 2009 that women should be able to endure some physical abuse in marriage. "If it's not requiring her to sin but simply hurting her, then I think she endures verbal abuse for a season, and she endures perhaps being smacked one night, and then she seeks help from the church."[27] Piper is clear that simply being hurt does not warrant a woman's refusal to submit to her husband's authority. Women are sometimes called to sacrifice themselves for the sake of their marriage. A wife who finds herself in this situation should call the church, not the police.

THE WAY HOME

All of the Titus 2 literature, whether on the fringe or in the mainstream, decries feminism for attacking God-given gender roles and, therefore, causing the breakdown of biblical womanhood and the proper Christian family. Some of the literature claims that feminism is more than a movement: it is a false religion. For example, almost every chapter of *Biblical Womanhood in the Home* identifies feminism as the greatest threat to biblical womanhood. Feminists spread a false doctrine of equality between men and women. As Susan Hunt explains in her chapter, "How to Raise Feminine Daughters," "the feminist philosophy says that equality means sameness and insists on independence from husbands and family. Now the daughters of those feminists are confused."[28] Feminists' desire for equality, she believes, clouds the reality that men and women have different roles and different needs. Women who believe that they do not need men, she concludes, are confused, lonely, and unhappy. Similarly, Carolyn Mahaney, in her chapter, "Femininity: Developing a Biblical Perspective" writes: "The feminist doctrine of our time upholds the notion that femininity is a matter of cultural conditioning. Many feminists argue that the only essential difference between men and women is our anatomy, but Genesis teaches otherwise."[29] Mahaney argues that, biologically, women have the desire to nurture children, a desire that is fulfilled with the help of a man who can support her.

The contributors to *Biblical Womanhood in the Home* credit Mary Pride as their inspiration.[30] Pride is well-known for her presentations at Titus 2 conferences and workshops, but even more so for her landmark book, *The Way Home: Beyond Feminism, Back to Reality*. First published in 1985, the book and her personal story provide a blueprint for female submission in conservative Christian marriage. The thesis of *The Way Home* is that women must reclaim biblical womanhood by honoring the value of work in the home. Pride argues that Titus 2:3–5 spells out everything a woman needs to know about gender roles. The feminist movement has duped women into thinking that liberation and happiness come from blurring those roles.

Pride identifies two serious problems with feminist equality. First, most evangelical churches have embraced feminism and are therefore subverting biblical principles. Second, "feminism is a totally self-consistent system aimed at rejecting God's role for women." Pride claims that feminism does not simply operate alongside of religion, or inform religious practices and values, it is in and of itself a distinct religion. While she reproaches American culture for endorsing a non-biblical view of womanhood, she reserves her most vehement criticism for those evangelical churches that support feminist goals. "The Christian churches in America had actually paved the way for feminism to succeed, even as preachers orated about the sanctity of motherhood!" She warns that promoting family planning, female ordination, and scheduling church meetings in evenings (during family time) ensures "role obliteration is the coming thing in evangelical, and even fundamentalist, circles." The way to combat this, according to Pride, is for women to reclaim "homeworking" (not simply staying at home) and to call evangelical churches to task for undermining and ultimately devaluing women's biblical roles.[31]

"Homeworking" not only allows women to fulfill their biblical roles, it also provides them with opportunities to build God's kingdom. In the chapter, "Forward to Ministry," Pride argues that nurturing children, serving others, providing hospitality, comforting others, and doing the "dirty work" or chores, are opportunities to evangelize in their homes and to the world. Not surprisingly, Pride valorizes Edith Schaeffer's work at L'Abri as an essential component of her husband's ministry. Schaeffer had not planned to open her home to hundreds of travelers. But, as an accomplished homemaker she proved up to the task. Pride notes, "I feel certain that Mrs. Schaeffer could never have handled the L'Abri ministry if she had not first gone through the midnight feedings, the cooking, the cleaning, and picking up spills with her own children." Her work feeding and cleaning for so many visitors constituted a form of ministry that, Pride believes, "influenced millions of people and led thousands to the Lord." Pride credits Schaeffer's excellent hospitality for keeping people at L'Abri long enough to benefit from Francis's sermons. She writes, "A friend of ours who has been at L'Abri told us seriously that, as he saw it, as many people were brought to the Lord through Mrs. Schaeffer's cinnamon buns as through Dr. Schaeffer's sermons!" (The same anecdote appears in other Titus 2 literature.) Any home cooked meal might be the way to a man's heart, but Schaeffer's cinnamon rolls were the route to his soul.[32]

Edith Schaeffer's example, in Pride's opinion, offers a biblical rebuttal to the call for female ordination. Creating a Christian home and submitting to the leadership of a Christian husband is a scripturally sound form of female witnessing to the world. In fact, Pride believes that it is a loftier goal than preaching. "Those agitating for ordination for women are throwing away with both hands the biggest ministry we could ever have in favor of a mere second-rate shadow." The Schaeffers proved that a successful ministry relies on the proper roles for husband and wife. Female ordination, from Pride's perspective, is both unbiblical and unworthy of the efforts of true Christian women. "I am going to show how homeworking and being subject to your husband combine to form a fantastic ministry. Why arm-wrestle a preacher for his pulpit when you can have a *church in your home?*" (emphasis in the original).[33]

Pride's authority comes from personal experience. Before her marriage and conversion to conservative Christianity she pursued an engineering career and called herself a "radical feminist." She read Mary Daly, attended feminist conferences, and identified with the struggle of female professionals. She is an apostate from feminism and draws on insider knowledge. Feminism, she says, is a big con game. It does not empower women. It offers the false promise that women can attain happiness and security on their own, without men. This "con game" leaves women vulnerable and depressed. In essence, she argues that feminism, with its "anti-natal" ideas, denies women's unique biological roles as mothers. It has promoted a form of gender equality based on crass career aspirations and the rejection of the inherent differences between men and women. This approach, she argues, leads to depression, divorce, social anarchy, and the worship of a "false religion." Her greatest disdain, however, is reserved for evangelicals who she asserts have abandoned inerrancy and promoted "modern" roles for women, especially evangelical women who call themselves "biblical feminists." Pride insists that "biblical feminists" are a tremendous threat to Christian families and cause societal deterioration.[34]

Pride's point is the evangelical engagement with culture that fosters feminism in the churches deeply affects women's abilities to live up to their biblical roles as defined through Scripture. One topic particularly vexing to Pride is the evangelical promotion of sex for pleasure. In her chapter "The Joy of Unkinky Sex," Pride mocks well-known evangelical sex authors discussed earlier for highlighting sexual pleasure at the expense of childbearing and unity within marriage. "We now have our own breed of evangelical sexperts whose advice reads like a watered-down version of the original pagan sex manuals." She takes a swipe at Marabel Morgan mocking an imaginary Christian couple, Harry and Sally, who were sent to an "intimacy workshop" by a Christian psychiatrist. At the workshop the couple learned about sexual problems they didn't know they had, and when the wife tried out an infamous technique suggested in Morgan's book to arouse her spouse, it ended in her humiliation. "And when Sally came to the door dressed in Saran Wrap, as she tearfully told the psychiatrist, 'Harry just laughed at me.'" Male Christian psychiatrists and self-proclaimed sex experts rely too heavily on secular views of sexuality that cater to men's base sexual desires. According to Pride, these views degrade women, are unbiblical, and ultimately lead to marital disaster.[35]

Pride argues that the secular emphasis on igniting desire in your spouse will eventually lead men to turn away from their wives, in some cases toward "perversion." In a reference most likely aimed at Marabel Morgan she explains this progression.[36] "Fallen human nature enjoys perversion. Therefore, Christian women who dress up like prostitutes in various kinky ways to excite their husbands need to seriously consider what they are trying to do. Do you want to train your husband to respond sexually to kinky dress, or to you?" Where, she asks, will the husband look next when the wife no longer excites him? Similar to her scorn for evangelicals' embrace of feminism, Pride contends that the promotion of secular sexual values within Christian marriage will lead to an attack on the family and female biblical roles.[37]

How ludicrous it seems for grown men and women, parents of children to scuff through sex manuals in search of kinky new kicks. But the implications are actually very serious. The new evangelical perspective on sex is an unwitting denial of God's basic plan for marriage and leads directly into role obliteration. The couple hopping into bed with a sex manual in one hand and a pen and pad of paper in the other may not be aware of it, but in the very middle of their most united experience the root of their marriage is being attacked.[38]

Pride stresses that evangelicals should ignore sex manuals in favor of the Bible—and only the PG parts. Rather than focus on the Song of Solomon, she emphasizes instead Genesis 1:28, "God blessed them and said to them, 'Be fruitful and increase in number; fill the earth and subdue it.'" Pride points out that the first humans were created in God's image as distinct male and female beings and were commanded to produce offspring. That is the biblical purpose of sex within marriage.

Books like *The Way Home* directly challenge secular and mainstream evangelical culture's views of sexuality in three distinct ways. First, helpmeet literature disconnects marriage from romance and sex for pleasure. Second, helpmeet literature argues that that older women are responsible for imparting sexual knowledge to younger women. Finally, helpmeet literature instructs wives to submit sexually to their husbands.

NO PRINCE CHARMING

The writers of helpmeet literature make no fairy-tale promises. They do not claim that women who practice purity and wait for a godly husband will eventually find Prince Charming. Nor is there an emphasis on God sending the perfect spouse. On the contrary, many writers devote their attention to discussing the difficulties and importance of submission to disagreeable spouses. What is at stake for most of the writers is not prosperity or utilizing each spouse's talents to help the family thrive. Rather, the goal is for each spouse to maintain their scriptural gender role despite disharmony or hardship. The working assumption is that the majority of husbands are difficult. Nonetheless, wives must submit to them to receive their eternal reward. Many writers highlight episodes of betrayal and disappointment in their own marriages as examples of opportunities for women to submit to unlikeable husbands as a demonstration of submission to God.

One problem often addressed in this literature is the unhappy predicament of having a husband who is incapable of competent leadership. When faced with such a situation, wives who can do better may be tempted to assume control. This is unacceptable precisely because it causes women to step out of their God-given roles. This rule holds true even when a husband's actions might lead to financial ruin and a wife is fully capable of correcting the problem. As Debi Pearl explains, "If you successfully do the job of leading the family, you will not find satisfaction in it. *It is far better that the job be done poorly by your husband than to be done well by you*" (emphasis in the original). Similarly, Martha Peace writes: "You may be smarter, wiser, or more gifted than your husband, but you are still to respect the position God has given him. You are like the soldier who stands at attention, salutes, and says, 'Yes Sir!' to his superior officers." The men in this literature are rarely portrayed as noble princes who have valiantly saved virtuous princesses from distress and embarked on a fairy-tale life together. They are fallible and sometimes loathsome men whose God-given role is to lead the family. The question for the writers is not whether women are intelligent or capable, but whether they will submit voluntarily to their husbands even under trying circumstances. Their willingness to fulfill that biblical role is a daily demonstration of their faith in God and an example to others.[39]

Helpmeet authors explain that, contrary to purity literature discussed in chapter 1, the notion of a fairy-tale marriage with Prince Charming is not biblical. The desire to have a romantic husband who seeks to fulfill his wife's dreams, they explain, is the product of secular culture that creates false expectations and leads to marital ruin. Any wife who expects Prince Charming is holding her husband to an impossible standard. It is also a view of marriage that does not prioritize sacrifice. Mary Pride argues that evangelicals have mistakenly emphasized companionship, sexual intimacy, and equality as the cornerstones of a successful Christian marriage. By publishing fairy-tale books about virgins waiting for God to send Prince Charming or, on the other side of the spectrum, promoting ideas of equality in marriage, evangelicals have bought into a warped secular view of marriage that leaves both spouses confused and unhappy. Marriage is not a fairy tale.

One need not look any further than the first book of the Bible for proof that marriage requires women to work for men. Pride points out that seeking equality and romance in godly marriage is a misinterpretation of Genesis 2:18, where God creates Eve to be a companion to Adam. "This analysis may sound good, but it directly contradicts the Bible passage....God did say, 'It is not good for the man to be alone,' but the *reason* he gave was that Adam needed a helper. God could have given Adam a *dog* if all Adam needed was a companion. God could have given Adam *another man* if companionship was all Adam needed." Similarly, romance and sexual satisfaction are not strong foundations for Christian marriage. Pride notes "Jacob and Isaac's lives with their wives were not all romance. In fact, Jacob stayed married to Leah, whom he disliked quite strongly, until she died." Sexual intimacy and romance are possible in Christian marriage, but as Pride summarizes: "Romance is the blossom on the flower of marriage, not the root. It is beautiful, it is a gift of God, but marriage *can* survive without it." Ultimately, she explains, any attempt to turn a perfectly good Christian marriage into a romantic marriage will end in divorce. The reason is that the desire for romance is selfish and shifts the couple's focus from their shared interests (children, home, etc.) to personal satisfaction. Pride is troubled by so-called companion marriages promoted by "biblical feminists" who share all of the financial and household duties with their spouses. She terms this type of relationship the "contract theory of marriage." Couples who strive for equality and romance in marriage will fail, according to Pride, because those efforts are selfish and unbiblical.[40]

What is the purpose of Christian marriage? According to Pride, "the biblical reason for marriage is to produce fruit for God. Marriage is to produce children, and to make the earth fruitful for God. Christian marriage, in other words, is God-centered (producing what God wants) rather than me-or us-centered (meeting my or our desires)."[41] The love of marriage, she continues, is a "brotherly" love; it is a type of love based on reason, not emotion. While children are the fruit of marriage, Pride concedes that they are a hindrance to romance. Other evangelical sex and marriage manuals discuss practical ways for couples to find alone time and rekindle passion that was presumably lit prior to their having children. In Pride's view, romantic love is neither necessary nor a priority for a healthy marriage. The goal of marriage is for the husband and the wife to find happiness by fulfilling their distinct roles in the important work of raising godly children to populate the kingdom of God.

FEMALE KNOWLEDGE

One of the purposes of Titus 2 ministries is to highlight the biblical mandate for older women to instruct younger ones. This is contrary to mainstream evangelical writers' reliance on secular male "experts" in matters of female anatomy, sexuality, childrearing, and gender roles. Some Titus 2 authors are contemptuous of those authorized by secular standards such as PhDs. In many cases, these misguided male experts are held responsible for female unhappiness in marriage, for providing inaccurate information, and for promoting gender role confusion. Debi Pearl, in *Created to Be His Help Meet,* insists that only older women can instruct younger women in their biblical gender roles. "God commands older women to teach the younger women the wonders of wifehood." Similarly, Mary Pride emphasizes, "God says the younger women should get their training from older women, not PhDs (Titus 2:4). Could it be that we *mothers* are the real experts on mothering?" Pride argues that the best way to decide who should train women, especially as mothers, is to look at the evidence of their households and their children. "Does an older woman have godly children? Well then, we can listen to her with a good degree of confidence. The returns are in. Whatever she did, at least it didn't hurt. Since she is just a wife and mother like us, we won't be overawed into taking her teachings as gospel without testing them against the Bible. She is not only a *teacher*, but a *model*." This is an indictment not just of secular culture but also of the evangelical psychologists and counselors such as Dr. James Dobson, who created "Focus on the Family" to dispense advice on all aspects of family life including childrearing, motherhood, sexuality, and marital counseling. "There are many books written by men, 'scholars' that undermine the beauty of a woman's help meet position. They do so by casting doubt on the Bible itself. They talk in elaborate and 'learned' terms about 'the original languages' and the 'cultural settings' in which the words of Scripture were written." According to Pride, Pearl, and others, this contradicts the inerrant and obvious meaning of Titus 2, that women are biblically commanded to instruct other women.[42]

Advice from older women is not limited to the topics of godly behavior or childrearing. Older women should provide sexual advice as well. The popular Titus 2 blog "Warrior Wives" promotes this view, departing from other helpmeet literature by welcoming advice on sexual techniques and practices. Often this advice is solicited from older women. For example, an advice column called "The Future of Sex: Advice from an Older Woman" warns young wives not to "idolize" sex but to create emotional connections with their husbands. Although this approach might go too far for Mary Pride, the author takes seriously the need for some Titus 2 women to welcome sex in marriage. She provides helpful tips for sexual satisfaction as women age, including drinking water for vaginal lubrication, engaging in foreplay, "and if your husband hasn't learned what a clitoris is, now is the time." Younger women are encouraged to learn about their sexual anatomy to help them gain or maintain sexual desire for their husbands. The implicit assumption is that wives are obligated to have sex in marriage. The problem addressed is the reality that many women seek to avoid it. Advice from older women who have found themselves in similar circumstances can prove useful.

But this is not an evangelical version of *Our Bodies, Our Selves*. The goal is not female sexual empowerment. When dispensing advice to young wives, the author highlights male sexual concerns. "I think the most important thing I'd want younger women to know is that the issues of erectile dysfunction or whatever are extremely sensitive and a wife should be very careful about whom she confides in. She needs to be patient and loving."[43] Another guest column written by "Pearl," of "Pearl's Oysterbed," also emphasizes female sexual awareness (find your clitoris) and the power of sexual intimacy in long marriages.[44] "If I'd only known in the early years how wonderful a *consistent* sex life is for marriage! I hope this empowers you beautiful readers. You probably already have a good thing with your mister, but you can have an incredible marriage and family as a by-product of consistent sexual intimacy."[45] Wives need sexual knowledge to learn to desire their husbands. Because they are required to satisfy their husbands' sexual needs, it makes sense to help them find ways to enjoy that responsibility. A cheerful wife and a sexually satisfied husband will ensure a happy biblical marriage.

Sex is a marital obligation. For warrior wives who just don't feel like having sex with their husbands, the site's main blogger encourages women to submit to their husbands' sexual needs and provides some advice from the early, rocky years of her marriage. "You can pray that God will bless your 'sex session'. You can pray that he would bring the desire to you. I can testify to that. I've sometimes felt like, *I just can't do this. This isn't going to be enjoyable. I REALLY DON'T WANT TO!!!!* And then I've quieted my spirit and prayed. God wants sex to be good! He made it for our enjoyment! He made it to strengthen marriage!"[46] Unlike other evangelical sex manuals, the message in this advice column is that although God wants marital sex to be good, even when it is bad, this author (and many other proponents of biblical womanhood) insists you should do it anyway. Practicing submission in all aspects of her marriage, especially in sex, has made her a warrior wife and brought her closer to her husband and to God.

SEXUAL MINISTRY

Of all of the admonitions given in helpmeet literature, the most countercultural and challenging to mainstream evangelical sensibilities is undoubtedly the mandate of sexual submission to one's husband. If Prince Charming never arrived, if the husband turns out to be a detestable oaf who is bringing the family to financial or emotional ruin, there is little recourse. The wife's primary obligation remains to serve her husband in all ways, especially sexually.

In the most conservative helpmeet literature, sexual submission is non-negotiable. Martha Peace contends, "God's will for every Christian wife is that her most important ministry be to her husband (Gen 2:18). After a wife's own personal relationship with the Lord Jesus Christ, nothing else should have greater priority."[47] This ministry includes sexual requirements that must be met by the wife regardless of her feelings about either sex or her spouse. Debi Pearl captures the ministering side of sexuality: "It is your duty to fulfill his sexual needs. His faithful responsibility to you, and yours to him are both equally important, and we wives must give an account before God for our faithfulness in this area. I call it 'ministering' to my husband. He says I am a mighty fine minister."[48] Frequent sexual ministering, in Pearl's view, is a way for wives to practice faithfulness to Christ.

The reason that women should have frequent and cheerful sex with their husbands, the helpmeet writers explain, is that men are created by God with the need to have their sex drives fulfilled. Women, on the other hand, are designed specifically to satisfy their husbands' sexual needs. It is a sin against God and disruptive to the community when a wife refuses to satisfy her husband. "God created man with a regular need for a woman, and God commanded the man's wife to see to it that his need is met. Do yourself and everyone else a favor, and devote at least 15 minutes every few days to *totally* pleasing your man."[49] Pearl insists that it does not matter if the wife is uninterested in sex—what matters is meeting the husband's physical needs.

Sex is a tangible way for a wife to show her love and submission to her husband. "No woman really loves her husband if she does not please him in this most important area seek to. If you are not interested in sex, then at least be interested in him enough to give *him* good sex....Hopefully you just didn't realize that your lack of sexual interest in your husband was a sin, but now you know. . . . God grants the marriage partner full access to his spouse's body for sexual gratification. And remember, indifference is unwillingness." A reluctant wife is equivalent to a sinful, disobedient wife. Rather than complaining that her marriage is sexually unsatisfying or lacks romance, a wife should focus on this unique form of ministry that she alone can perform. "But if a woman views sex as a ministry to her husband, then it is a selfless act of benevolence. She need not wait until she is stimulated

to desire eroticism; she need only seek to fulfill her husband's needs."
Wifely sexual submission and good housekeeping are in fact the only
legitimate forms of female ministry to men.[50]

Frank Schaeffer relates in his memoir that his mother, Edith, was
open about sexually submitting to her husband every night of their
long marriage. Schaeffer recalls an off-the-cuff conversation with his
mother after reading a Bible story at bedtime. "Your father demands
sexual intercourse *every single night* and has since the day we married."
His mother explained that she did not want to give the false impression
that she disliked sex with his father, "It's just that because Fran has a
Daily Need, I have to go with him on *every single speaking trip*. I hate
leaving you alone so often, even in a good cause." In this confession,
Edith admits to prioritizing her sexual responsibility to her husband
over her motherly responsibility to her son. Francis is apparently not
responsible for what he might do to satisfy his daily sexual needs if he
is left alone for one night.[51]

Titus 2 women would recognize this sexual sacrifice as the wife's
duty, but Edith Schaeffer did not embrace their rejection of birth control. Sexually satisfying her husband did not mean ignoring the risk of
pregnancy. Frank describes his mother as faithfully using a diaphragm
(and sharing that information with him) and often expressing pity for
Catholics living in the darkness because of theological error and lack
of family planning.[52] This was before her husband, Francis, made his
famous call for all conservative Christians (including Catholics) to
unite in "co-belligerency" to fight the legalization of abortion.

This was also before the rise of Mary Pride as a conservative
evangelical spokesperson for homemaking, homeschooling, and raising large numbers of children. Frank claims that Pride ridiculed his
mother's well-known advice about dressing provocatively for one's
husband. Pride also denounced Edith's stance on contraception. After
reading *The Way Home*, a book Frank helped to publish, Frank reports
his mother's response to Pride: "Where on earth did you dig up This
Unfortunate Woman?"[53] In many respects Edith Schaeffer serves as
a model of Christian submission in marriage. But, her firm embrace
of family planning is overlooked in the glowing references to her in

"helpmeet" literature. Rather, among the most conservative writers, the Titus 2 ideal remains to refuse all forms of contraception and thus demonstrate the rejection of secular and lukewarm Christian values.

PRO-NATALISTS: A FULL QUIVER

The most visible pro-natal, conservative evangelical group that emphasizes large families and strict biblical gender roles is the Quiverfull Movement, a subsection of what is sometimes referred to as the Christian Patriarchy Movement. Quiverfull families take their name from Psalm 127:3–5 "Children are a heritage from the LORD, offspring a reward from him. Like arrows in the hands of a warrior are children born in one's youth. Blessed is the man whose quiver is full of them. They will not be put to shame when they contend with their opponents in court." Children are understood to be a blessing bestowed by God on believing parents. The primary goal of marriage is to receive this blessing. Quiverfull parents raise large families, attend small fundamentalist churches or home churches, follow biblical guidelines for male headship of families, and homeschool their children.[54]

Quiverfull families resist many secular American norms, especially regarding family size. But while they reject secular values, they have not retreated from American culture. On the contrary, they seek to transform it. They advocate evangelizing the world by raising large numbers of conservative Christian children ("arrows") who will have an impact on the future demographics and politics of the nation. Birthing children is a concrete way to build the kingdom of God. "A family raising three of four children to follow Christ can have a great impact for Him. But what about a family raising nine for his glory? Let's consider this—by having more children we can actually be contributing to world evangelism."[55] According to Quiverfull literature, Christian parents who limit the number of children they have are, whether they know it or not, helping Satan.

It's a numbers game. The secular acceptance of contraception is evil because it decreases the number of godly children who will do battle for Christ. Members of the Quiverfull Movement insist that God is responsible for determining the number of pregnancies in families and any interference with conception is both selfish and contrary to God's will.[56] Contraception, according to Quiverfull writers, is more detrimental to building God's kingdom than abortion because it limits the possibility of conception every month. "If the Christian Church had not listened to the humanistic lies of the enemy and limited their families, the army of God would be more powerful in this endtime hour. The enemy's camp would be trembling. Instead they are laughing. Has contraception limited the army of God even more effectively than abortion?"[57] Contraception, in their view, is one of Satan's most effective weapons.

The rejection of any method of birth control is based on the belief that it interferes with God's authority and constitutes a form of abortion. This is in contrast to mainstream evangelicals who embraced family planning in the 1960s. Quiverfull women are instructed that they should always be sexually available to their husbands and that reproduction should remain the focus of sexual intercourse. What sets the Quiverfull writers apart from other Protestant pro-natalists (like the Torodes mentioned at the beginning of this chapter), is their assertion that the offspring of godly sexual encounters are intended to build God's army on earth. "We must always strive to remember that we are not really at home here. We are at war. Now recall that one of the terms God uses for children is 'arrows.' The arrows of a warrior are not used for rototilling, kneading dough, or meteorology—they are weapons of war."[58] In Quiverfull writings, women warriors sacrifice their physical bodies through continual reproduction in order to bring about the kingdom of God.[59] Not only are women saved through childbearing, but the kingdom of God will be saved as well.

While many Titus 2 women take a pro-natalist stance, the Quiverfull Movement holds radical views on women's roles and sexuality. For them, any type of contraception—especially the Pill, but also including IUDs and barrier methods such as condoms and diaphragms—constitutes a type of abortion. Some of these methods, they argue, are not simply obstructing conception but are aborting a fertilized egg every time they are used during ovulation. According to Quiverfull writers, many Christian parents are ignorant of this fact: "[m]any Christians are unaware that they are not only engaging in an unbiblical practice of preventing 'blessings,' but that some of the very practices they embrace have abortifacient consequences. How sad to think that someday we will get to Heaven and learn of untold millions of children that were inadvertently aborted by their Christian parents—all because of a lack of faith and ignorance." The anti-contraception rhetoric in some of the literature reaches extreme levels. In *Be Fruitful and Multiply*, for example, the author compares contraception to genocide. "In short, the death toll from the IUD and the Pill exceeds that of the Nazi Holocaust—each year—in the United States alone."[60]

Pro-natalists also oppose "sinful" surgical procedures such as tubal ligations and vasectomies, claiming they are not only ungodly they are also unhealthy. Rachel Scott explains that, besides inhibiting pregnancy, these two surgical procedures can pose serious health risks and cause emotional pain. For example, vasectomies, according to Scott, "bring forth great physical pain, decrease your libido or sexual pleasure, mess up your immune system, get in the way of raising your own children, and even prevent you from ever meeting or enjoying your grandchildren!" Scott recommends that couples who regret these procedures should seek a reversal through surgery or supernatural intervention. In either case, the first step to healing is repentance. "When a couple recognizes that they have sinned by trying to control this area and then attempts a reversal, it is important that they go through steps of repentance." Healing in the area of reproduction is available to those who seek God's forgiveness and believe in the possibility of restored health. Scott reminds her readers that God wants to heal all forms of infertility. "God loves the barren and wants them to be able to have the children that He desires for them to have. He wants to see husbands and wives made complete again and He wants to restore what the enemy has stolen from them through sterilizations, the pill, the IUD, and miscarriages." Although Scott affirms that barrenness is a curse from God and sterilization is a sin against God, both states of infertility can be reversed through the process of repentance and divine intervention.[61]

Unlike the Torodes, who promoted Natural Family Planning (NFP), Quiverfull writers reject any effort to place human control over reproduction. "When a couple realizes God's true part in conception, along with other truths for the Word, they realize that NFP is simple needless tinkering with a system He already controls lock, stock, and baby."[62] Quiverfull writers also take NFP to task for refusing women the experience of being sexually active during ovulation, a time in the female cycle when they believe women are most desirous of sex. "I believe we must be honest that NFP is not completely 'natural.' First, it denies the wife the intimacy she would naturally desire with her husband. Second, it is a deliberate attempt to thwart God's natural design for intimacy in which the potential for life and the act of love are mutually inextricable throughout the fertile season of a woman's life. For these reasons we must conclude that NFP contradicts God's natural order for divine creation and His stated will that we be fruitful and multiply."[63] Craig Houghton, author of *Family UNplanning,* agrees with this position. "NFP is hardly natural if we use it to circumvent the reproductive system that the LORD has put into place. The most natural thing to do would be to let Nature take its course, and once again allow God to be sovereign in this area of our lives."[64]

Two of the most cited and authoritative books in the movement are *A Full Quiver: Family Planning and the Lordship of Christ* by Rick and Jan Hess, and Nancy Campbell's *Be Fruitful and Multiply: What the Bible Says about Having Children.* The Hesses argue that there is no scriptural evidence that supports contraception. On the contrary, they highlight scriptural passages that demonstrate God's power to confer or withhold the "blessing" of children. Similarly, they claim that there is no strictly biological evidence for infertility. For example, the Hesses refer to Hannah's barrenness in 1 Samuel 1:6 and provide their interpretation. "God did not say that Hannah was barren because she had a tipped uterus, blocked Fallopian tubes, endometriosis, or irregular periods. The Great Physician proclaims quite matter-of-factly His diagnosis of the cause of barrenness. He had closed her womb; i.e., He was not giving conception."[65] The theme that God chooses to "open" and "close" wombs continues throughout their book and is used to explain infertility in most Quiverfull literature. In *Be Fruitful and Multiply*, Nancy Campbell cites several passages to support her belief that barrenness is a curse from God.[66] "In the Word of God, fruitfulness of the womb is always considered a blessing. Barrenness was considered a curse, a shame and a disgrace. God's blessing on His people was multiplication. When they sinned and He had to bring judgment, it was usually by thinning their numbers."[67] Why, she asks, would any woman choose this disgrace through contraception, hysterectomies, or even waiting too long to have children? Ultimately, a couple's effort to control conception is futile because God determines the number of children for each family. A righteous family will accept God's authority in this matter and welcome as many children as God provides.

One of the tragic failings of the contemporary Christian church, according to Quiverfull writings, is the acceptance of family planning. "Our world is being deceived by its ruler, Satan, into thinking that children are a threat or at best a horrible inconvenience. Even the church is being led astray by those who adulterate or handle dishonestly the Word of God." The Hesses believe that more evangelicals would adopt their pro-natalist position if they had not been scared away by the anti-baby propaganda of secular culture, propaganda that is echoed in mainstream evangelical churches. Fears of overpopulation, depletion of natural resources, food shortages, they argue, rely on questionable facts and skewed research. Similarly, the Hesses note that one of the most common fears they hear is the cost of raising multiple children. Concerns regarding the expense of children, they explain, are ultimately God's responsibility and not parents'. "Do we really believe that we provide for our children? We cannot in our own strength even provide for our own needs today. No father is the sole provider for his family, without God. That would be a most unbiblical position and that is why Jesus taught us to pray for the provision of our daily needs in Matthew 6:11, 'Give us this day our daily bread.'" The acceptance of a large family is neither a sign of personal achievement nor material abundance. It is a visible act of faith.[68]

An unwillingness to trust God and receive children as blessings has far-reaching implications. "A bad attitude towards children brings a curse. A miserly attitude towards children makes God miserly towards us. But an openhearted, generous desire for and appreciation of children as God's gifts inclines God to trust us with many *more* good gifts—gifts that we have not even seen for over 150 years now and can scarcely imagine."[69] The choice to trust God will not only bring temporal blessings but will have future—and ultimately eternal—consequences. As Nancy Campbell explains: "To bear children is to lay up a treasure in heaven. God is not only interested in populating earth, but in populating eternity. Parenthood has eternal rewards."[70]

The biggest immediate threat to large, godly families is the medical health professions. In this literature, medical science and public health initiatives are blamed for transforming myths about pregnancy into facts. Sadly, according to the Hesses, most American evangelicals have embraced these myths. Two cultural "myths" that the Hesses dismiss are the fear of health risks stemming from multiple births and pregnancies at advanced ages. In general, they dispute the notion that any pregnancy should be labeled "high risk." Pregnancy is natural and, in their opinion, rarely risky for women. The term "high risk pregnancy," they contend, is the product of a generation of OB/GYNs who have been fooled by inaccurate studies that begin with the mistaken premise that pregnancy is an illness. The Hesses suggest that the best course of action for any pregnancy is for the family to employ a midwife. Rachel Scott agrees, noting that midwives are legitimate because they are mentioned in the Bible (Gen. 35:17) and they take a more "natural" approach to childbirth rather than relying on epidurals and C-sections administered in hospitals.[71] Not everyone has access to a midwife. If enlisting the help of a midwife is not possible, the family ought to find a doctor who is pro-life, who has many children, and "though we would not make it an absolute criterion, how good it would be if he patterned his practice after the Great Physician."[72] Presumably a midwife or an approved doctor would be less likely to focus on the potential risks of pregnancy to the mother.

Quiverfull writers emphasize that pregnancy is a natural state for women. Therefore, if the woman is living according to God's commandments, pregnancy, even at an advanced age, carries little risk. Contraception, on the other hand, is very harmful to women's and men's health. Rachel Scott believes that if people were better informed of the health risks, they would be less likely to use contraception. "The pill, the IUD, birth control injections, sterilizations, and so on have been linked to such health problems as every form of reproductive cancer, heavy menstrual bleeding, emotional hysteria, weight gain, headaches, mood swings, autoimmune diseases, heart disease, blood clots, and even death." Furthermore, birth control, she argues, has created new complications during menopause. Women in biblical times, Scott explains, were shielded from difficulties during menopause because their reproductive organs had been so well exercised throughout their lives. "Scripture does not speak of women who had these kinds of complications. The Bible speaks of menopausal women in a peaceful way. In fact if these types of problems were occurring to the masses like they are today, wouldn't the Bible have mentioned at least one menopausal complication?"[73] All female reproductive health concerns appear to be the product of contraception, sin, or both.[74]

The second cultural myth that the Hesses seek to disprove is that women who get pregnant when they are older are risking their own health and their babies'. The Hesses and others are careful to assert that pregnancy is healthy for women because it is a natural state and because there are numerous examples of women in the Bible who gave birth later in life. Rachel Scott writes, "I believe that if God did not want women to bear children over the age of thirty-five, then He would not have given their bodies the ability to do so. In God's eyes, when is a woman ever too old? He allowed Elizabeth and Sarah to give birth in later years and we know that women over thirty-five have been successfully birthing children for six thousand years." In fact, Scott argues, "I believe that it's clear that God intended for people to birth children until their early to mid-fifties when their bodies complete menopause."

If Sarah could give Abraham Isaac at the age of 90, godly women should welcome pregnancy at 55.[75]

Nancy Campbell, on the other hand, encourages women to have their first child when they are young. She argues that early childbearing and nursing reduces long-term health risks for women. Campbell is happy to use medical and social scientific research when it supports her theological agenda. She cites medical studies that claim women who have children before the age of eighteen and women who breastfeed are less likely to develop breast cancer. The research she quotes also demonstrates the negative health consequences for women who delay pregnancy. "Studies also reveal that women who bear their first child before age twenty-two are less likely than others to develop ovarian cancer. Those who delay pregnancy are more prone to have endometriosis which is known as the 'career woman's disease.' "[76] Rather than deny the possibility of reproductive health problems, like the Hesses, she provides medical studies that state the risks and benefits to reinforce her biblical view. The Hesses suggest that scientific studies provide false information regarding the health risks of multiple pregnancies. Campbell, on the other hand, presents medical research to support the health benefits of multiple pregnancies for young mothers. From her perspective, science is uncovering the truth of God's design for humanity. In Campbell's words, "The Word of God is always ahead of science."[77] In the end, scientific truths support biblical truths about female reproductive bodies.

In Quiverfull literature, the only circumstance in which one should avoid pregnancy is if the condition is certain to be fatal. The Hesses claim that if pregnancy will be fatal a woman must be very sick or, in their words, *really* "at death's door." There does not appear to be a provision in the book for a woman who is generally healthy but whose health would be threatened by a pregnancy. If pregnancy is physically dangerous to the woman, then she is already gravely ill. This view has profound consequences for any couple and their marriage. In extreme, legitimate medical cases, the Hesses advise celibacy.

"In other words, a Christian man, convinced of a fatal pregnancy would sublimate his sexual desires to his wife's good and display true, self-sacrificial love. Sex, under such circumstances, assuming that a serious health problem *really* exists, would be simply untamed lust and not 'doing unto others as ye would have them do unto ye.'" This view neither acknowledges female sexual desire nor allows for the couple to use contraception. The clear message is that if pregnancy is not possible, the couple should refrain from sexual activity. "We would not discount all medical testimony about the hazards of pregnancy for women with serious physical conditions. But serious physical conditions have a way of discouraging sexual activity, or even (in some cases) making it physically impossible. If God has put it in your heart to desire your husband sexually, and into his heart to desire you, could He perhaps have put it into His plan to care for the result?" Within the Quiverfull world this creates a difficult situation in which a couple is given the choice to either ignore serious risks to the wife's health or remain in a sexless marriage. There is no provision for marital sexual pleasure without the possibility of conception.[78]

Many outsiders criticize the Quiverfull Movement for its poor treatment of women and children. Hilary McFarland, blogger and author of *Quivering Daughters*, is a former insider. McFarland claims that in authoritarian and "patriocentric" families assaults happened often and are the logical result of unlimited paternal power and the sexual "submission theology" that is preached to women. Men, McFarland explains, are able to exert abusive power over women and young girls who are shamed into silence and thus rarely report sexual assaults. "Unfortunately, there is little accountability within many patriocentric homes, and grave opportunity for abuse of authority. And while many, no doubt, succeed leading their families well, there is a growing under-culture of pain and tragedy within this branch of conservative Christianity. And in the effort to follow formulaic teaching, many families experience the serious fruits of a father-centric system."[79]

McFarland's book and blog created a stir among women who support the Quiverfull lifestyle.[80] The blog, "Steadfast Daughters," is devoted to exposing the weaknesses of McFarland's book and her movement to liberate women from abusive situations in authoritarian families. The contributors to "Steadfast Daughters" affirm what they call "real biblical patriarchy" and condemn the actions of a few tyrannical, misguided men. The women note that the term "abuse" is often overused and that tyrannical men are found in all sorts of homes—their presence is neither unique nor more prevalent in biblical patriarchal families. And yet, in families where older women instruct young women that it is a sin to refuse to sexually submit to their husbands, it is hard to prove any form of abuse, especially rape.

The debates over domestic abuse in Quiverfull families have led some prominent writers to distance themselves from the term "Quiverfull." Stacy McDonald, author of *The Passionate Housewife* and the blog "Your Sacred Calling," seeks to give Quiverfull a more general, positive definition and, specifically, to reject the image that women in Quiverfull families are abused. While she denies being part of any specific movement, her views are consistent with Quiverfull teachings. Although she promotes large families, she rejects the view that fertility is a contest and that following a list of rules is equivalent to living a biblical lifestyle. In an entry entitled "Jesus-Full" posted on her blog and reposted on "Steadfast Daughters," McDonald states her case. "So, stop focusing on the rules. Don't get so caught up in the details! Start focusing on the blessing that comes from denying yourself and submitting to God and the details will take care of themselves. Am I 'quiverfull?' No, I think I'd rather be 'Jesus-full.'"[81]

The popular TV show "19 Kids and Counting," which follows the Duggar family, increased media attention on the Quiverfull movement, causing many supporters of the movement, including McDonald, to separate themselves from the lifestyle depicted on the show.[82] In the afterword of the twenty-fifth-anniversary edition of *The Way Home*, even Mary Pride, who wrote the foreword to *A Full Quiver*, distanced herself from popular stereotypes of the Quiverfull movement. While she still affirms that sex should always be open to reproduction, she rejects the focus on female fertility cycles. "We are also not supposed to be militantly seeking to conceive. For example, to confine sex solely to a woman's optimal fertile dates is clearly unbiblical." She also objects to the tendency among Quiverfull families to view the "blessing" of many children as a reflection of their own righteousness and effort. "Christian marriage is not a baby derby. We are not trying to have as many babies as possible through our own efforts. We are certainly not *proud* about how many children we have—as if we created them ourselves!" Finally, she criticizes men in the movement for "micromanaging" their wives in domestic matters. According to Pride, men are the leaders of the family, but women are the CEOs in the kitchen and nursery.[83]

Pride not only criticizes Quiverfull, she also takes aim at purity balls. She agrees that the idea of fathers taking an interest in daughters is natural; however, Pride insists it is not biblical to suggest that a girl's success and happiness relies on what she observes and learns from her father. Although many proponents of biblical womanhood recognize that their husbands are not Prince Charming, they sometimes still employ dreams of a fairy-tale marriage through attendance at purity balls to encourage purity and submission to fathers among their young daughters. Pride is deeply unhappy with those who participate in purity balls because of the emphasis on the Dads "dating" their daughters. "I think the idea of fathers treating their daughters like 'junior wives' is extremely dangerous, for all sorts of obvious reasons. Dating her? Putting a ring on her finger? Having her act as a hands-on personal attendant? This imagery is disturbing to say the least."[84] Pride finds no biblical evidence that godly men ever engaged in such practices and highlights the relationships that were forged between mothers and daughters in the Bible, with daughters serving mothers. While Pride is valorized among many in the Quiverfull movement for her vision of biblical female roles, domesticity, pro-natalism, motherhood, and homeschooling, she parts ways with them on many of their more radical positions on sexuality, female subservience, and father–daughter relationships. Women might be saved through childbearing, but even Pride can see that godliness can turn to abuse when husbands and fathers over-step their biblical roles. When sexuality and salvation are taken to patriarchal extremes,

righteous women and children are not only called on to sacrifice themselves, but they are also placed in eternal jeopardy.

CONCLUSION

I began this chapter with a book by the Torodes, *Open Embrace*.
A blurb on the cover describes the book as a "bold critique of modern
ideas about sex, marriage, and contraception." Protesting secular culture, the Torodes promoted Natural Family Planning as the Christian
way to have sex. They took aim at Christians who use contraception
and believe that sex for pleasure is biblical. The Torodes' "open womb"
idea that sexual intercourse should always be open to conception pits
them against other evangelicals. Marital sex, moreover, is not just about
sex. For the Torodes, marital sex is bound up with ideas about motherhood, the proper role of a biblical wife, and salvation.

Although the Torodes practiced Natural Family Planning,
pro-natalists go a step further and reject all efforts to interfere with
conception. Evangelical pro-natalists consider the sexual practices and
gender roles of other married evangelicals too "worldly." The emphasis on sexual pleasure in marriage, the use of contraception, women
working outside of the home, and, in some churches, the acceptance of
female preaching, are all considered unbiblical by pro-natalists. Secular
culture's reach, they contend, has extended deep into the pews and up
into the pulpits and has led evangelicals astray from biblical mandates.
These worldly evangelicals, who seem to have accommodated to culture, are no longer living witnesses to the truth of Scripture. The "good
news" that they preach is culture, not Christ.

American secular culture is blamed for much of the worldly misinformation accepted by lax evangelicals. The most dangerous force
decried in all of the literature, however, is the feminist movement.
Feminism, in these writings, is responsible for the creation, distribu-
tion, and acceptance of contraception. The feminists who hawked
their contraceptive pills to vulnerable Christian women, the argument
goes, made unfounded claims that limiting family size provides true

empowerment and freedom. Feminists, and their championing of contraception, are the primary menace to godly families. Feminism takes women out of the home and creates friction within couples. Feminists turn sex into self-gratification instead of self-sacrifice. Feminists believe women should be in the clergy rather than fulfilling their call to ministry in the home. Feminists define sexual submission as rape, a crime that is punished in civil courts not handled in the home or at church. For all of these reasons, feminism is identified as the root cause of the attack on biblical womanhood, sanctified sex, and godly families. It is more than a secular philosophy, the authors claim, it is heresy. The pro-natalists see themselves as Christians witnessing to Christ in a godless culture that promotes feminism, a pagan religion.

The tension between Christianity and culture that is played out in these writings is also about self-definition. Who is the most pious believer? What are the visible signs of faith? How does a true believer act out faith? The pro-natalist books are about how a group of Christians interact with secular culture on the topics of sexuality, reproduction, and gender roles. On those topics they position themselves against secular culture and against other evangelicals. Any evangelical can accept Christ as savior. True believers visibly demonstrate their faith through large families and the knowledge that marriage is about self-sacrifice and not sexual pleasure. Among the saved, sacrificial sexuality will further the kingdom of God.

One of the striking aspects of the pro-natalist movement is it appears to be limited almost entirely to white evangelicals. Among all of the literature that is available in print and on the Internet, there are few examples of non-Anglo families that promote the Quiverfull lifestyle. There are many non-Anglo women who support biblical womanhood. What is noteworthy is that they do not promote the "open womb" approach to fulfilling their scriptural roles as women, wives, and mothers. In fact, non-Anglo women who promote Titus 2 lifestyles tend to generalize about wives' specific roles and focus on women's unique, God-given abilities.

The books and websites we have examined thus far all presume a predominantly white readership. This is apparent through the choice of images, language, examples, and textual cues. The equating of evangeli-calism with whiteness is not only a problem in popular texts about sex-uality but also reflects a larger lacuna in the scholarship of American evangelicalism. In the next chapter, I turn to texts that consciously address a non-Anglo evangelical audience on matters of sexuality and salvation.

CHAPTER FIVE

SEXUAL HEALING

INTRODUCTION

Dressed in a bright pink, long-skirted suit and preaching to a jam-packed arena of cheering women, Prophetess Juanita Bynum delivered her now-famous "No More Sheets" sermon. During nearly an hour of vigorous preaching, she spoke in tongues, wiped sweat from her brow, and exposed her own imperfect life as a cautionary tale for her audience. Bynum spoke passionately about sin, sexuality, marriage, singleness, and biblical womanhood. Toward the end of the oration she declared that single women make poor marriage decisions because they are needy and want to be rescued from financial debt. "Let me tell you how messed up you are, because you know what, by now you oughta have at least one piece of property in your name." Women, Bynum proclaims, think marriage is about fulfilling romantic desires. "You don't want a man, you want sex! You don't want a husband, you want a midnight rendezvous." If you want to attract a godly man, Bynum pleads with her listeners, be a Proverbs 31 woman. For Bynum, a biblical woman is financially independent, has a savings account to offer to her fiancé, and understands that: "Marriage is not sex. Marriage is ministry." The exuberant response of the crowd showed that her message was heard loud and clear.[1]

Bynum's view of sexuality and salvation is one that most evangelicals would recognize and applaud. She quotes the Bible, affirms male leadership and female submission in marriage, highlights the individual believer's daily struggle with faith and action, and calls on the power of the Holy Spirit to guide her. What distinguishes Bynum's approach from almost all the other evangelical media examined in this book is not her theology. It is not the message; it is the messenger. She preaches openly about sexual sins and makes assumptions about the unbiblical sexual practices of her audience. Unlike most of the authors and preachers we have discussed, she uses herself as a negative example rather than holding herself up as a model of perfection. Although Bynum does not say it explicitly, she does not seek to address a universal evangelical audience. Her words are powerful because they resonate with born-again African American women. Their sexual lives and faith journeys may or may not be similar Bynum's, but her words, her humor, and her biblically based advice are obviously recognizable and affirming to them. Although Bynum is clearly a gifted orator, it is hard to imagine this exact sermon having the same effect on a predominantly white audience.

RACE, EVANGELICALISM, AND SEXUALITY

What does Bynum's appeal tell us about American evangelical views of sexuality and salvation? More broadly, what might it tell us about American evangelicalism? Although the books we have examined thus far are marketed to evangelicals broadly, the illustrations, examples, and language make it clear that the target audience is white. Moreover, the authors relate "whiteness" to purity, godliness, and beauty. For example, the majority of the princess themed children's books we discussed characterize the fair princess as "lily white." Only a few children's princess books include illustrations of children of color. The purity literature aimed at born-again teens overwhelmingly depicts young Anglos. Here again, radiance and purity is often depicted as "stainless" and "lily white." Even the marital sex manuals follow the same pattern; if there's a couple on the cover or in the illustrations, odds are they are white. Titus 2 ministries purport to be for all Christian women, but the most prominent spokeswomen are, with few exceptions, white.[2] I have yet to find a non-Anglo family that publicly identifies with the Quiverfull Movement.[3] There likely are nonwhite Quiverfull families, but they do not represent the public image of the movement.

Anyone who is interested in reading about sexuality from a born-again perspective might find helpful information in these writings. And yet, even a cursory glance at the illustrations, book covers, authors' photos, and authors' biographies, it is apparent that the majority of bestsellers are written by white authors. There are books and blogs about sexuality and salvation geared to evangelical people of color. Typically the books are not put out by the big evangelical publishing houses like Thomas Nelson, Tyndale, and Zondervan. Although their ideas about sexuality, gender roles, and marriage are similar to those of their white counterparts, these writers do not claim to speak to all evangelicals. Their writings target the specific life experiences of nonwhite evangelicals. Any Bible-believing Christian might read the literature, but unlike the white writers, these authors tend not to expect a universal appeal. This divide is symptomatic of a much more widespread problem within evangelicalism.

It is difficult to know how many African Americans identify as evangelicals.[4] While evangelicalism in the United States is theologically, socially, and ritually diverse and hard to categorize, it is even trickier for African Americans. As a scholarly category, "evangelicalism" has traditionally meant "white evangelicalism," and many black, Latino, and Asian evangelicals do not fit neatly into it. Many people think of African American Christianity primarily in terms of the historic Black Church denominations—the African Methodist Episcopal Church, black Methodists, black Baptists—which are generally lumped in with liberal Protestantism. Yet, many African Americans were involved in the founding of conservative evangelical movements. Some early twentieth-century movements, like Pentecostalism, were multi-racial at their inception and only later became segregated. But these early movements changed over time. According to A. G. Miller, many African American evangelicals believed that white evangelicals were not concerned with evangelizing African Americans. Nor were they willing to accept African American leadership.[5] African American fundamentalist groups, such as the black Plymouth Brethren and the Christian and Missionary Alliance, banded together to form the National Black Evangelical Association (NBEA). Its aim was to develop black evangelical leadership and promote fundamentalism among African American Christians. For many years these Christians worked alongside white evangelicals, sharing conservative theological viewpoints, but neither worshipping in the same places nor sharing leadership roles.

African American Pentecostals, who adhered to fundamentalist tenets of biblical literalism, also joined the NBEA, but differed from the other NBEA evangelicals because of their emphasis on the experience of gifts of the Holy Spirit. Black Pentecostals brought to the NBEA a tradition of being entirely independent of white churches. The founding of the NBEA was the first step in the growth of separate African American evangelical groups that were often at odds with the traditional Black Church. These groups would later grow to include new movements such as Neo-Pentecostalism, with which Juanita Bynum is closely associated.

In popular media, conservative African American Christians have been most visible in televangelism, especially those pastors connected to megachurches. In his groundbreaking book *Watch This!*, Jonathan Walton demonstrates that up until recently, these figures remained a real scholarly blind spot.[6] This is in part because conservative religious broadcasters in the twentieth century were predominantly white. Popular contemporary religious media personalities like T. D. Jakes, Eddie Long, and Creflo Dollar have defied these categories. "The history of evangelicalism and religious broadcasting in America," Walton argues, "extends beyond the narrow confines of white Christian conservatism. Similarly, black Christian thought and practice in America transcend a definitional identity structured by civil rights and social justice." His analysis of the racial politics of televangelism applies equally well to evangelical writings about sex.[7]

Although male pastors are more visible and powerful, there is room for female voices in arenas beyond the pulpit. Women are often featured at singles seminars or women's events sponsored by a church. This is where speakers like Juanita Bynum are able to find their place in the African American evangelical discussion of sexuality and salvation.

NO MORE SHEETS

Prophetess Juanita Bynum built her ministry on preaching honestly about sexuality and spirituality to a predominantly African American female audience. She became a national figure after she delivered a sermon at one of Bishop T. D. Jakes's singles conferences in Dallas in 1998. The now-famous "No More Sheets" sermon brought over 17,000 people to their feet and was soon reproduced and circulated via video and books, and later preached again and again at other seminars.[8] Bynum's straight talk about sexuality among born-again women is explicit, emotional, and at times funny. She offers a deeply personal account of her sexual struggles as a single Christian woman. As she delivers the sermon, Bynum wraps a series sheets around her body and then removes them one by one. The sheets represent the emotional and spiritual burden of extra-marital sex with multiple partners, and by unwinding them Bynum lets go of spiritual attachments to each lover.[9] She describes, in graphic detail, her yearning for sexual intimacy and the spiritual consequences of her actions. Her message to the audience is that single, born-again women should not deny that they have sexual desires, but should direct those desires toward a spiritual relationship with God. Single women are urged to make a covenant with the Holy Spirit to sanctify their bodies, allowing them to attain spiritual satisfaction in a relationship beyond the physical world. This is not easy, Bynum warns; she knows her listeners' desires and struggles, and she models herself as someone who has experienced a full range of sexual misconduct and now seeks to live a holy life.

"No More Sheets" is a remarkable testimony because of Bynum's ability to connect with her audience, especially regarding the need for women to be honest about sex with themselves and with each other. Throughout her sermon she prefaces statements with "I got be honest with you," and "y'all can beg to differ if you want, but..." She punctuates statements with the call, "Can I find one honest women here?"[10] Honesty about sexuality, for Bynum, is essential for salvation. Living a dishonest sexual life breaks the relationship with God and will only lead to misery and heartbreak. The only honest route to happiness, now and eternally, is to reclaim celibacy through an exclusive relationship with God until you are ready for marriage. This process, Bynum warns, cannot be rushed. The time-table for marriage is set by God.

Bynum's "No More Sheets" sermon echoes many of the themes found in evangelical writing aimed at white audiences. Bynum affirms celibacy prior to marriage by promoting a covenantal relationship with God. But, unlike most of the chastity literature aimed at teens and young women, she admits that sometimes maintaining purity does not lead to a happy marriage. Bynum confesses "I have had the experience of being single, and being a virgin, and waiting for God for a mate, and then the whole trauma of getting the wrong mate." Playing by the rules, she explains, is not always enough. And after a marriage fails, how does one become single again? These are issues, Bynum contends, that the church does not want to address even though so many God-fearing women find themselves in the same circumstances. "And if the church don't get real with the people of God," Bynum warns, "we gonna lose a whole lot of folk." This is where Bynum finds her niche. Her ministry aims to reconnect sexuality to spirituality among adult single women, many of whom have had prior sexual relationships. Her target audience is born-again African American women who, she believes, respond to her message because they can relate to her life experiences.[11]

Single women, whether divorced, widowed, separated, or never married, Bynum argues, must let go of former sexual attachments and love God before they can love a man. Bynum takes issue with the platitudes given in most books and seminars for evangelical singles. She does not assume that everyone in her audience has been sexually pure and she does not pretend that chastity is easy for the righteous. "I have bought just about every book I could think of on being single. And how to be single, and how to walk single, and none of it really helped me until I began to experience the single life." In this way she distinguishes herself as an authentic voice for adult single women. She is particularly critical of advice given by experts who are not single. "Y'all can beg to differ with me if you want to. But I find it very difficult to listen to anybody preach to me about being single when they got a pair of thighs in their bed every night!" Bynum's ability to connect with her audience is based on her willingness to disclose her sexual past, giving her the authority that comes from personal experience. She is not above her audience, judging their actions; she is on the same journey, making the same mistakes and trying to change.[12]

Bynum believes that her sexual struggles are connected to spiritual warfare. Echoing the themes found in deliverance literature, Bynum claims that "once you have had sex with a man, then what happens according to the realm of the spirit, the spirit of that man, steps into your body." Every person with whom Bynum has had sex, she believes, she still carries a part of them "the man's residue" with her. Although she does not refer to medical knowledge of sexually transmitted diseases as demons or the notions of inherited genetic damage caused by sexual acts, she does affirm that spirits merge during sexual intercourse and spiritual attachments remain until they are replaced by a renewed commitment to God. In her testimony she describes the disappointment of leading a chaste, single life, but never finding a man who is interested in marriage. "And I asked the Lord, 'well why am I not married?' And he said to me, 'you been married too many times.' He said, 'every time you slept with somebody, you married them, and that person became your husband.'" In other words, "You're not married because you're not single." In effect, sexual intercourse forms spiritual marriages and she remains spiritually married to many people. Bynum's refrain, "no more sheets," chanted over and over again at the end of the sermon, reminds her listeners that true singleness is only achieved when women sever previous sexual ties and join together with God.[13]

Bynum tells women that they must "get their house in order" before they seek marriage. She does not directly make reference to the concept of wives as "helpmeets," but she does echo Titus 2 literature. For example, she states, "Marriage is not sex, marriage is ministry and unless you are prepared to minister to the men of God, don't mess over them." Although her remarks are in general emphasizing a woman's role to submit to the authority of her husband; her approach to achieving the role of helpmeet is distinct from the literature examined in the previous chapter.[14]

Bynum urges women to become economically independent and to improve their own lives. Bynum states that she (like many others) has been seduced by the promise of material goods, like a new couch or a new car. She gently mocks women (including herself) who brag about boyfriends who "buy me this or buy me that." Her advice is: "buy it yourself!"[15] In a 2001 interview published in *Essence* magazine, Bynum explained that her lack of financial independence combined with her desire for material comforts made her dependent on men who did not value her. The first step toward finding a worthy man was to become financially independent. "And I no longer need a man who will buy me a new dress or furniture. I've got lamps, I've got a couch, I've got a stove. I don't have to subject myself to a man's disrespect simply because he bought me a living-room set."[16] This approach is a clear departure from evangelical marriage guides that focus on men providing material goods and women submitting to the needs and desires of men. Financial independence helps women respect themselves and make wise choices.

In order to be ready for the role of helpmeet in marriage, Bynum explains, women need to have their finances under control and should be able to choose a husband based on spiritual qualities not financial needs or desires. Financial independence also makes them more appealing to godly men. Bynum puts it this way, "when you are ready to get married, what are you bringing to the table, Miss sister-thing?"[17] Financial security enables women to make a wise choice of a husband, and being debt-free demonstrates that she can serve as a biblical helpmeet because it is evidence that she can manage her household. Upholding the ideal of virginity prior to marriage is not highlighted. Entering a marriage with the necessary skills to fulfill the biblical role of wife is essential. Unlike much of the helpmeet literature, Bynum does not focus on the merits of older seasoned women mentoring younger naïve women. She addresses her audience as peers and presumes that they have a similar life experience.

Bynum's straight talk about sex, using her own physical body as an example, struck a chord with her listeners, and has inspired many writers and preachers to follow in her footsteps, publishing their own books, blogs, and running workshops dedicated to single adult women. Although Bynum's message is for all Bible-believing women, her main audience is African American women. Why is that? Her message relies on a conservative interpretation of Scripture that is consistent with most evangelical teaching about sexuality and salvation. She approves of chastity prior to marriage, biblical roles within marriage, and a belief that sexuality is related to God's plan for salvation. Why did she headline at T. D. Jakes's singles conferences and not James Dobson's singles seminars? American evangelicals have always been amenable to adapting the gospel message to different audiences. But, in this historical moment, with global communication and multiple forms of media, as well as a rapidly changing US population, why is there still racial segregation among evangelicals who promote the same theological message about sexuality?

Bynum's appeal, in part, stems from the combination of a theologically conservative message with meaningful language and anecdotes that resonate with the social circumstances of her audience. Bynum fills a niche in much the same way as Mark Driscoll does for a different demographic. They are both born-again Christians who speak honestly and directly about sexuality to their particular constituents. While the overall message may be the same, the people listening do not share the same pews. In part that is due to the differences between the charismatic and Reform side of evangelicalism. But, it is also because the "good news" preached by evangelicals accommodates the life experiences of believers. Those distinct experiences, lived through the history of American racial disharmony, lead black and white evangelicals to different churches. Although sexuality may be universal, preaching and writing about sexuality and salvation in American evangelicalism, like so many other topics, remains segregated.

THE LADY, HER LOVER, AND HER LORD

There are many African American evangelical men and women who write about sexuality, but perhaps the best known is Bishop T. D. Jakes of Dallas, Texas. Jakes's career as a Neo-Pentecostal preacher and a national media figure was built on his ministry to women. Specifically, Jakes's straight talk on sexual assault and domestic violence has endeared him to countless women who have been affected by his call to speak openly and to release women from the shame of crimes committed against them. In Jakes's preaching and writings, victims of sexual assault have not fallen into sin, they are wounded women who can find their beauty and value through a relationship with a loving God. Jakes has written many books geared toward both men and women, but I will focus primarily on the latter.[18]

Jakes's willingness to discuss sexual abuse is related to his theology, which emphasizes a loving God who provides healing and forgiveness. Jakes grew up in a Pentecostal church and in a family that struggled financially and emotionally. Jakes began preaching in his late teens and, after many years of building and relocating a small interracial church, he settled in Charleston, West Virginia. There he began a popular women's bible study program called "Woman Thou Art Loosed!" His reputation as an excellent preacher grew, he received invitations to preach at large events, he was broadcast on Christian TV, and by the time *Woman Thou Art Loosed!* was published in book form in 1993, he was a star in the African American evangelical world. Three years later he relocated to Dallas and renamed his congregation Potter's House Church.[19]

Unlike traditional Pentecostal preachers, Jakes's sermons and books do not focus on rules-based living and damnation. He presents a compassionate God who wants individuals to achieve personal fulfillment. This is not a prosperity gospel (although Jakes is not opposed to wealth) that equates health and wealth with godliness, it is a theology that acknowledges that God can act in your life to affect your future regardless of your past or present circumstances. According to Jonathan Walton, the three themes of Jakes's ministry are God's compassion, individual reconciliation with God, and personal fulfillment. African American women, Walton argues, are his dominant audience partly because of his focus on overcoming the past through faith in a loving God and forging healthy relationships through self-love and care.[20] Walton contends that Jakes has built his ministerial success on speaking about critical issues that affect African American women's lives.[21] Jakes affirms women's capabilities in all social and work environments and backs this up by including women on his ministerial staff. But this does not mean that he thinks men and women are the same. Jakes insists that males and females are created by God to be unique and distinct and that those natural and spiritual qualities must be maintained.

In many ways, Jakes's writings on gender roles and sexuality are similar to the writings of conservative white evangelicals. In *Woman Thou Art Loosed!* Jakes explains: "By nature woman is a receiver. She is not physically designed to be a giver. Her sexual and emotional fulfillment becomes somewhat dependent on the giving of her male counterpart (in regard to intimate relationships)."[22] Jakes uses a metaphor to describe the physical and emotional connection between men and women. "Nearly every home in America is wired for electricity. Walls are covered with receptacles which deliver the electric current. In order to take advantage of the power, something must be plugged into the receptacle. The receptacle is female and the plug is male....Women are open by nature and design. Men are closed. You must be careful what you allow to plug into you and draw strength from you. The wrong plugs may seek your help and drain your power."[23] Physical differences are directly related to emotional needs and desires. These anatomical differences are created by God.

Jakes affirms the role of married women as "helpmeets" to their husbands. This complementarian understanding of marriage as well as the unique and "innate" qualities of men and women, Jakes believes, is confirmed by the story of creation. "The woman was made, fashioned out of the man, to be a help meet. Through their union they find wholeness in each other. She helps him meet and accomplish his task." As in white evangelical writings, the role of the husband is to serve as a protector of the wife, a commitment that is both biblical and necessary to ensure the sanctity of the marriage. "He has designed that those who plug into a woman sexually will have a covenant with that woman. God never intended for humanity to have casual sex. His design always included the commitment of a covenant. He purposed that a man who has sexual relations with a woman would be committed to that same woman for life. Nothing short of this commitment meets His standard. God wants you covered like an outlet is covered, in order that no one tamper with your intended purpose. The married woman is covered by her husband." Therefore, sex within marriage is part of a biblical contract that balances female submission with male protection.[24]

Sex, for Jakes, is an integral part of marriage and is essential for a man's emotional well-being. In his book *He-Motions*, Jakes affirms that sex is designed by God and is an act of worship. Like many evangelical sex manuals, Jakes makes the point that sex allows a married couple to participate in the divine act of creation. "It is through this glorious worshipful joining that God invites a man and his wife to partake in the awesome act of creation; with Him, bride and groom collaborate to give life to our children and legacy to our existence." Sex also creates a spiritual union between spouses. "But it is more than body meeting body. Good sex, divinely ordained sex, is a blissful soul union. Sex makes a man feel loved." Specifically, sex provides an opportunity for men to express emotions. "For a man, being sexual brings him center stage with his emotions. Sex provides an outlet for him to confront his emotions and express them to his wife in the most private settings. He learns that it's okay for him to feel, to share, to be intimate—both outside of bed as well as in the passion of physically loving his wife." Wives, Jakes believes, can support their husbands' egos by initiating sex and showing them that they are desired. In this respect, Jakes is more like Tim LaHaye than like Debi Pearl; while a godly marriage needs sex, it shouldn't be a chore. "Sex is not a duty or a reward; it is a part of your ministry to him and to yourself." Good sex, according to Jakes fulfills different needs in men and women, but it is essential for both.[25]

Finally, like white evangelical writers, Jakes stresses that single women should remain chaste and dedicate their single years to creating a strong relationship with God. Jakes believes that this will make a woman more attractive to men and will translate to serving her future husband. "Some of you do not understand the benefits of being single. In reality, while you're not married you really ought to be involved with God. When you get married, you direct all of the training that you had while you were unmarried toward your spouse."[26]

In this, Jakes echoes Sarah Mally's and Leslie Ludy's focus on the intimate relationship with the heavenly prince as the primary relationship for single evangelical young women. Mally and Ludy at times use deeply intimate language to depict the power of that primary romantic bond. Jakes gets even more explicit because he is addressing adult single women. "The Lord wants to make sweet love to you. I'm not being carnal, I'm being real. He wants to hold you. He wants you to come in at the end of the day and say, 'Oh Lord, I could hardly make it today....Hold me, touch me, strengthen me. Let me hold You. Let me bless You. I've set the night aside for us. Tonight is our night....My body is Yours. Nobody touches me but You. I am holy in body and in spirit. I am not committing adultery in our relationship. My body is Yours."[27] The language Jakes uses to describe the relationship between single women and God is much more erotic than Prophetess Bynum's. Yet, it is closer in form and substance (though not the explicit language) to the literature geared toward young white evangelical women.

Despite the general similarities to white evangelical literature, there are important differences. *Woman Thou Art Loosed!* is not a sex manual and does not include information about sexual techniques. It is also not a book that aims to produce fear of the physical and spiritual dangers of premarital sex. Unlike much of the chastity literature or deliverance manuals, there is no discussion of the irreparable damage that sexual sin will cause a future spouse or generations to come. Jakes does not suggest that sexual transgressions are demonic or that physical diseases have a spiritual component. He neither condemns the use of contraceptives nor promotes large families as a path to salvation. On the contrary, Jakes presents a view of sexuality and spirituality that acknowledges sexual experiences that are either ignored in the white evangelical literature or set apart as exceptional cases. What is noteworthy about Jakes is that he does not shame women for past sexual indiscretion. In his writings, Jakes does not give women sexual tests to pass or fail or reputations to maintain or lose; everyone has the ability to be sexually redeemed and to start again.

Jakes writes extensively about sexual abuse and the need for clergy and churchgoers to help people heal from the trauma. This is another stark difference from white evangelical writings on sexuality examined in previous chapters, which tend to ignore or refute sexual assault. Jakes is particularly interested in recognizing that women and children who are sexually assaulted should not be blamed and should understand that they are not defined by the assaults against them. Even women who are not the victims of assault should not be defined by their past sexual actions. There is always a chance at a new spiritual and sexual beginning. Men, Jakes believes, must be held accountable for sexual violence. This is a stark difference from John Piper's claim that within marriage women should be prepared to suffer "being smacked" by their husband. An example of Jakes's approach are his comments and questions relating to John 8, the passage in the New Testament that discusses an adulterous woman. "Have you ever wondered where the man was who had been committing adultery with this woman? She had been caught in the very act. Surely they knew who the man was. There still seems to be a double standard today when it comes to sexual sin. Often we look down on a woman because of her past but overlook who she is now. Jesus, however, knew the power of a second chance."[28] Jakes says nothing about women tempting men by immodest clothing and flirting or excusing men from improper sexual behavior because of their inability to control their "natural" sexual desires. Women are equally accountable for sexual transgressions, but they are not the scapegoats and they are never to blame for sexual assault.

Throughout *Woman Thou Art Loosed!*, Jakes makes claims that many people struggle with past sexual sins that were made against them or that they knowingly made. Rather than hold up sexual sin as an extreme case, he reassures his readers that they are not alone and that they can overcome those transgressions through Christ. This is a very different approach to sexuality than the one found in the purity literature, which presents virginity as something that can be lost forever and leaves a terrible stain that will negatively impact the rest of women's lives. In those books, women are taught that it is their responsibility to guard against men's natural instincts and, if they are sexually violated, their spiritual and emotional worth is diminished forever. Jakes disagrees: "Jesus took your abuse upon Himself on the cross of Calvary. He paid for your shame. He made a way for you to be clean again. He took your indiscretions and sins upon Himself and died in your place....When you accept Him you become clean and holy. You are made pure. Don't think you were alone, though; everyone struggles with the same kinds of sins as you, whether you they show it on the outside or not."[29]

Jakes writes that, ideally, everyone should be chaste prior to marriage, but recognizes that voluntary premarital sex and sexual abuse occur among his readers. Chastity, while a goal, is not a test that can be failed once and forever. Jakes clearly believes that people can redeem their sexuality by asking forgiveness and can recover from sexual abuse. One reason for this approach is that his presumed audience is adult, single women. The chastity literature examined earlier presents a common perception depicted in white evangelical sex literature that single women are young, living at home or in college, and have never been married. All the discussions about parental involvement in choosing a spouse and waiting patiently for God to bring a husband become less relevant to women living independently, working, and perhaps raising children on their own.

Most of the purity writers in the white evangelical camp tend to think of single women as young women. There is very little attention given to older single women because the assumption is that among evangelicals they are the exception, not the rule. Elisabeth Eliot, who is widowed, gives advice to single older women, but even her writings depict unmarried evangelical women as Christian heroines or women on an unusual and lonely path. Because white evangelical purity writings are geared toward youth, the princess theme makes a certain amount of sense. It evokes a girl in the bloom of her youth seeking counsel from interested parents and waiting for a handsome, virile young knight to arrive. Her prince is not a middle-aged insurance salesman with a gym membership and high cholesterol issues. Princess dreams are for the young.

In Jakes's writings, women are not characterized as young princesses; rather, they are queens. His audience consists primarily of women seeking purity of mind, soul, and body. The fairy-tale narrative of God sending a prince, which so much of white evangelical writing geared at single women has relied on, is not geared to the women reading Jakes's books and listening to his sermons. His response to waiting for Prince Charming is: "You are God's woman. You are not called to sit by the window waiting on God to send you a husband. You had better have some faith yourself and believe God down in your own spirit."[30] Women, in Jakes's view, are not cloistered princesses waiting patiently to be saved, they are God's queens ready to ascend the throne.

Jakes affirms the goal of a complementarian marriage and the role of a wife as a helpmeet, but he does not project an image of the home or family that is common among conservative white evangelicals who promote biblical womanhood. Jakes believes that women's strength comes from their femininity and that they should embrace their unique, God-given qualities. He does not extend that vision to a mandate that the only way she can fulfill her role as helpmeet is to be a stay-at-home mother who homeschools her children. Jakes neither claims that wives who earn a salary will hurt their husbands' egos, nor does he suggest that godly mothers keep their children out of the public schools. In fact, there is no mention of motherhood as the route to godliness. Women are enjoined to create a strong personal relationship with God and, if they marry, they should be helpmeets to their husbands. The details of that help are not focused on motherhood, the politics of contraception, or on the importance of a single-income household.

Jakes's approach to female sexuality is unique compared to white evangelical male authors and other conservative African American male preachers and writers. Yet, in terms of ideals and gender roles his approach is consistent with theirs. For example, his emphasis on forging a relationship with God while single runs throughout evangelical sex literature aimed at young men and women. Similarly, the stress on women restraining their bodies through clothing and behavior to keep themselves pure and not ignite the "natural desires" in men is also a commonly employed strategy for maintaining individual holiness and social order. However, controlling African American female bodies with the language of sin and salvation is particularly poignant given the history of African American women in the United States.

Although Jakes insists that his female congregants are queens and have sanctified bodies that they can control, this has not been the case for much of the history of African American women. In an article on faith-based ministries for single black Christian women, Monique Moultrie explains that restraining African American women's bodies has resonance in American history in general, and specifically in the history of the black church. While African American women's bodies were exploited during slavery and throughout American history, many black churches over-compensated for the hostile culture by holding church-going women to a high standard of modesty and purity. On the individual and institutional level (in churches), African American women, Moultrie explains, are encouraged to maintain respectability by disciplining the body to downplay their sexuality. The churches' efforts today focus on prohibiting premarital sex and homosexuality and while they apply to both men and women, the stigma of illicit sexuality typically falls on women. "This restraint led to policing of black female bodies and sexualities through codes of silence and public shaming."[31] Jakes's ministry seeks to maintain the standard of purity while removing the stigma of illicit sex as he urges women to transform themselves through a relationship with Christ.

Titus 2 ministries appeal to many African American evangelical women because of the emphasis on being a godly woman. Typically, Titus 2 ministries focus on the qualities of a biblical woman, who should be chaste, sensible, trustworthy, hospitable, domestic, as well as on the importance of older women teaching younger women how to behave in their God-given roles as wives and mothers. The majority of Titus 2 ministries stress that women can best fulfill their calling from within the home, serving their husbands and training their children. Among the most conservative groups, biblical womanhood requires full submission of the female body to God's will, letting Him determine the number of children in the family. Among members of the Quiverfull movement the rejection of all forms of birth control, even the rhythm method, is paired with a theology of hierarchal submission and protection that begins with God and ends in the family unit. This is a relatively small, overwhelmingly white group of evangelicals. The ideal Titus 2 woman, regardless of race, is in a two-parent household. But Biblical womanhood is a flexible category that can include single, married, divorced, and widowed women who may or may not be mothers and homemakers. What holds these diverse women together is an assertion that Scripture teaches that women are valuable, unique creations who have a set of biblical guidelines for behavior that identify them as godly.

All women who engage in Titus 2 religious bodily practices have to negotiate the ideal of purity with the reality of sexual desire and sexual violence. But, as anthropologist Marla F. Frederick has noted, that tension is exacerbated for African American women in light of the racial history of slavery in the United States. "While white women share this history of rape, teen pregnancy, and physical abuse, black women's experiences of sexuality are shadowed by a history of ownership, exploitation and forced pregnancy for the sake of profit." In her ethnographic research on women in a rural North Carolina county, Frederick found that some of the women she interviewed modified their views on sexuality and faith over time and that their interpretations of the relationship between sexual desires and religious convictions varied. Although their answers to questions on this topic were not uniform, they tended to view their bodies as temples, sacred spaces that allowed for intimate communion with God.[32] Sex, for many of these women, was a careful negotiation between belief and practice. And biblical ideals often do not match reality. As Frederick found, those negotiating that gap did not abandon their faith when their practices were at odds with biblical mandates. While the women in her study affirmed their church's teachings about sex being enjoyed only within heterosexual marriage, their individual life stories suggest that they made autonomous choices about sexuality. "Nevertheless," Frederick concludes, "the women all maintain that the ideal of sexual intimacy within the covenant of marriage is best." But sexual intimacy outside of the parameters of biblical marriage challenges and reframes faith. "Thus while the tenets of faith establish a set of ground rules for intimacy, faith expressions are often challenged by the realities of singleness and the compromises necessary within marriage."[33] Although the majority of the women Frederick interviewed were theologically conservative, their experiences with racism and their collective knowledge about historical injustice led them toward politically liberal views of social justice. Thus, they were balancing two religious trajectories within African American communities and weighing their biblical ideals against their everyday realities.

Biblical womanhood sets up an ideal that is easier for some women to meet than others. On the extreme edges of Titus 2 ministries, women are married and economically dependent on their spouses. They raise many children and spend the majority of their time in the home. But this is not the only vision of biblical womanhood available to believers. Many born-again Christians, including African Americans, are shaping biblical womanhood to match the realities and contingencies of everyday life in the American economy and culture. In the preaching of T. D. Jakes and the words of Juanita Bynum, women's bodies are reclaimed as sacred because they are fashioned by God. Any past sexual experience that has polluted the body can be overcome through the transformative act of dedicating the soul to God. There is no sin, no sexual transgression that definitively cuts off a believer from God. There is always another chance at redemption and the believer always has the opportunity to sanctify the body.

CONCLUSION

Does it matter that the universal claims about biblical sex written primarily by white evangelicals are not relevant for all evangelicals? Is the category of evangelical so flexible or contested (depending on your opinion) that niche marketing and preaching is the only meaningful way to reach the diverse faithful? Because evangelicalism emphasizes the individual's personal relationship with Christ, it might make sense that believers are addressed according to their particular life circumstances.

There is an enormous amount of niche marketing of evangelical products from personal finance to healthy eating. Why not sex?

In his seminars on "Sex and the Gospel," pastor Blake Wilson of Crossover Bible Fellowship in Houston tells the audience made up primarily of young people that sex is spiritual warfare. In a 2013 interview with the *Christian Post* he explained: "Many people don't realize that sex is actually an issue of warfare, because the devil knows that God is trying to reproduce His image through procreation, the original purpose, and to raise up godly offspring. That's why I believe that the enemy has the issue under such attack from the very beginning of the Bible. So as a result, the man [starts] living according to his own sexual agenda, versus God's biblical blueprint." The problem, he believes, is that many Bible-believers are not comfortable talking about sex. But the Bible has a blueprint for sexuality that protects the faithful from the pain of sexual immorality. "It was never God's design for people to have sexually transmitted diseases. It was not God's design for people to raise children with no fathers." Besides STDs and children born out of wedlock, the number of girls losing their virginity prior to marriage is a visible sign of Satan's effort in the cosmic battle with God. Pastor Wilson believes that sexual immorality is sinful, but he is careful to avoid placing the blame only on the individual. He claims that because the church has not addressed sexuality believers have not been able to make wise sexual decisions.

Pastor Wilson, like Juanita Bynum and T. D. Jakes, holds theologically conservative values about sexuality and salvation but appears much more forgiving of sexual misdeeds than are the predominantly white evangelicals we discussed in previous chapters. What distinguishes these born-again Christians is their straight talk about sexuality, their acceptance of the gap between biblical ideals and sexual realities of believers' lives, and their hope for personal transformation and spiritual healing. There are frank conversations about sexual abuse but very little blaming of the victims or suggesting that their worth is compromised because of abuse. Their self-esteem might be damaged but that hurt can be healed through therapy and a relationship with God. The overall message about sexuality and salvation is that

God intended believers to enjoy sex within heterosexual marriage and although sex outside of marriage is not biblical, it, like all sin, can be overcome.

These writers and speakers uphold conservative biblical sexual values but they recognize that the faithful may not always live up to ideals. This is particularly true for born-again women. Rather than instructing women to wait for their Prince Charming or to rely on the protection of fathers and brothers, women are told to become independent and take care of themselves before they look for a husband. Women in these writings are not shamed for sexual sins, nor are they taught that they are responsible for sexual crimes against them. There is acknowledgment that sexual assault occurs and hope that women can be healed of the pain of the abuse. While women are told that in marriage they are to be a helpmeet to their husbands, the route to marriage is independence and maturity. Sex within marriage should create unity and fulfill both spouses.

It would be a mistake to claim that all of the writing and preaching by African American evangelicals presents a positive view of female sexuality and authority. What I suggest is that in many of these writings, the expectation of living up to strict biblical sexual ideals and the shaming that has repercussions for a lifetime (and eternity), are often softened. In the end, this is perhaps a more hopeful, or at least a more realistic, sexual gospel. When it comes to sexuality, a believer's salvation is not at stake if one falls into sin. There is always forgiveness and redemption. There is always another chance to reclaim the body and recommit the soul. Past sins, sexual or otherwise, can be overcome. The individual is not forever stained or discarded like a piece of chewed up gum for being sexually impure. Sexual healing is possible and salvation is available to those who believe.

AFTERWORD

In September 2013, guest writer Ashley Moore wrote a short essay
for the *Christianity Today* blog "Her-meneutics" entitled "We Don't
Need Sexual Healing." Moore took inspiration from the 2012 film
"The Sessions," in which Helen Hunt plays a sexual surrogate—
someone who provides sexual intimacy as therapy to people who
are physically incapable or are otherwise unlikely to experience sex.
Moore argued that therapeutic sex is unbiblical. Sexual pleasure is a
strong human desire, she claimed, but it is not a human right; it is a
divine gift. While her conclusion is predictable—that it is ungodly to
pay for sex under any circumstances—her decision to speak boldly
against a marginal sexual practice portrayed in a movie demonstrates
the extent to which believers find meaning in engaging with and taking a stand against sexual practices allowed, or at least portrayed, in
secular culture.

The theory behind sexual surrogacy is that sexual intimacy and
pleasure are important human experiences that can be both healing
and empowering. It is part of a larger therapeutic program of well-
ness. And while it is hardly a common practice, and the writer is
responding to a fictional portrayal in a movie, both the practice and
the response bring into sharp relief some of the questions raised in
this book. What does the Bible have to say about sexuality and how
should born-again believers fit those mandates into their daily lives?
If heterosexual desire is understood to be biblical and natural, why
is it constantly scrutinized and debated? Where are the boundaries of
acceptable sex? Why does talking about sex quickly become a form
of witnessing? How do born-again Christians engage with American

culture? When it comes to sexuality, should they resist secular culture or accommodate it?

Central to all these questions is the assumption that although everyone has sexual desires, there are biblical rules governing who can experience sex. Evangelicals contend that sexual desire was created by God, affirmed in Scripture, and is an integral part of heterosexual marriage. Sexual pleasure serves to unite married couples, it produces offspring, and it can strengthen the mystical relationship with the divine. The details are up for debate. Some evangelicals believe that it is the duty of the wife to sexually satisfy her husband. Others argue that both husband and wife should enjoy sex. There are some who reject birth control as a direct interference with God's plan for individuals and families. Others contend that family planning is essential for excellent sex and happy marriages. As seen throughout this book, the specifics about permitted marital sexual practices are contested. While there are arguments about sexual practices, evangelicals agree that sex should only occur within heterosexual marriage. Married evangelicals who claim to enjoy excellent marital sex simultaneously witness to the truth of the Bible and participate in secular conversations about the importance of sexual pleasure.

For evangelical youth, purity literature and the larger purity movement encourage young men and women to remain chaste in body, mind, and soul. Young people are told that they are standing up for Christ and resisting America's sexualized culture by claiming virginity as a countercultural, radical stance. The purity enterprise uses secular cultural tools such as concerts, rallies, t-shirts, merchandise, social networking, etc., to grab and hold teens' attention by being relevant and accessible. Purity writers emphasize that sexual desire is natural and that it is difficult to refrain from sexual activity prior to marriage. Moore reiterates this point by writing: "Sexual desire—intense, demanding, and immediate—is a very real thing. Trust me, I am horribly aware of that. But, as much as it pains me to say this, it's not a right or requirement." While evangelical youth remain unmarried, their pure bodies are witnesses against a permissive secular culture that degrades sexuality. If they do eventually get married, they are promised that the pay-off for chastity is fabulous sex.

If sex within a sanctified marriage is fabulous, why do evangelicals continue to buy books about sexual technique and practices? Clearly, many born-again married Christians believe that they should be sexually satisfied, but they need instructions. If sex is natural and given by God, why is it difficult? The evangelical sex manual industry keeps churning out books to answer this question. It is one thing for the authors of sex manuals to define the parameters of what they think is biblically sanctioned sex. It is another thing to have to teach believers how to enjoy marital sex. There seems to be a wide gap between the ideal preached during the chastity years and the sex practiced during the married years. The evangelical sex manual writers seek to bridge the gap between the ideal and the real. In the process they walk a line between promoting their approach to sex as distinct from secular sex manuals and arguing that their approach has much in common with secular sex manuals. Sex according to biblical ideals is always good, but often human reality can make it unsatisfying. In some literature wives are blamed for "letting themselves go" or not attending to their husbands' needs. The logic is that this inattention leads believing husbands to have their sexual needs met by other women or through pornography. Work schedules, childrearing, and invasive technology (such as TVs, computers, iPhones) all compete for believers' attention and cause distance between spouses. Whatever the reasons, it seems obvious that although evangelicals make the case to American secular culture that they have the best sex, they continue to keep pace with secular readers in the market for sexual advice in marriage.

For those born-again Christians who never marry, celibacy remains the only option. Although a single life is often portrayed as the unusual exception, it is a reality for some of the faithful. If marriage is designed by God, why would some believers never find a spouse? In this case the sexual surrogacy article adds an interesting twist. How do people who are physically or cognitively challenged and may not be able to find a spouse and participate in sexual union fit in the design for biblical marriage? In other words, what happens to people who do not match the marital sexual mold? Here there are no easy answers. Moore makes an interesting move—she employs the equally difficult example of Jesus, the unmarried, celibate, divine human. It is very unusual for evangelicals to mention Jesus when discussing specific sexual practices (like surrogacy). The Holy Spirit is often invoked, and sometimes God. But Jesus, though called on in purity literature as the perfect boyfriend, rarely enters the marital bedroom. It is noteworthy, therefore, that Moore must turn to the ideal of Jesus to reject sexual surrogacy and encourage celibacy. "Jesus Christ walked this earth for 33 years, unmarried and undefiled, spotless, stainless, and, to be frank, sexless. He lived a perfect human life—a fulfilling life—but God didn't work sex and marriage into the short life plan of Jesus on earth, and Jesus didn't demand it." Rather than finding room for a believer with physical or cognitive limitations to experience sex, they, like everyone else, are forever forbidden unless they are married. Among the saved, there are no sexual exceptions.

The disappointment of never achieving a fairy-tale marriage, compounded with the realization that a believer will never experience sexual pleasure, is solved by the example of Jesus. It does not answer the question of why some of the faithful fall into the unmarried and forever celibate category. Moore seems particularly cruel as she washes her hands of this issue. "I know—it is easy for me to say. I'm only in my mid-20s, and my odds of living a celibate life are pretty low. It's an odd, uncomfortable thing to point out the 'rules' in God's word for people in a situation I will probably never find myself in. Telling anyone that celibacy seems like the best biblical model makes me feel uncomfortable, and a teensy bit nauseous." And yet, that has not stopped countless evangelicals from prescribing sexual ideals for people and situations that they themselves may not understand. Talking about sex allows evangelicals to take difficult stands, especially if what they say is perceived as unpopular, or out of step with the values of empathy and freedom portrayed in secular culture. Those who do not fit the biblical model are seen as marginal ("my odds of living a celibate life are pretty low") and can be explained away as "exceptions." They are portrayed as outliers to the wide circle of the blessed. They are not, however, outside the boundaries of being used as examples to affirm the author's own purity and courage to speak out against secular culture.

Sexual surrogacy is an uncommon therapeutic process that is a strange choice for discussion on an evangelical women's blog. That is the point. Writing, thinking, talking, expounding on sexuality is never just about sex. American evangelicals talk a lot about sex and a lot about salvation. In the process, they are working through their relationship with American culture. This is an active engagement that sometimes takes the mode of resistance and other times accommodation. When talking, writing, and preaching about sex, American evangelicals define what makes them exceptional and also what makes them like everyone else. Depending on the topic and the writer, they can be at odds or in complete agreement with what they perceive to be the majority opinion in the United States. In some instances, when it comes to sexuality, evangelicals argue with each other, claiming that one group has accommodated culture too far or has become too radical in their practices. In all cases, whether resisting or accommodating secular culture, sexuality provides the opportunity to witness to faith and demonstrate one's salvation to the wider culture.

American evangelicals engage in the cultural conversations about sexuality that reflect the theological, social, and racial diversity of the movement. Rather than denying the sexual body, evangelical sex writers present distinct visions of how sexual acts and rituals can be productive for individual and world salvation. Although there is diversity among evangelicals, born-again believers affirm that heterosexual sex is natural, it is sanctioned by God, and should be practiced only in marriage. Born-again Christians embody their faith by refraining from prohibited sexual acts or participating in sanctioned ones. The prescriptive literature about sexuality creates models for every stage of a believer's life. Born-again Christians are told that if they follow the biblical rules about sexuality their lives and their marriages will be blessed. But it offers little to those among the faithful who do not achieve the biblical model.

Sexuality is just one mode of engaging with American culture. Talking about sexuality allows evangelicals to carve an identity for themselves that sets them apart from secular American culture, even as they fervently embrace many aspects of that same culture. For evangelicals, sex is not just about sex but also about salvation. It is not just about the body but ultimately about the soul. And it is not just about the individual but also about the world. Through sex, evangelicals affirm their faith, testify to non-believers, and, they contend, further the kingdom of God.

NOTES

INTRODUCTION

1. Ed and Lisa Young, *Sexperiment: 7 Days to Lasting Intimacy with your Spouse* (Nashville, TN: Faithwords, 2012).

2. The Defense of Marriage Act (DOMA) was enacted on September 21, 1996. It was a federal law that allowed states to refuse to recognize same-sex marriages granted under the law in other states. In 2013 the Supreme Court of the United States ruled section 3 of DOMA unconstitutional.

3. Peter Brown, *The Body and Society: Men, Women, and Sexual Renunciation in Early Christianity* (New York: Columbia University Press, 1988); David Brakke, *Demons and the Making of the Monk* (Cambridge, MA: Harvard University Press, 2006); Carolyn Walker Bynum, *Fragmentation and Redemption: Essays on Gender and the Human Body in Medieval Religion* (New York: Zone Books, 1992).

4. Richard Godbeer, *Sexual Revolution in Early America* (Baltimore, MD: Johns Hopkins Press, 2004); Lawrence Foster, *Religion and Sexuality: The Shakers, The Mormons, and the Oneida Perfectionists* (Champaign: University of Illinois Press, 1984).

5. R. Marie Griffith, *Born Again Bodies: Flesh and Spirit in American Christianity* (Berkeley and Los Angeles: University of California Press, 2004); Leigh Eric Schmidt, *Hearing Things: Religion, Illusion, and the American Enlightenment* (Cambridge, MA: Harvard University Press, 2002); Ann Taves, *Fits, Trances, and Visions: Experiencing Religion and Explaining Experience from Wesley to James* (Princeton: Princeton University Press, 1999); Heather D. Curtis, *Faith in the Great Physician: Suffering and Divine Healing in American Culture, 1860–1900* (Baltimore, MD: Johns Hopkins Press, 2007).

6. Lynne Gerber, *Seeking the Straight and Narrow: Weight Loss and Sexual Reorientation in Evangelical America* (Chicago: University of Chicago Press, 2011).

7. For example, see the National Association for Research and Therapy for Homosexuality at http://narth.com.

8. Tanya Erzen, *Straight to Jesus: Sexual and Christian Conversions in the Ex-Gay Movement* (Berkeley and Los Angeles: University of California Press, 2006); Gerber, *Seeking the Straight and Narrow*; Janet Jakobsen and Ann Pellegrini, *Love the Sin: Sexual Regulation and the Limits of Religious Tolerance* (New York: New York University Press, 2003).

9. For a chastity rally website with tour schedule, see: http://www.silver-ringthing.com. For Christian domestic discipline: http://www.christiandomesticdiscipline.com. For evangelical marital aids websites, see: http://www.covenantspice.com. For an evangelical pro-natalist group, see: http://www.quiverfull.com. For a pastor's guide to sex, read Mark and Grace Driscoll's *Real Marriage: The Truth about Sex, Friendship and Life Together* (Nashville, TN: Thomas Nelson, 2012). For advice on how a helpmeet wife should relate to her husband, see the blog: http://joyfulhelpmeetathome.webs.com. All of the sources mentioned above are representative of many other sites, blogs, and books.

CHAPTER I

1. A bride price in antiquity is the amount of money or property paid by the groom's family to the bride's family. There is mention of this practice in the Bible found in Exodus and Deuteronomy.

2. "The Virgin Daughters," *The Cutting Edge*, Channel 4 Television Corporation, (UK: 25 September 2008)

3. Nancy Gibbs, "The Pursuit of Teen Girl Purity," *Time*, July 17, 2008, http://www.time.com/time/magazine/article/0,9171,1823930,00.html; Jennifer Baumgardner, "Would You Pledge Your Virginity to Your Father?" *Glamour*, January 1, 2007, http://www.glamour.com; Neela Banerjee, "Dancing Away the Night with a Higher Purpose," *New York Times*, May 19, 2008, http://www.nytimes.com/2008/05/19/us/19purity.html; Amanda Robb, "Father Knows

Best," *Marie Claire*, August 7, 2007, http://www.marieclaire.com/
sex-love/relationship-issues/articles/father-marriage; "Purity Balls,"
The Today Show, September 16, 2008, http://video.google.com/vide
oplay?docid=4762184037273160599; "Daddy–Daughter Pledge of
Chastity," *Good Morning America*, June 28, 2007, http://abcnews.
go.com/GMA/story?id=3325449&page=1; "Purity Balls" aired on
TLC November 2008.

4. "The Pledge," Generations of Light, http://www.generationsoflight.
com/html/thepledge.html.

5. Generations of Light, http://www.generationsoflight.com/html/
index.html.

6. Breanna Fahs, "Daddy's Little Girl: On the Perils of Chastity Clubs,
Purity Balls, and Ritualized Abstinence," *Frontiers: A Journal of
Women's Studies* 31, no. 3 (2010): 116–142, 133.

7. Baumgardner, "Would You Pledge Your Virginity to Your Father?"

8. See, for example, Alex and Brett Harris's 2011 The Rebelution Tour,
http://www.therebelution.com/about/alex_and_brett.htm. The twins
are younger brothers to author Joshua Harris who has written many
courtship and purity books including *I Kissed Dating Goodbye*, rev.
ed. (Colorado Springs, CO: Multnomah Books, 2003). Alex and
Brett have written *Do Hard Things: A Teenage Rebellion against
Low Expectations* (Colorado Springs, CO: Multnomah Books,
2008).

9. Jennie Bishop, *The Princess and the Kiss: A Story of God's Gift
of Purity* (Anderson, IN: Warner Press, 1999). Similar titles can
be found and purchased on purity websites such as Generations
of Virtue (http://www.generationsofvirtue.org). Examples of
princess-themed purity literature aimed at girls ages 5 and under
include: Karen Kingsbury, *The Princess and the Three Knights*
(Grand Rapids, MI: Zonderkidz, 2009); Angela Elwell Hunt, *The
True Princess* (Lake Mary, FL: Charismakids, 2005). Other books
continue on the princess theme but emphasize manners or "godly"
female character traits such as virtue, honesty, gentleness, faithfulness. For an example of a princess story that emphasizes "godly"
character reinforced by scriptural passages, see Kathryn O'Brien,
I'd be Your Princess: A Royal Tale of Godly Character (Cincinnati,
OH: Standard Publishing Co., 2004). For an example of manners

being taught through biblical principles and a princess character, see Emilie Barnes, *A Little Princess in the Making: A Royal Guide to Becoming a Girl of Grace* (Eugene, OR: Harvest House, 2007); Jacqueline Johnson, *Princess Joy's Birthday Blessing* (Grand Rapids, MI: Zonderkidz, 2011). It is noteworthy that in all of the children's books the princesses are depicted as Anglo and often with blonde hair.

10. There are a number of books that are written for boys that use the princess theme to encourage purity among boys. For example, see Bishop's companion book, *The Squire and the Scroll: A Tale of the Rewards of a Pure Heart* (Anderson, IN: Warner Press, 2004).

11. Bishop, *The Princess and the Kiss*, 7.

12. O'Brien, *I'd be Your Princess*; Cindy Morgan, *Dance Me, Daddy* (Grand Rapids, MI: Zonderkidz, 2009).

13. Sheila Walsh, *Gigi, God's Little Princess* (Nashville, TN: Thomas Nelson, 2005).

14. Dannah Gresh, *8 Great Dates for Moms and Daughters: How to Talk about True Beauty, God's Fashion, and. . . Modesty* (Eugene, OR: Harvest House Publishers, 2010) does not emphasize the princess theme but represents this focus on the mother–daughter relationship for girls in the 8–12 age group.

15. Jackie Kendall, *Lady in Waiting for Little Girls: Strengthening the Heart of Your Princess* (Birmingham, AL: New Hope Publishers, 2009).

16. Kelly Chapman, *Princess with a Purpose* (Eugene, OR: Harvest House Publishers, 2010).

17. Sheila Walsh, *God's Little Princess Devotional Bible: Bible Storybook*, rpt. ed. (Nashville, TN: Thomas Nelson, 2006); Sheila Walsh, *Sweet Dreams Princess: God's Little Princess Bedtime Bible Stories* (Nashville, TN: Thomas Nelson, 2008); Sheri Rose Shepherd, *His Little Princess: Treasured Letters from your King* (Colorado Springs, CO: Multnomah Books, 2006); Jeannie Bishop, *Life Lessons from the Princess and the Kiss* (Niles, MI: Revive our Hearts, 2004).

18. Andy Holmes, *My Princess Bible* (Nashville, TN: Tyndale House Publishers, 2010).

19. *Princess Bible: Pink* (Nashville, TN: Thomas Nelson, 2007).

20. Lisa E. Samson, *Apples of Gold: A Parable of Purity* (Colorado Springs, CO: Waterbrook Press, 2001), 99.

21. Ibid., 99, 100.

22. Sarah Mally, *Before You Meet Prince Charming: A Guide to Radiant Purity* (Greensburg, IN: Winters Publishing, 2006), 23.

23. Ibid., 151, 112, 153.

24. Ibid., 130, 76.

25. Beth Shively, "'Can-Do' or 'Set-Apart'?: Contemporary Christian Courtship and the Rejection of Girl Power," Midwest American Academy of Religion, Rock Island, IL (March 2010). Shively argues that Mally uses the language of girl power to assert empowerment through submission.

26. Mally, *Before You Meet Prince Charming*, 40, 80, 22.

27. Ibid., 135.

28. Ibid., 158.

29. Ibid., 207–208, 211.

30. Ibid., 185.

31. Leslie Ludy's On-Line Living Room, http://www.setapartgirl.com.

32. Leslie Ludy, *Set-Apart Femininity* (Eugene, OR: Harvest House Press, 2008), 11.

33. Leslie Ludy, *Answering the Guy Questions: The Set-Apart Girl's Guide to Relating to the Opposite Sex* (Eugene, OR: Harvest House Publishers, 2009), 41–42.

34. Ludy, *Set-Apart*, 53.

35. Ibid., 45, 69–70.

36. The modest dressing movement has grown over the past ten years, particularly through websites, blogs, and fashion conferences. For examples, see Pure Fashion (http://www.purefashion.com), Sierra Brooke (http://www.sierrabrooke.com), Shari Brendel's Fashion Meets Faith website (http://www.sharibraendel.com) for books, events, speaking engagements, and a free online color analysis. Dannah Gresh runs the "Modesty Project" through her site Secret Keeper Girl (http://www.secretkeepergirl.com). She provides a petition for the fashion industry to create age-appropriate clothing for girls and her site sponsors "shop 'til you drop" events when girls and mothers shop at approved stores that do not sell clothes that sexualize young girls. For an extensive modest clothing directory including

modesty blogs from various religious traditions: http://www.living-modest.com.

37. Wendy Shalit, *A Return to Modesty: Discovering the Lost Virtue* (New York: Free Press, 1999). Shalit has also written *The Good Girl Revolution: Young Rebels with Self-Esteem and High Standards* (New York: Ballantine Books, 2008) and manages the blog http://blogs.modestlyyours.net/.

38. Annie Wesche, "Beautiful Provision: When God Claims a Closet," *Setapartgirl Magazine*, May/June 2011, 82–87.

39. Leslie Ludy, "What Kind of Swimwear Is Appropriate for a Set-Apart Young Woman?" May/June 2011, 88–90.

40. Ibid., 60.

41. Ibid., 111.

42. Ibid., 118–119.

43. For more information on Christian Charm Courses, see Emily Hunter, Jody Capeheart, Angela Carnathan, and Amy Kendrick Pierson, *The New Christian Charm Course: Student Book* (Eugene, OR: Harvest House Publishers, 2009).

44. Dannah Gresh, *And the Bride Wore White: Seven Secrets to Sexual Purity* (Chicago: Moody Publishers, 2004), 68. Shannon Ethridge and Stephen Arterburn, *Every Young Woman's Battle: Guarding Your Mind, Heart and Body in a Sex-Saturated World* (Colorado Springs, CO: Waterbrook Press, 2004), 144. According to purity authors, the most essential reason for a young man to be considered marriage material is a sincere belief in salvation through Jesus.

45. Lifeway Christian Resources, "True Love Waits," http://www.lifeway.com/Article/true-love-waits.

46. True Love Waits sells rings, wristbands, necklaces, t-shirts, and a variety of other accessories listed under "forgiven jewelry." The group also suggests that pledgers purchase James Jackson's TLW's bible study, *Revolutionary Purity* and *The Path to Purity: A Family Guide*. The True Love Waits material tends to capitalize on teens being countercultural when they pledge purity.

47. Lifeway Christian Resources, "True Love Waits," http://www.lifeway.com/Article/true-love-waits.

48. Christine J. Gardner, *Making Chastity Sexy: The Rhetoric of Evangelical Abstinence Campaigns* (Berkeley: University of California Press, 2011).

49. For more on Silver Ring Thing: Sara Moslener, "Don't Act Now! Selling Christian Abstinence in the Religious Marketplace," in *God in the Details: American Religion and Popular Culture*, edited by Eric Mazur and Karen McCarthy (New York: Routledge Press, 2009), 197–218.

50. Medical News Today, "Many Teens Who Take 'Virginity Pledges' Substitute Other High-Risk Behavior for Intercourse," http://www.medicalnewstoday.com. Pledgers tend not to use condoms and engage in sexual behavior such as oral and anal sex because they don't view that as losing their virginity.

51. Janet E. Rosenbaum, "Patient Teenagers?: Virginity Pledges as a Marker for Lower Sexual Activity," *Pediatrics* 123, no. 1 (January 2009): 110–120.

52. Mark D. Regnerus, *Forbidden Fruit: Sex and Religion in the Lives of American Teenagers* (New York: Oxford University Press, 2007). Regnerus draws his statistics from his own research the National Survey of Youth and Religion as well as other studies such as the federal National Longitudinal Study of Adolescent Health.

53. The emphasis on a purity lifestyle has emerged over the past few years in response to a growing perception that evangelicals who joined chastity clubs define virginity as refraining from heterosexual vaginal intercourse.

54. Jim Burns, *The Purity Code: God's Plan for Sex and Your Body* (Minneapolis, MN: Bethany House, 2008), 16.

55. Ludy, *Set-Apart Femininity*, 28.

56. Heather Hendershot, *Shaking the World for Jesus: Media and Conservative Evangelical Culture* (Chicago: University of Chicago Press, 2004), 87–113.

57. Ibid., 103–106.

58. Similar to Michel Foucault's emphasis on the "task of telling" through confession, young women whose bodies are pure are continually called on to examine their innermost thoughts and desires. Michel Foucault, *The History of Sexuality*, vol. 1, *An Introduction* (New York: Vantage Books, 1980), 22.

59. See, for example, Kris Vallotton, *Purity: The New Moral Revolution* (Shoppensburg, PA: Destiny Image, 2008), 128; DiMarco, *Technical Virgin: How Far is Too Far?* (Grand Rapids, MI: Fleming H. Revell, 2006), 86.

60. DiMarco, *Technical Virgin*, 11, 44, 70, 28.

61. Ludy, *Answering the Guy Question*, 117.

62. Elisabeth Elliot, *Quest for Love: True Stories of Passion and Purity* (Grand Rapids, MI: Fleming H. Revell, 1996), 180.

63. Gresh, *And the Bride Wore White*, 69.

64. Elliot, *Quest for Love*, 249.

65. Ethridge and Arterburn, *Every Young Woman's Battle*, 102.

66. Ibid., 140.

67. There are a few courting novels that are often recommended in the place of romantic fiction. For example, see Mr. and Mrs. Stephen B. Castleberry, *Jeff McLean: His Courtship* (Poplar, WI: Castleberry Farms Press, 1998).

68. Ethridge and Arterburn, *Every Young Woman's Battle*, 143.

69. Gresh, *And the Bride Wore White*, 116.

70. Fahs also highlights the exclusion of mothers in purity balls. Fahs, "Daddy's Little Girls," 134.

71. For example, Gresh, who also accepts dating prior to marriage, balances the mother and father's involvement in guiding daughters in their efforts to maintain purity and choose a godly husband (Gresh, *And the Bride Wore White*, 116). This is part of her distinctive emphasis on mother–daughter relationships at a younger age through her Secret Keeper books, website, and events aimed at girls age 8–12. Secret Keeper Girls, http://www.secretkeepergirl.com.

72. Josh Harris, *Boy Meets Girl: Say Hello to Courtship* (Colorado Springs, CO: Multnomah Press, 2005).

73. Ludy, *Set-Apart*, 116.

74. Gresh, *And the Bride Wore White*, 141.

75. Meg Meeker, *Strong Fathers, Strong Daughter: 10 Secrets Every Father Should Know* (Washington, DC: Regnery Publishing, 2006); Meg Meeker, *Epidemic: How Teen Sex Is Killing Our Kids* (Washington, DC: Lifeline Press, 2002). Meeker makes a direct connection between a strong father–daughter relationship and young women remaining abstinent.

76. Gresh, *And the Bride Wore White*, 142. Another concern raised by the promise of purity involves infertility. Many of the purity authors bolster their claims on the prevalence of STDs associated with premarital sex. They often argue that STDs lead to depression and sometimes infertility. Young women who follow purity rules are all but assured that they will not be infertile. This is an area that requires further research.

77. According to the 2008 Barna Report, 78 percent of American adults have been married, 84 percent of American "born again" Christians report to have been married. Among all American adults who have been married, one-third have had one divorce, that statistic is the same for people who identify as born-again Christians (33%). http://www.barna.org/barna-update/article/15-familykids/42-new-marriage-and-divorce-statistics-released.

78. Mally, *Before You Meet Prince Charming*, 235.

79. Elliot, *Quest for Love*, 198, 199.

80. Ibid., 250. "If marriage is not God's plan for you, may He give you grace to receive singleness as a gift to be embraced and offered back to Him with thanksgiving. Throughout Christian history single men and women have, by the living sacrifice of their aloneness, blessed the Church and found the fulfillment that spiritual parenthood offers."

81. Kris Vallotton, *Purity: The New Moral Revolution* (Shippensburg, PA: Destiny Image Publishers, Inc., 2008), 122.

82. Lakita Garth, *The Naked Truth* (Ventura, CA: Regal Books, 2007).

83. *Virgin Tales*, DVD, directed by Mirjam von Arx, (2012; Zurich, Switzerland: Ican Films Gmbh).

CHAPTER 2

1. Tim LaHaye and Beverly LaHaye, *The Act of Marriage: The Beauty of Sexual Love*, rev. ed. (Grand Rapids, MI: Zondervan, 1998), 37.

2. It should be noted, however, that Comfort's 1972 book focuses on heterosexual sexual activity and deems homosexuality as a lesser and immature form of sexual behavior.

3. For general information on early twentieth-century secular sex manuals, see Peter Laipson, "'Kiss Without Shame, For She Desires It': Sexual Foreplay in American Marital Advice Literature 1900–1920," *Journal*

of *Social History* 29, no. 3 (spring 1996): 507–525; Barbara Epstein, "Family, Sexual Morality, and Popular Movements in Turn-of-the-Century America," in *Powers of Desire: The Politics of Sexuality*, edited by Ann Snitow, Christine Stansell, and Sharon Thompson (New York: New York University Press, 1983); John D'Emilio and Estelle B. Freedman, *Intimate Matters: A History of Sexuality in America* (New York: Harper & Row, 1988); Barbara Ehrenreich, Elizabeth Hess, and Gloria Jacobs, eds., *Re-Making Love: The Feminization of Sex* (New York: Anchor Press, 1986); Carol S. Vance, ed., *Pleasure and Danger: Exploring Female Sexuality* (Boston: Routledge and Keegan Paul, 1984); Michael Gordon, "From an Unfortunate Necessity to a Cult of Mutual Orgasm: Sex in American Marital Education Literature, 1830–1940," in *Studies in the Sociology of Sex*, edited by James M. Henslin (New York: Appleton-Century-Crofts, 1971), 53–77; Michael Gordon, "Sex Manuals: Past and Present," *Medical Aspects of Human Sexuality* 5, no. 9 (September 1971): 20–37; M. E. Melody and Linda M. Peterson, *Teaching America about Sex: Marriage Guides and Sex Manuals from the Late Victorians to Dr. Ruth* (New York: New York University Press, 1999).

4. Thomas H. Van De Velde, M.D., *Ideal Marriage: Its Physiology and Technique*, trans. by Stelle Browne, rev ed. (New York: Random House, 1966), 244.

5. For general information on post–World War II secular sex manuals, see Gordon, "Sex Manuals: Past and Present"; Michael Gordon and Penelope J. Shankweiler, "Different Equals Less: Female Sexuality in Recent Marriage Manuals," *Journal of Marriage and the Family* 33, no. 3 (August 1971): 459–466; Martin S. Weinberg, Rochelle Ganz Swensson, and Sue Kiefer Hammersmith, "Sexual Autonomy and the Status of Women: Models of Female Sexuality in U.S. Sex Manuals from 1950–1980," *Social Problems* 30, no. 3 (February 1983): 312–324; Melody and Peterson, *Teaching America about Sex.*

6. Edward Podolsky, *Sex Technique for Husband and Wife* (New York: Cadillac Publishing Co., 1949), 70.

7. Alex Comfort, *The Joy of Sex: A Gourmet Guide to Love Making* (New York: Simon and Schuster, 1972). For readers who have never seen the first publication of this book, the illustrations will shock you mostly because of how our cultural representations of beauty have

changed. It is impossible to imagine a best-selling sex manual today that would picture lovers as unshaved and untoned. Indeed, recent editions of *The Joy of Sex* have updated the illustrations to match our current taste in bodily beauty.

8. It is noteworthy that Comfort uses the same couple throughout his text. A larger theme of this book is that sexual freedom comes from experimentation with your committed heterosexual lover not by constant exchanging of partners or through homosexual sex.

9. Meryl Altman, "Everything They Always Wanted You to Know: The Ideology of Popular Sex Literature," in *Pleasure and Danger: Exploring Female Sexuality*, edited by Carole S. Vance (Boston: Routledge, 1984), 116–117. Altman in this section refers specifically to Dr. David Reuben's 1969 *Everything You Always Wanted to Know about Sex (*But Were Afraid to Ask)*, but the article surveys a number of sex manuals including Alex Comfort's *The Joy of Sex*. The reference to Michel Foucault's term "speaker's benefit" comes from Michel Foucault, *The History of Sexuality,* vol. 1, *An Introduction*, trans. by Robert Hurley (New York: Vintage Press, 1980), 6.

10. Marabel Morgan, *The Total Woman* (Old Tappan, NJ: Fleming H. Revell, 1973); Marabel Morgan, *Total Joy* (Old Tappan, NJ: Fleming H. Revell, 1976); James Dobson, *What Women Wish Their Husbands Knew about Women* (Wheaton: IL: Tyndale House Publishers, 1975); LaHaye, *The Act of Marriage*. There is little secondary literature written specifically about evangelical sex manuals. The best overall summary is Patricia M. Lennon, "Bible Believers Have Better Sex: Popular Sexology and Gender Ideology in Biblical Marriage" (MA thesis, Department of Religious Studies, Indiana University, 1993). Other secondary sources include: Peter Gardella, "Sex and Submission in the Spirit," in *Religions of the United States in Practice*, vol. 2, edited by Colleen McDannell, Princeton Readings in Religions (Princeton: Princeton University Press, 2001), 173–193; Ehrenreich, Hess, and Jacobs, *Re-Making Love*; Kenneth L. Woodward with Eloise Salholz, "The Bible in the Bedroom," *Newsweek*, February 1, 1982, 71; Mark Oppenheimer, "In the Biblical Sense: A Guide to the Booming Christian Sex-Advice Industry," posted Tuesday, November 20, 1999, at 12:30 A.M. PT, http://slate.msn.com; Michael McMahon, "Come, All Ye Faithful,"

The Spectator (London), vol. 283, December 15–25, 1999, 18–19. Publishing statistics taken from Lennon, "Bible Believers," 5.

11. All quotations from the Bible are from the *New International Version®*.

12. Kevin Leman, *Sheet Music: Uncovering the Secrets of Sexual Intimacy in Marriage* (Wheaton, IL: Tyndale House, 2003), 47.

13. LaHaye, *The Act of Marriage*, 71. The LaHayes make the point that the sexual education they advocate is not taught in the public schools but through books like theirs that stress the Christian approach to sexual education.

14. Ibid., 102.

15. Ibid., 91.

16. Some exceptions include: *Love Life for Every Married Couple: How to Fall in Love and Stay in Love*, written by Ed Wheat and Gloria Okes Perkins who are not married; *Sexuality*, by Letha Dawson Scanzoni; and *Holy Sex: God's Purpose and Plan for Our Sexuality*, co-authored by two men, Terry Wier and Mark Carruth.

17. Ed Wheat and Gaye Wheat, *Intended for Pleasure: Sex Technique and Sexual Fulfillment in Christian Marriage*, 3rd edn. (Grand Rapids, MI: Fleming H. Revell, 1997), 148–162.

18. Leman, *Sheet Music*, 113.

19. Dobson, *What Women Wish*, 114.

20. LaHaye, *The Act of Marriage*, 34.

21. For example, Clifford and Joyce Penner trained at the Masters and Johnson Institute. Clifford and Joyce Penner, *The Gift of Sex: A Guide to Enjoying God's Gift of Sexual Intimacy* (Dallas, TX: Dallas Word Publishing, 1981).

22. I thank Ms. Allison Andre for doing this in the spring of 2004. She drove around mid-Michigan (Lansing, East Lansing, Ann Arbor, and Detroit) and visited dozens of Christian bookstores.

23. Herbert J. Miles, *Sexual Happiness in Marriage: A Positive Approach to the Details You Should Know to Achieve a Healthy and Satisfying Sexual Partnership* (Grand Rapids, MI: Zondervan, 1967), 89–91.

24. Ibid., 95–96.

25. LaHaye, *The Act of Marriage*, 96.

26. Leman, *Sheet Music*, 69–70.

27. Miles, *Sexual Happiness*, 100.

28. Alan Rusbridger, *A Concise History of the Sex Manual, 1886–1986* (London: Faber and Faber, 1986), 21.

29. Podolsky, *Sex Technique for Husband and Wife*, 60.

30. Ed Wheat and Gaye Wheat, *Intended for Pleasure: Fulfillment in a Christian Marriage*, rev. ed. (Grand Rapids, MI: Fleming, 1999), 98.

31. The illustrations are centrally situated at the midpoint of the book.

32. Douglas E. Rosenau, *A Celebration of Sex* (Nashville, TN: Thomas Nelson Publishers, 1994), 150.

33. Ibid., 248, 157.

34. LaHaye, *The Act of Marriage*, 44.

35. Tim LaHaye, *How to Be Happy Though Married* (Wheaton, IL: Tyndale House, 1968).

36. Ed Wheat and Gaye Wheat, *Intended for Pleasure: Sex Technique and Sexual Fulfillment in Christian Marriage*, 3rd edn. (Grand Rapids: Fleming H. Revell, 1997), 93, 135.

37. John Piper, *What's the Difference? Manhood and Womanhood Defined According to the Bible* (Wheaton, IL: Crossways Books, 1990), 26.

38. James Dobson, *What Wives Wish their Husbands Knew about Women* (Wheaton, IL: Tyndale, 1975), 115.

39. Rosenau, *A Celebration of Sex*, 88.

40. Morgan, *The Total Woman*, 117, 97.

41. Martin E. Marty, "Fundies and the Fetishes," *The Christian Century*, December 8, 1976, 1111.

42. Joyce Maynard, "The Liberation of Total Woman," *New York Times Magazine*, September 28, 1975, 47; Claire Safran, "Can the Total Woman 'Magic' Work for You?" *Redbook*, February 1976, 90.

43. Gardella, "Sex and Submission in the Spirit," 174–175.

44. Morgan, *The Total Woman*, 163, 127, 20.

45. Mark Driscoll and Grace Driscoll, *Real Marriage: The Truth about Sex, Friendship, and Life Together* (Nashville, TN: Thomas Nelson, 2012).

46. Molly Worten, "Who Would Jesus Smack Down?" *New York Times Magazine*, January 6, 2009.

47. For example, see Driscoll's sermon preached in Edinburgh, Scotland, in 2007, "Sex, a Study of the Good Bits from Song of Solomon," in which he argues that oral sex is biblical. The sermon is not posted on

his website, http://marshill.com, but is easily available through word search on the Internet.

48. Susan Wise Bauer, "Talking about REAL Marriage: Advice from the Driscolls," *Books and Culture: A Christian Review*, January 2, 2012.

49. For example, see Fuller Theological Seminary blogger David Moore's review of the book posted on January 6, 2012: http://the-burnerblog.com/arts/books/how-to-avoid-satan-himself-laying-in-the-space-between-you-and-other-loose-ends-from-questions-fr om-real-marriage.

50. Driscoll, *Real Marriage*, 117.

51. Ibid., 189, 180.

52. The most commonly quoted Scriptures to support the claim of the sanctity of sex are: Genesis 1:25–31; Song of Solomon 2:3–17, 4:1–7; Hebrews 13:4; Proverbs 5:18–19; 1 Corinthians 7:2–9.

CHAPTER 3

1. The *Denver Post* ran regular articles on the Haggard case between November 6, 2006, and February 9, 2007. The articles are accessible through http://Denverpost.com. The quotes are taken directly from the *Denver Post* articles. Haggard's evangelical peers quickly responded. An oversight committee of local clergy reviewed the allegations and sent him to a "restoration" program in Phoenix, Arizona, run by two evangelical pastors: Jack Hayford of The Church on the Way in Van Nuys, California, and Tommy Barnett of First Assembly of God in Phoenix, Arizona. The high-profile James Dobson of Focus on the Family—a national evangelical group based in the same city as New Life Church—was invited to participate but declined.

2. Some familiar with the evangelical Ex-Gay movement, whether or not they agree with reparative therapy to "cure" people of their homosexuality, point out that "reprogramming" takes a lifetime; there is no quick fix, even for the most ardent believer.

3. One of the participants in the "restoration," the Reverend Jack Hayford founded The Church on the Way in Van Nuys, CA, and The King's College and Seminary. He has written dozens of books and hundreds of hymns. In the media reporting about Haggard's restoration, there was no direct link made to deliverance, although

Hayford affirmed that prayer and counseling was part of the private sessions. It is reasonable to assume that deliverance was part of the restoration based on information about his ministry posted on his website. There are three examples of deliverance listed on his website. First, under "Related Ministries," Hayford lists Cleansing Stream Ministries and explains it "is committed to partnering with pastors and churches in teaching and training leaders and maturing believers in personal cleansing, deliverance, and spiritual warfare so they can be released to serve, minister, and disciple others in the Body of Christ" (http://www.cleansingstream.org). Second, under "The Library" and then "Frequently Asked Questions," Hayford answers "What is a demon?" and provides several links to resources about the influence of evil spirits on believers. Third, under "OSPN" (Online School of Pastoral Nurture), there is a sample page of "Pastor Hayford on Deliverance: How the Ministry of Deliverance is to be Conveyed" (http://www.jackhayford.com/ospn_sample_pages/deliverance.html).

4. Terry Wier and Mark Carruth, *Holy Sex: God's Purpose and Plan for Our Sexuality* (New Kensington, PA: Whitaker House, 1999).

5. David Brakke, *Demons and the Making of the Monk: Spiritual Combat in Early Christianity* (Cambridge, MA: Harvard University Press, 2006); David Frankfurter, *Evil Incarnate: Rumors of Demonic Conspiracy and Satanic Abuse in History* (Princeton, NJ: Princeton University Press, 2008).

6. Elizabeth Reiss, *Damned Women: Saints and Sinners in Puritan New England* (Ithaca, NY: Cornell University Press, 1999); Walter Stephens, *Demon Lovers: Witchcraft, Sex, and the Crisis of Belief* (Chicago: University of Chicago Press, 2002); Charles Zika, *Exorcising Our Demons: Magic, Witchcraft, and Visual Culture in Early Modern Europe* (Leiden: Brill, 2003).

7. Angus McLaren, *Twentieth-century Sexuality: A History* (Malden, MA: Wiley-Blackwell Publishers, 1999); Albert R. Mohler, Jr., "Is Your Baby Gay? What if You Could Know? What if you could do Something about It?" http://albertmohler.com/blog_read.php?id=891.

8. Disability activists have become increasingly concerned regarding genetic testing and counseling. Many argue that there is an

implicit eugenics program underlining the concern to identify "normal" and "abnormal" genes. For example, the American College of Obstetricians and Gynecologists changed its recommended guidelines in January 2007 to encourage all pregnant women (not just those over 35 years old) to undergo genetic screening for chromosomal irregularities such as Down syndrome. For more on the ethics of genetic testing, see Ruth Hubbard, *The Politics of Women's Biology* (New Brunswick, NJ: Rutgers University Press, 1990); Lisa Blumberg, "The Politics of Prenatal Testing and Selective Abortion," in *Women and Disabilities: Reproduction and Motherhood*, special issue of *Sexuality and Disability Journal* 12, no. 2 (1994): 135–153. Adrienne Asch, "The Human Genome and Disability Rights," *Disability Rag and Resource* January/February (1994): 12–13; C. Mansfield et al., "Termination Rates after Prenatal Diagnosis of Down Syndrome, Spina Bifida, Amencephaly, Turner and Kliefelter Syndromes: A Systematic Literature Review," *Prenatal Diagnosis* 19, no. 9 (1999): 808–812.

9. Tim Allen Gardner, *Sacred Sex: A Spiritual Celebration of Oneness in Marriage* (Colorado Springs, CO: Waterbrook Press, 2002); C. J. Mahaney, *Sex, Romance, and the Glory of God: What Every Christian Husband Needs to Know* (Wheaton, IL: Crossway Books, 2004); Gary and Betsy Ricucci, *Love that Lasts: When Marriage Meets Grace* (Wheaton, IL: Crossway Books, 2006).

10. Alex Comfort, *The Joy of Sex: A Gourmet Guide to Lovemaking* (New York: Crown Press, 1972).

11. Gardner, *Sacred Sex*, 5.

12. R. Marie Griffith's analysis of Christian diet books in *Born-Again Bodies* shows that the fitness of the born-again body can be construed as directly or indirectly affecting an individual's relationship with the divine.

13. Gardner, *Sacred Sex*, 48–49.

14. Donald Basham, *Deliver Us from Evil: A Pastor's Reluctant Encounters with the Powers of Darkness* (Grand Rapids, MI; Chosen Books, 1972); Frank Hammond and Ida Mae Hammond, *Pigs in the Parlor: A Practical Guide to Deliverance* (Kirkwood, MO: Christina Books, 1973); Francis MacNutt, *Healing* (Notre Dame, IN: Ave Maria Press, 1974); Kenneth McAll, *Healing*

the Family Tree (London: Sheldon Press, 1982); Alex W. Konya, *Demons: A Biblically Based Perspective* (Schaumburg, IL: Regular Baptist Press, 1990); Derek Prince, *They Shall Expel Demons—Your Invisible Enemies* (Grand Rapids, MI: Chosen Books, 1998).

15. Merrill F. Unger, *What Demons Can Do to Saints* (Chicago: Moody Press, 1977), 109.

16. Michael W. Cuneo, *American Exorcism: Expelling Demons in the Land of Plenty* (New York: Doubleday Press, 2001). Cuneo contends that the rise in interest and practice of deliverance is consistent with the growth in the therapeutic approach to self-transformation and healing that became more mainstream in American culture during this time. "Despite being cloaked in the time-orphaned language of demons and supernatural evil, deliverance was surprisingly at home in the brightly lit, fulfillment-on-demand culture of post-sixties America" (126). Cuneo also credits the 1971 publication of William Peter Blatty's recounting of a child's possession in *The Exorcist* and the release of the 1973 film *The Exorcist* with adding to the cultural appetite and demand for demon deliverance.

17. Grant Wacker, *Heaven Below: Early Pentecostalism and American Culture* (Cambridge, MA: Harvard University Press, 2001), 92. The belief that demons caused illness was common knowledge among late nineteenth-century holiness people and from the beginnings of Pentecostalism in the twentieth century. "Everyone knew that evil spirits caused most illnesses. Therefore in many cases divine healing involved exorcism of the tormenting spirit."

18. Hank Hanegraaff, *The Covering: God's Plan to Protect You from Evil* (Nashville, TN: W. Publishing Group, 2002), 110.

19. Cuneo, *American Exorcism*, 42–49.

20. Ibid., 46.

21. M. Scott Peck, *Glimpses of the Devil: A Psychiatrist's Personal Accounts of Possession, Exorcism and Redemption* (New York: Free Press, 2005).

22. Jim Logan, *Reclaiming Surrendered Ground: Protecting Your Family from Spiritual Attacks* (Chicago: Moody Press, 1995), 147.

23. Prince, *They Shall Expel Demons*, 192–202; Derek Prince, *Rules of Engagement: Preparing for Your Role in the Spiritual Battle* (Grand Rapids, MI: Chosen Books, 2006), 111.

24. The military organization and personification of demons is represented well in Frank E. Peretti's popular apocalyptic novels. In *This Present Darkness* (Wheaton, IL: Crossway Books, 1986) and the sequel *Piercing the Darkness* (Wheaton, IL: Crossway Books, 1989) a battalion of demons fights heroic angels over the eternal souls of humankind. Angels are supported by the prayers of the faithful who provide "prayer coverage" while demon soldiers employ evil tactics to infiltrate and control society. Jay Howard notes that the main conduits for demonic control in Peretti novels are meditative practices and channeling in New Age Religions, educational institutions, the media, the government, and corporations. These arenas are crawling with demons seeking to control children and their faithful parents. Against all encroaching odds the forces of good, gathered in small communities, wage war through personal salvation and prayer. Jay R. Howard, "Vilifying the Enemy: The Christian Right and the Novels of Frank Peretti," *The Journal of Popular Culture*, 28, no. 3 (1994): 193–206.

25. Hammond, *Pigs in the Parlor*, 3.

26. Matthew 12:43–45: "When the unclean spirit has gone out of a person, it wanders through waterless regions looking for a resting place, but it finds none. Then it says, 'I will return to my house from which I came.' When it comes it finds it empty, swept, and put in order. Then it goes and brings along seven other spirits more evil than itself, and they enter and live there; and the last state of that person is worse than the first. So it will be also with this evil generation."

27. Hammond, *Pigs in the Parlor*, 2.

28. Mark 16:17: "And these signs will accompany those who believe: In my name they will drive out demons; they will speak in new tongues."

29. Hammond, *Pigs in the Parlor*, 8.

30. Ibid., 24, 26, 28–30.

31. Ibid., 125.

32. Many deliverance manuals follow this model of parental rejection leading to demonic affliction. Some authors such as Derek Prince go so far as to argue that prenatal rejection can cause demonic affliction on a fetus. Besides prenatal demonization through exposure to parental "false religions" such as Buddhism and Hinduism, Prince writes: "Other negative forces may also affect an unborn child and

expose it to demonic influences. A mother may resent or even hate the baby in her womb. Perhaps the mother is not married or the father is unfaithful and irresponsible, or the mother may simply not want the child....This (lack of love) will turn in to a deeper wound: rejection. Many babies are born with the spirit of rejection already in them" (Prince, *They Shall Expel Demons*, 104–105).

33. Ibid., 214, 212.
34. Rodger K. Bufford, *Counseling and the Demonic: A How-to Approach* (Dallas, TX: Word Books, 1988), 109.
35. Wier and Carruth, *Holy Sex*, 77, 79.
36. 1 John 3:9: "No one who is born of God will continue to sin, because God's seed remains in them; they cannot go on sinning, because they have been born of God."
37. Wier and Carruth, *Holy Sex*, 83.
38. Ibid., 111.
39. Ibid., 85.
40. Ibid., 83.
41. Bufford, *Counseling and the Demonic*, 109; Logan, *Reclaiming Surrendered Ground*, 107, 110–111; C. Fred Dickson, *Demon Possession and the Christian* (Chicago: Moody Press, 1987), 219–221.
42. Wier and Carruth, *Holy Sex*, 49.
43. Kenneth McAll, *Healing the Family Tree* (London: Sheldon Press, 1982), 7.
44. Wier and Carruth, *Holy Sex*, 87, 86.
45. Tim F. LaHaye and Jerry B. Jenkins, *The Left Behind* series published by Tyndale Press. Sixteen books in all (the first published in 1995), the series follows a Christian apocalyptic end times narrative including the rapture and tribulation.
46. Wier and Carruth, *Holy Sex*, 12.
47. Cuneo, *American Exorcism*, 272–273.

CHAPTER 4

1. 1 Timothy 2:15: "But women will be saved through childbearing—if they continue in faith, love and holiness with propriety."

2. Sam and Bethany Torode, *Open Embrace: A Protestant Couple Rethinks Contraception* (Grand Rapsids, MI: Eerdmans Publishing Company, 2002), 24–25.

3. Mark Oppenheimer, "An Evolving Plan View of Natural Family Planning," *New York Times*, July 8, 2011.

4. Torode, *Open Embrace*, 25, xiv.

5. Ibid., 36–37.

6. Ibid., 37, 25, 39–40.

7. Ibid., 92–93.

8. Oppenheimer, "An Evolving View." The Torodes requested that the publisher Eerdmans stop printing the book, but to date it is still available in paperback via Amazon and other websites.

9. Torode, *Open Embrace*, 89.

10. Some of the most popular websites and blogs are: Ladies Against Feminism, http://www.ladiesagainstfeminism.com; Titus 2 Joy, http://titus2joy.blogspot.com; Visionary Daughters, http://visionary-daughters.com; Your Sacred Calling, http://yoursacredcalling.com/blog; Raising Homemakers, http://raisinghomemakers.com; At the Well, http://www.titus2atthewell.com; Titus 2, http://www.titus2.com; True Woman, http://www.truewoman.com; Girls Gone Wise, http://www.girlsgonewise.com; Above Rubies, http://aboverubies.org.

11. Kathryn Joyce, *Quiverfull: Inside the Christian Patriarchy Movement* (Boston: Beacon Press, 2009), 53.

12. Nancy Leigh DeMoss, ed., *Biblical Womanhood in the Home* (Wheaton, IL: Crossways Books, 2002), 17.

13. Genesis 2:18; Proverbs 31; Ephesians 5:21; 1 Peter 3:1.

14. http://titus2women.webs.com/apps/blog/entries/show/7525434-woman-wife-mother-. Posted June 26, 2011, at 10:30 A.M.

15. Joyce, *Quiverfull*, 53.

16. Martha Peace, *The Excellent Wife: A Biblical Perspective* (Bemidji, MD: Focus Publishing, Inc., 1995, 1999).

17. Joyce, *Quiverfull*, 42–43.

18. Schaeffer's appeal does not extend to everyone who adopts a complementarian approach to biblical womanhood, this is especially evident among younger evangelical women. In a response to a popular book by Rachel Held Evans, *A Year of Biblical Womanhood* (Nashville,

TN: Thomas Nelson Press, 2012), the blogger Mary Kassian of "Girls Gone Wise" states that she laughed out loud when she read the Edith Schaeffer inspired the movement. She writes, "'The Hidden Art of Homemaking'???!! I just about fell off my chair. The book was written seventeen years before the inception of CBMW and about twenty years before we adopted the term 'complementarian.' I have never even heard of it." http://www.girlsgonewise.com.

19. Molly Worthen, "Not Your Father's L'Abri," *Christianity Today*, March 2008.

20. Edith Schaeffer, *Hidden Art of Homemaking* (Wheaton, IL: Tyndale House, 1971).

21. Frank Schaeffer, *Sex, Mom, and God: How the Bible's Strange Take on Sex Led to Crazy Politics—and How I Learned to Love Women (and Jesus) Anyway* (Cambridge, MA: Da Capo Press, 2011), 15.

22. It was based on the earlier "Danvers Statement" first published by the Council on Biblical Manhood and Womanhood a decade earlier.

23. Peace, *The Excellent Wife*, 54.

24. Debi Pearl, *Created to Be His Help Meet: Discover How God Can Make your Marriage Glorious* (Pleasantville, TN: No Greater Joy Ministries, 2004).

25. Ibid., 50, 32.

26. Mary Kassian, "Girls Gone Wise," http://www.girlsgonewise.com.

27. The full response can be viewed on http://www.youtube.com/watch?v=3OkUPc2NLrM. Piper has since amended his statement on December 19, 2012, to include that a woman may in some cases contact the police (not simply have the abuse handled at home or with church elders).

28. DeMoss, *Biblical Womanhood*, 151.

29. Ibid., 23.

30. Pride wrote the introduction to the edited collection.

31. Mary Pride, *The Way Home: Beyond Feminism, Back to Reality*, 25th Anniversary Edition (Fenton, MO: Home Life Books, 2010), pp. xxii–xxiii.

32. Ibid., 191, 202.

33. Ibid., 202, 197.

34. Ibid., 3, 4, 13.

35. Ibid., 24, 25.

36. Frank Schaeffer believes that this reference was a critique aimed at his mother's (Edith Schaeffer) well-known advice that a happy marriage depended on a Christian wife owning black lingerie. Although Pride praises Schaeffer throughout *The Way Home* as a model Christian homemaker, she did not agree with Schaeffer's ideas regarding sexuality and reproduction. Schaeffer, *Sex, Mom, God*, 163.

37. Pride, *The Way Home*, 29.

38. Pride, *The Way Home*, 25.

39. Pearl, *Created to Be His Help Meet*, 23; Peace, *The Excellent Wife*, 109.

40. Pride, *The Way Home*, 16, 17, 19.

41. Ibid., 20.

42. Pearl, *Created to Be His Help Meet*, 15, 51; Pride, *The Way Home*, 111. Note that Pride assumes that older Christian women do not hold advanced degrees, although she earned a Masters in Computer Systems Engineering.

43. http://www.thewarriorwives.com/2012/09/titus-2-sex-advice-what-to-expect-later.html, posted September 11, 2012.

44. "Pearl's Oysterbed: Encouraging the low libido wife. Helping her understand men, marriage, sex. . . and maybe a lot about herself along the way," http://www.oysterbed7.com.

45. http://www.thewarriorwives.com/2012/08/what-i-wish-id-known-about-sex.html#.UDzJudZlSgo, posted August 28, 2012.

46. http://www.thewarriorwives.com/2012/08/whos-in-charge-of-sex.html, posted August 15, 2012. The author of this entry admits in a previous post that if she had known better she probably would not have married her husband whom she claims has betrayed her many times.

47. Peace, *The Excellent Wife*, 4.

48. Pearl, *Created to Be His Help Meet,* 169.

49. Ibid., 168.

50. Ibid., 164, 167, 169.

51. Schaeffer, *Sex, Mom, and God,* 75–76. This refers to the biblical story found in 2 Samuel 11 and 12 about King David's lust for Bathsheba who he saw bathing on a rooftop. The king had sex with Bathsheba, even though she was married to Uriah the Hittite, who was off fighting a war for David. After Bathsheba became pregnant, David had Uriah killed by putting him on the front line of battle.

52. Schaeffer, *Sex, Mom, and God,* 9.

53. Ibid., 163.

54. http://ati.iblp.org/ati; http://www.aceministries.com/homeschool; http://www.visionforum.com. Homeschooling is part of the larger call for a return to the patriarchal order of biblical culture in which parents are mandated by God to educate their children. There are many homeschooling materials available for Quiverfull families, the most popular come from Bill Gothard's Institute in Basic Life Principles (the Advanced Training Institute International), A.C.E. Homeschool, and the Vision Forum Ministries.

55. Rick and Jan Hess, *A Full Quiver: Family Planning and the Lordship of Christ* (Brentwood, TN: Wolgemuth & Hyatt Publishers, Inc., 1989), 169.

56. Joyce, *Quiverfull*, pp. ix–xi.

57. Nancy Campbell, *Be Fruitful and Multiply: What the Bible Says about Having Children* (San Antonio, TX: Vision Forum Ministries, 2003), 80.

58. Hess, *A Full Quiver*, 169.

59. Joyce, *Quiverfull*, 134. The number of people who identify as "Quiverfull" is uncertain. Joyce puts it at the low tens of thousands noting that many more identify with the movement without claiming the name.

60. Campbell, *Be Fruitful and Multiply*, 11, 175.

61. Rachel Giove Scott, *Birthing God's Mighty Warriors* (Maitland, FL: Xulon Press, 2004), 304, 305, 309.

62. Hess, *A Full Quiver*, 94.

63. Campbell, *Be Fruitful and Multiply*, 112.

64. Craig Houghton, *Family UNplanning: A Guide for Christian Couples Seeking God's Truth on Having Children* (Maitland, FL: Xulon Press, 2007), 49.

65. Hess, *A Full Quiver*, 19.

66. Leviticus 26:21–22, Deuteronomy 28:62, Psalm 106:14–15, Ezekiel 19:10–14.

67. Campbell, *Be Fruitful and Multiply*, 45.

68. Hess, *A Full Quiver*, 38, 79.

69. Ibid., 65.

70. Campbell, *Be Fruitful and Multiply*, 98.

71. Scott, *Birthing God's Mighty Warriors*, 299.

72. Hess, *A Full Quiver*, 98. The "Great Physician" is a reference to Jesus who in the Gospels of the New Testament is recognized as both a spiritual and physical healer.

73. Scott, *Birthing God's Mighty Warriors*, 292.

74. Ibid., 279, 292.

75. Ibid., 340–341, 342.

76. Campbell, *Be Fruitful and Multiply*, 108.

77. Ibid., 109.

78. Hess, *A Full Quiver*, 102–103.

79. Hilary McFarland, *Quivering Daughters: Hope and Healing for the Daughters of Patriarchy* (Dallas, TX: Darklight Press, 2010), 48.

80. The blog "Quivering Daughters" is no longer active. Its stated purpose was to encourage healing for women addressing emotional and spiritual abuse from authoritarian families. The archives remain available at: http://www.quiveringdaughters.com.

81. http://yoursacredcalling.com/blog/2010/11/979. Republished from November 2009.

82. The reality show "19 and Counting" began following the Duggar family in September 2008. The Duggar family also hosts a website, http://www.duggarfamily.com, and the parents Michelle and Jim Bob Duggar have published the book, *The Duggars: 20 and Counting!* (New York: Howard Books, 2008).

83. Pride, *The Way Home*, 218–219. Pride specifically references journalist Kathleen Joyce's 2009 book, *Quiverfull: Inside the Christian Patriarchy Movement*.

84. Pride, *The Way Home*, 220.

CHAPTER 5

1. The 95-minute sermon can be viewed on YouTube in seven 13.53-minute segments at: http://www.youtube.com/watch?v=3CIMGNKebSo. This version of the "No More Sheets" video was uploaded to YouTube on August 3, 2010.

2. For a few examples, see "Meet the Ladies" on the website "Titus 2 Women," http://www.thetitus2women.com, or peruse the photos of the writers on the blog "At the Well," http://www.titus2atthewell.com. The website that claims to be the official Titus 2 website is run

by the Maxwell family and can be accessed here: http://www.titus2. com/about-the-maxwells.html.

3. This does not mean that they do not exist; it means that they are not visible in the popular literature.

4. Albert G. Miller, "The Rise of African-American Evangelicalism in American Culture," in *Perspectives on American Religion and Culture*, edited by Peter W. Williams (New York: Blackwell Press, 1999), 259–269.

5. Ibid., 265.

6. An exception to this statement is a book published after Walton's. Kate Bowler, *Blessed: A History of the American Prosperity Gospel* (New York: Oxford University Press, 2013).

7. Jonathan L. Walton, *Watch This! The Ethics and Aesthetics of Black Televangelism* (New York: New York University Press, 2009), 45.

8. Michelle Burford, "Carnal Knowledge," *Essence* (May 2001): 185.

9. http://www.youtube.com/watch?v=3CIMGNKebSo.

10. "No More Sheets," http://www.youtube.com/watch?v=3CIMGN KebSo.

11. "No More Sheets," http://www.youtube.com/watch?v=3CIMGN KebSo; Burford, "Carnal Knowledge," 222.

12. "No More Sheets," http://www.youtube.com/watch?v=3CIMGN KebSo.

13. Burford, "Carnal Knowledge," 222; "No More Sheets" http://www. youtube.com/watch?v=3CIMGNKebSo.

14. "No More Sheets," http://www.youtube.com/watch?v=3CIMGN KebSo. It is worthwhile to mention that Bynum does not discuss issues such as birth control, homeschooling, or logistics of running a large household that are found in much of the helpmeet literature written by white women. These topics may or may not be significant to her audience. Those types of details are not the point of her sermon and therefore it is not surprising that they are absent.

15. "No More Sheets," http://www.youtube.com/watch?v=3CIMGN KebSo.

16. Burford, "Carnal Knowledge," 222.

17. "No More Sheets," http://www.youtube.com/watch?v=3CIMGN KebSo.

18. T. D. Jakes has published over 50 books (many are revised or new editions). His books that are directly related women include: *Promises*

from God to a Single Women (New York: Putnam, 2005); *Beside Every Good Man: Loving Myself While Standing by Him* (Brentwood, TN: Warner Faith, 2004); *God's Leading Ladies: Out of the Shadows into the Light* (New York: Putnam, 2004); *Loose That Man and Let Him Go!* (Ada, MI: Bethany House, 2003); *Lady, Her Lover, and Her Lord* (New York: Putnam, 2000); *His Lady: Sacred Promises for God's Woman* (New York: Putnam, 1999); *T. D. Jakes Speaks to Women! Deliverance for the Past, Healing for the Present* (Ada, MI: Bethany House, 1996); *Daddy Loves His Girls* (Lake Mary, FL: Charisma House, 1996); *Woman Thou Art Loosed!* (Shippensburg, PA: Destiny Image, 1994).

19. Jonathan Walton, *Watch This! The Ethics and Aesthetics of Black Televangelism* (New York: New York University Press, 2009), 104–107.

20. Ibid., 108.

21. Ibid., 118. Walton estimates that hundreds of thousands of women watch his broadcasts, attend seminars, and purchase his books. He also states that Jakes "is arguably one of the first male African American preachers of his stature to openly and consistently acknowledge women as a focal point of his ministry and God's concern" (ibid., 119).

22. Jakes, *Woman Thou Art Loosed!*, 12.

23. Ibid., 67.

24. Ibid., 67–68.

25. T. D. Jakes, *He-Motions: Even Strong Men Struggle* (New York: Putnam's Sons, 2004), 249, 254.

26. Jakes, *Woman Thou Art Loosed!*, 91.

27. Ibid., 93.

28. Ibid., 43.

29. Ibid., 178.

30. Ibid., 82.

31. Monique Moultrie, "After the Thrill is Gone: Married to the Holy Spirit but Still Sleeping Alone," *Pneuma* 33 (2011): 237–253, 240, 239.

32. Marla F. Frederick, *Between Sundays: Black Women and Everyday Struggles of Faith* (Berkeley and Los Angeles: University of California Press, 2003), 187, 190.

33. Ibid., 197.

REFERENCES

PRIMARY SOURCES

Above Rubies. "Above Rubies." 2013. http://aboverubies.org.

Accelerated Christian Education, Inc. "Homeschool." 2013. http://www.aceministries.com/homeschool/.

Ackerberg, John, and John Welson. *The Facts on Homosexuality: Scientific Research and Biblical Authority: Can Homosexuals Really Change?* Eugene, OR: Harvest House, 1994.

Alcorn, Randy. *Does the Birth Control Pill Cause Abortions?* 10th ed., rev. Sandy, OR: Eternal Perspective Ministries, 2011.

At the Well. "At the Well: Titus 2:4–5." 2013. http://www.titus2atthewell.com/.

Barnes, Emilie. *A Little Princess in the Making: A Royal Guide to Becoming a Girl of Grace.* Eugene, OR: Harvest House, 2007.

Basham, Donald. *Deliver Us from Evil.* Grand Rapids, MI: Chosen Books, 1972.

Bishop, Jennie. *Life Lessons from the Princess and the Kiss.* Niles, MI: Revive Our Hearts, 2004.

———. *The Princess and the Kiss: A Story of God's Gift of Purity.* Anderson, IN: Warner Press, 1999.

———. *The Squire and the Scroll: A Tale of the Rewards of a Pure Heart.* Anderson, IN: Warner Press, 2004.

Botkin, Anna Sofia, and Elizabeth Botkin. "Visionary Daughters." 2013. http://visionarydaughters.com/.

Bufford, Rodger K. "Counseling and the Demonic: A How-to Approach." In *Resources for Christian Counseling*, vol. 17, edited by R. Collins Gary. Dallas, TX: Word Books, 1988.

Burns, Jim. *The Purity Code: God's Plan for Sex and Your Body.* Minneapolis, MN: Bethany House, 2008.

Bynum, Juanita. *No More Sheets: The Truth about Sex.* Lanham, MD: Pneuma Life Publishing, 1998.

Campbell, Nancy. *Be Fruitful and Multiply: What the Bible Says about Having Children.* San Antonio, TX: Vision Forum Ministries, 2003.

Chapman, Kelly. *Princess with a Purpose.* Eugene, OR: Harvest House, 2010.

Comfort, Alex. *The Joy of Sex: A Gourmet Guide to Love Making.* New York: Simon and Schuster, 1972.

Davies, Bob, and Lori Rentzel. *Coming Out of Homo-Sexuality: New Freedom for Men and Women.* Downers Grove, IL: InterVarsity Press, 1993.

DeMoss, Nancy Leigh, ed. *Biblical Womanhood in the Home.* Wheaton, IL: Crossway Books, 2002.

Dickson, C. Fred. *Demon Possession and the Christian.* Chicago: Moody Press, 1987.

DiMarco, Hayley. *Technical Virgin: How Far is Too Far?* Grand Rapids, MI: Fleming H. Revell, 2006.

Dobson, James. *What Women Wish Their Husbands Knew about Women.* Wheaton, IL: Tyndale House Publishers, 1975.

Driscoll, Mark, and Grace Driscoll. *Real Marriage: The Truth about Sex, Friendship, and Life Together.* Nashville, TN: Thomas Nelson, 2012.

Duggar, Jim Bob, and Michelle Duggar. *The Duggars: 20 and Counting!* New York: Howard Books, 2008.

Duggar Family. *The Duggar Family.* http://www.duggarfamily.com.

Elliot, Elisabeth. *Quest for Love: True Stories of Passion and Purity.* Grand Rapids, MI: Fleming H. Revell, 1996.

Ethridge, Shannon, and Stephen Arterburn. *Every Young Woman's Battle: Guarding Your Mind, Heart, and Body in a Sex-Saturated World.* Colorado Springs, CO: Waterbrook Press, 2004.

Evans, Rachel Held. *A Year of Biblical Womanhood: How a Liberated Woman Found Herself Sitting on Her Roof, Covering Her Head, and Calling Her Husband "Master."* Nashville, TN: Thomas Nelson Press, 2012.

Gardner, Tim Allen. *Sacred Sex: A Spiritual Celebration of Oneness in Marriage.* Colorado Springs, CO: Waterbrook Press, 2002.

Garth, Lakita. *The Naked Truth: About Sex, Love and Relationships.* Ventura, CA: Regal Books, 2007.

Generations of Light. "The Pledge." http://www.generationsoflight.com/html/thepledge.html.

Gill, John Thomas. *How to Hold Your Husband: A Frank Psychoanalysis for a Happy Marriage.* Philadelphia, PA: Dorrance & Company, 1951.

Gresh, Dannah. *8 Great Dates for Moms and Daughters: How to Talk about True Beauty, Cool Fashion, and... Modesty!* Eugene, OR: Harvest House, 2010.

———. *And the Bride Wore White: Seven Secrets to Sexual Purity.* Chicago: Moody Publishers, 2004.

———. "Secret Keeper Girls." http://www.secretkeepergirl.com.

Hammond, Frank, and Ida Mae Hammond. *Pigs in the Parlor: A Practical Guide to Deliverance.* Kirkwood, MO: Impact Christian Books, 1973.

Hanegraaff, Hank. *The Covering: God's Plan to Protect You from Evil.* Nashville, TN: W. Publishing Group, 2002.

Harper, Michael. *Spiritual Warfare: Recognizing and Overcoming the Work of Evil Spirits.* Ann Arbor, MI: Servant Books, 1983.

Harris, Alex, and Brett Harris. *Do Hard Things: A Teenage Rebellion Against Low Expectations.* Colorado Springs, CO: Multnomah Books, 2008.

Harris, Joshua. *Boy Meets Girl: Say Hello to Courtship.* Portland, OR: Multnomah Press, 2000.

———. *Not Even a Hint: Guarding Your Heart Against Lust.* Portland, OR: Multnomah Press, 2003.

———. *I Kissed Dating Goodbye: A New Attitude Toward Relationships and Romance.* Portland, OR: Multnomah Press, 1997.

Hess, Rick, and Jan Hess. *A Full Quiver: Family Planning and the Lordship of Christ.* Brentwood, TN: Wolgemuth & Hyatt Publishers, Inc., 1989.

Holmes, Andy. *My Princess Bible.* Nashville, TN: Tyndale House Publishers, 2010.

Houghton, Craig. *Family UNplanning: A Guide for Christian Couples Seeking God's Truth on Having Children.* Maitland, FL: Xulon Press, 2007.

Hunt, Angela Elwell. *The True Princess.* Lake Mary, FL: Charismakids, 2005.

Hunter, Emily, Jody Capeheart, and Angela Carnathan. *The New Christian Charm Course: Today's Social Graces for Every Girl (Student Book)*. Eugene, OR: Harvest House Publishers, 2009.

Institute in Basic Life Principles. "Advanced Training Institute International: Equipping Youth and Families to Do Great Works!" 2011. http://ati.iblp.org/ati/.

Jakes, T. D. *He-Motions: Even Strong Men Struggle*. New York: Putnam's Sons, 2004.

———. *The Lady, Her Lover, and Her Lord*. New York: Berkley Books, 1998.

———. *Woman, Thou Art Loosed!* Shippensburg, PA: Treasure House, 1997.

Johnson, Jacqueline. *Princess Joy's Birthday Blessing*. Grand Rapids, MI: Zonderkidz, 2011.

Jones, Stanton L. *The Gay Debate*. Downers Grove, IL: InterVarsity Press, 1994.

Kassian, Mary A. "Girls Gone Wise." 2013. http://www.girlsgonewise.com/.

———. "Review of A Year of Biblical Womanhood." *Girls Gone Wise*, November 10, 2012. http://www.girlsgonewise.com/review-of-a-year-of-biblical-womanhood/.

Kendall, Jackie. *Lady in Waiting for Little Girls: Strengthening the Heart of Your Princess*. Birmingham, AL: New Hope Publishers, 2009.

Kingsbury, Karen. *The Princess and the Three Knights*. Grand Rapids, MI: Zonderkidz, 2009.

Konya, Alex W. *Demons: A Biblically Based Perspective*. Schaumburg, IL: Regular Baptist Press, 1990.

Ladies Against Feminism/Beautiful Womanhood. "Ladies Against Feminism." 2013. http://www.ladiesagainstfeminism.com/.

LaHaye, Tim. *How to Be Happy Though Married*. Wheaton, IL: Tyndale House, 1968.

———. *The Unhappy Gays: What Everyone Should Know about Homosexuality*. Wheaton, IL: Tyndale House, 1978.

LaHaye, Tim, and Beverly LaHaye. *The Act of Marriage: The Beauty of Sexual Love*. Grand Rapids, MI: Zondervan, 1976.

———. *The Act of Marriage: The Beauty of Sexual Love*. Rev. ed. Grand Rapids, MI: Zondervan, 1998.

Lawless, Chuck. *Discipled Warriors: Growing Healthy Churches that are Equipped for Spiritual Warfare*. Grand Rapids, MI: Kregel Publications, 2002.

Leman, Kevin. *Sheet Music: Uncovering the Secrets of Sexual Intimacy in Marriage*. Nashville, TN: Tyndale House, 2003.

Lifeway Christian Resources. "True Love Waits." http://www.lifeway.com/Article/true-love-waits.

Liswood, Rebecca. *A Marriage Doctor Speaks Her Mind about Sex*. New York: Dutton, 1961.

Logan, Jim. *Reclaiming Surrendered Ground: Protecting Your Family from Spiritual Attacks*. Chicago: Moody Press, 1995.

Ludy, Leslie. *Answering the Guy Questions: The Set-Apart Girl's Guide to Relating to the Opposite Sex*. Eugene, OR: Harvest House Publishers, 2009.

———. "Leslie Ludy's Online Living Room." http://www.setapartgirl.com.

———. *Set-Apart Femininity: God's Sacred Intent for Every Young Woman*. Eugene, OR: Harvest House Press, 2008.

———. "What Kind of Swimwear Is Appropriate for a Set-Apart Young Woman?" *Setapartgirl Magazine*, May/June 2011, 88–90.

MacNutt, Francis. *Deliverance from Evil Spirits: A Practical Manual*. Grand Rapids, MI: Chosen Books, 1995.

———. *Healing*. Notre Dame, IN: Ave Maria Press, 1974.

Mahaney, C. J. *Sex, Romance, and the Glory of God: What Every Christian Husband Needs to Know*. Wheaton, IL: Crossway Books, 2004.

Mally, Sarah. *Before You Meet Prince Charming: A Guide to Radiant Purity*. Greensburg, IN: Winters Publishing, 2006.

McAll, Kenneth. *Healing the Family Tree*. London: Sheldon Press, 1982.

McDonald, Stacy. "Jesus-full." *Your Sacred Calling: Inspiration for the Passionate Housewife* (blog). November 2009. http://yoursacredcalling.com/blog/2010/11/979.

McFarland, Hilary. *Quivering Daughters* (blog). 2011. http://www.quiveringdaughters.com.

———. *Quivering Daughters: Hope and Healing for the Daughters of Patriarchy*. Dallas, TX: Darklight Press, 2010.

Meeker, Meg. *Epidemic: How Teen Sex Is Killing Our Kids*. Washington, DC: Lifeline Press, 2002.

————. *Strong Fathers, Strong Daughters: 10 Secrets Every Father Should Know*. Washington, DC: Ballantine Books, 2006.

Miles, Herbert J. *Sexual Happiness in Marriage: A Positive Approach to the Details You Should Know to Achieve a Healthy and Satisfying Sexual Partnership*. Grand Rapids, MI: Zondervan, 1967.

Mohler, Albert R., Jr. "Is Your Baby Gay? What if Your Could Know?" http://albertmohler.com/blog_read.php?id=891.

Moore, Ashley. "We Don't Need Sexual Healing." *Her-meneutics*, September 23, 2013. http://www.christianitytoday.com/women/2013/september/why-we-dont-need-sexual-healing.html.

Morgan, Cindy. *Dance Me, Daddy*. Grand Rapids, MI: Zonderkidz, 2009.

Morgan, Marabel. *Total Joy*. Old Tappan, NJ: Fleming H. Revell, 1976.

————. *The Total Woman*. Old Tappan, NJ: Fleming H. Revell, 1973.

Need, Bettie. "Titus 2 Joy." 2012. http://titus2joy.blogspot.com/.

O'Brien, Kathryn. *I'd Be Your Princess: A Royal Tale of Godly Character*. Cincinnati, OH: Standard Publishing, 2004.

Peace, Martha. *The Excellent Wife: A Biblical Perspective*. Bemidji, MN: Focus Publishing, Inc., 1995.

Pearl. *Pearl's OysterBed: Encouraging the Low Libido Wife. Helping Her Understand Men, Marriage, Sex. . . and Maybe a lot about Herself along the Way* (blog). http://www.oysterbed7.com/.

————. "What I Wish I'd Known about Sex." *Warrior Wives* (blog), August 28, 2012. http://www.thewarriorwives.com/2012/08/what-i-wish-id-known-about-sex.html.

Pearl, Debi. *Created to Be His Help Meet: Discover How God Can Make Your Marriage Glorious*. Pleasantville, TN: No Greater Joy Ministries, 2004.

Peck, M. Scott. *Glimpses of the Devil: A Psychiatrist's Personal Accounts of Possession, Exorcism, and Redemption*. New York: Free Press, 2005.

————. *People of the Lie: The Hope for Healing Human Evil*. New York: Touchstone Press, 1983.

————. *The Road Less Traveled*. New York: Simon & Schuster, 1978.

Penner, Clifford, and Joyce Penner. *The Gift of Sex: A Guide to Enjoying God's Gift of Sexual Intimacy*. Dallas, TX: Dallas Word Publishing, 1981.

Pentecost, Dwight J. *Your Adversary, the Devil*. Grand Rapids, MI: Zondervan Publishing House, 1969.

Peretti, Frank E. *Piercing the Darkness*. Wheaton, IL: Crossway Books, 1989.

———. *This Present Darkness*. Wheaton, IL: Crossway Books, 1986.

Peterson, Robert. *Are Demons for Real?* Chicago: Moody Press, 1979.

Piper, John. "John Piper: Does a Woman Submit to Abuse?" Posted September 1, 2009. http://www.youtube.com/watch?v=3OkUPc2NLrM.

———. *What's the Difference? Manhood and Womanhood Defined According to the Bible*. Wheaton, IL: Crossway Books, 1990.

Podolsky, Edward. *Sex Technique for Husband and Wife*. New York: Cadillac Publishing Co., 1949.

Pride, Mary. *The Way Home: Beyond Feminism, Back to Reality*. 25th anniversary ed. Fenton, MO: Home Life Books, 2010.

Prince, Derek. *Rules of Engagement: Preparing for Your Role in the Spiritual Battle*. Grand Rapids, MI: Chosen Books, 2006.

———. *They Shall Expel Demons: What You Need to Know about Demons–Your Invisible Enemies*. Grand Rapids, MI: Chosen Books, 1998.

Princess Bible: Pink. Nashville, TN: Thomas Nelson, 2007.

Provan, Charles D. *The Bible and Birth Control*. Monongahela, PA: Zimmer Printing, 1989.

Raising Homemakers. "Raising Homemakers." 2013. http://raisinghomemakers.com.

Reuben, David. *Everything You Always Wanted to Know About Sex (*But Were Afraid to Ask)*. New York: Random House, 1969.

Revive Our Hearts. "True Woman." 2012. http://www.truewoman.com/.

Ricucci, Gary, and Betsy Ricucci. *Love that Lasts: When Marriage Meets Grace*. Wheaton, IL: Crossway Books, 2006.

Rosenau, Douglas E. *A Celebration of Sex: A Guide to Enjoying God's Gift of Married Sexual Pleasure*. Nashville, TN: Thomas Nelson, Inc., 1993.

Samson, Lisa E. *Apples of Gold: A Parable of Purity*. Colorado Springs, CO: Waterbrook Press, 2001.

Scanzoni, Letha Dawson. *Sexuality (Choices)*. Louisville, KY: Westminster John Knox Press, 1984.

Schaeffer, Edith. *The Hidden Art of Homemaking*. Wheaton, IL: Tyndale House, 1971.

Scott, Rachel Giove. *Birthing God's Mighty Warriors*. Maitland, FL: Xulon Press, 2004.

Shalit, Wendy. *The Good Girl Revolution: Young Rebels with Self-Esteem and High Standards*. New York: Ballantine Books, 2008.

———. *A Return to Modesty: Discovering the Lost Virtue*. New York: Free Press, 1999.

Shepherd, Sheri Rose. *His Little Princess: Treasured Letters from Your King*. Colorado Springs, CO: Multnomah Books, 2006.

Spence, Elizabeth. "The Future of Sex: Advice from an Older Woman." *Warrior Wives* (blog), September 11, 2012. http://www.thewarrior-wives.com/2012/09/titus-2-sex-advice-what-to-expect-later.html.

———. "Who's in Charge of Sex?" *Warrior Wives* (blog), August 15, 2012. http://www.thewarriorwives.com/2012/08/whos-in-charge-of-sex.html.

Titus2, Inc. "Titus2." 2013. http://www.titus2.com/.

Titus 2 Women's Ministry Network. "Woman, Wife, Mother." *Titus 2 Women*, June 26, 2011. http://titus2women.webs.com/apps/blog/entries/show/7525434-woman-wife-mother-.

Torode, Sam, and Bethany Torode. *Open Embrace: A Protestant Couple Rethinks Contraception*. Grand Rapids, MI: Wm. B. Eerdmans Publishing Co., 2002.

Unger, Merrill F. *What Demons Can Do to Saints*. Chicago: Moody Press, 1977.

Vallotton, Kris. *Purity: The New Moral Revolution*. Shippensburg, PA: Destiny Image, 2008.

Van De Velde, Thomas H. *Ideal Marriage: Its Physiology and Technique*. Rev. ed. Translated by Stelle Browne. New York: Random House, 1966.

Virgin Tales. DVD. Directed by Mirjam von Arx. 2012; Zurich, Switzerland: Ican Films Gmbh.

"The Virgin Daughters." *The Cutting Edge*. Channel 4 Television Corporation. UK: 25 September 2008.

The Vision Forum, Inc. "Vision Forum: Discipleship & Education for Christian Families." 2013. http://www.visionforum.com/.

Walsh, Sheila. *Gigi, God's Little Princess*. Nashville, TN: Thomas Nelson, 2005.

———. *God's Little Princess Devotional Bible: Bible Storybook*. Nashville, TN: Thomas Nelson, 2006.

———. *Sweet Dreams Princess: God's Little Princess Bedtime Bible Stories, Devotions, & Prayers*. Nashville, TN: Thomas Nelson, 2008.

Weber, Stu. *Tender Warrior: God's Intention for a Man*. Portland, OR: Multnomah, 1993.

Wesche, Annie. "Beautiful Provision: When God Claims a Closet." *Setapartgirl Magazine*, May/June 2011, 82–87.

Wessel, Helen. *The Joy of Natural Childbirth: Natural Childbirth and the Christian Family*. New York: HarperCollins, 1963.

Wheat, Ed, and Gloria Okes Perkins. *Love Life for Every Couple: How to Fall in Love and Stay in Love*. Rev. ed. Grand Rapids, MI: Zondervan, 1996.

Wheat, Ed, and Gaye Wheat. *Intended for Pleasure: Sex Technique and Sexual Fulfillment in Christian Marriage*. 3rd ed. Grand Rapids, MI: Fleming H. Revell, 1997.

Wier, Terry, and Mark Carruth. *Holy Sex: God's Purpose and Plan for Our Sexuality*. New Kensington, PA: Whitaker House, 1999.

Worthen, Anita, and Bob Davies. *Someone I Love is Gay: How Family and Friends Can Respond*. Downers Grove, IL: InterVarsity Press, 1996.

Young, Ed, and Lisa Young. *Sexperiment: 7 Days to Lasting Intimacy with Your Spouse*. Nashville, TN: Faithwords, 2012.

Young, Jeanna, and Jacqueline Johnson. *Princess Joy's Birthday Blessing*. Grand Rapids, MI: Zonderkidz, 2011.

SECONDARY SOURCES

Altman, Meryl. "Everything They Always Wanted You to Know: The Ideology of Popular Sex Literature." In *Pleasure and Danger: Exploring Female Sexuality*, edited by Carole S. Vance, 116–117. Boston: Routledge, 1984.

Asch, Adrienne. "The Human Genome and Disability Rights." *Disability Rag and Resource* (January/February 1994): 12–13.

Banerjee, Neela. "Dancing the Night Away, with a Higher Purpose." *New York Times*, May 19, 2008. http://www.nytimes.com/2008/05/19/us/19purity.html.

Banes, Sally, Sheldon Frank, and Tem Horwitz, eds. *Our National Passion: 200 Years of Sex in America*. Chicago: Follett Publishing Company, 1976.

Barna Group. "New Marriage and Divorce Statistics Released." March 31, 2008. http://www.barna.org/barna-update/article/15-familykids/42-new-marriage-and-divorce-statistics-released.

Bartkowski, John. *Remaking the Godly Marriage: Gender Negotiation in Evangelical Families*. New Brunswick, NJ: Rutgers University Press, 2001.

Battan, Jesse F. "'The Word Made Flesh': Language, Authority, and Sexual Desire in Late Nineteenth-Century America." *Journal of the History of Sexuality* 3, no. 2 (October 1992): 223–244.

Bauer, Susan Wise. "Talking about REAL Marriage: Advice from the Driscolls." *Books and Culture: A Christian Review*, January 2, 2012.

Baumgardner, Jennifer. "Would You Pledge Your Virginity to Your Father?" *Glamour*, January 1, 2007. http://www.glamour.com/sex-love-life/2007/01/purity-balls.

Bellafante, Ginia. "Single Evangelical in Need of Advice? Books Have Plenty." *New York Times*, July 19, 2004.

Bendroth, Margaret Lamberts. *Fundamentalism and Gender, 1875 to the Present*. New Haven, CT: Yale University Press, 1996.

Betts, John R. "Mind and Body in Early American Thought." *Journal of American History* 54, no. 4 (March 1968): 787–805.

Bivins, Jason C. *Religion of Fear: The Politics of Horror in Conservative Evangelicalism*. New York: Oxford University Press, 2008.

Blumberg, Lisa. "The Politics of Prenatal Testing and Selective Abortion." *Sexuality and Disability Journal* 12, no. 2 (1994): 135–153.

Brakke, David. *Demons and the Making of the Monk: Spiritual Combat in Early Christianity*. Cambridge, MA: Harvard University Press, 2006.

Brown, Peter. *The Body and Society: Men, Women, and Sexual Renunciation in Early Christianity*. New York: Columbia University Press, 1988.

Bullough, Vern L. "Early American Sex Manual, or, Aristotle Who?" *Early American Literature* 7, no. 3 (Winter 1973): 236–246.

Burford, Michelle. "Carnal Knowledge." *Essence*, May 2001.

Butler, Judith. *Gender Trouble: Feminism and the Subversion of Identity*. New York: Routledge, 1990.

Bynum, Carolyn Walker. *Fragmentation and Redemption: Essays on Gender and the Human Body in Medieval Religion*. New York: Zone Books, 1992.

Chidester, David. *Authentic Fakes: Religion and American Popular Culture.* Berkeley and Los Angeles: University of California Press, 2005.

Cuneo, Michael W. *American Exorcism.* New York: Doubleday, 2001.

Curtis, Heather D. *Faith in the Great Physician: Suffering and Divine Healing in American Culture, 1860–1900.* Baltimore, MD: Johns Hopkins University Press, 2007.

Davis, Dena S. "Religion, Genetics, and Sexual Orientation: The Jewish Tradition." *Kennedy Institute of Ethics Journal* 1, no. 2 (2008): 125–148.

DeBerg, Betty A. *Ungodly Women: Gender and the First Wave of American Fundamentalism.* Macon, GA: Mercer University Press, 2000.

Degler, Carl N. "What Ought to Be and What Was: Women's Sexuality in the Nineteenth-Century." *American Historical Review* 79, no. 5 (December 1974): 1467–1490.

D'Emilio, John, and Estelle B. Freedman. *Intimate Matters: A History of Sexuality in America.* New York: Harper & Row, 1988.

DeRogatis, Amy. "Born Again is a Sexual Term: Demons, STDs, and God's Healing Sperm." *Journal of the American Academy of Religion* 77, no. 2 (June 2009): 275–302.

———. "What Would Jesus Do? Sexuality and Salvation in Protestant Evangelical Sex Manuals, 1950s–Present." *Church History: Studies in Christianity and Culture* 74, no. 1 (March 2005): 97–137.

Ditzion, Sidney. *Marriage, Morals, and Sex in America: A History of Ideas.* New York: Bookman Associates, 1953.

Douglas, Kelly Brown. *Sexuality and the Black Church: A Womanist Perspective.* Maryknoll, NY: Orbis Books, 1999.

Dreger, Alice D. *Hermaphrodites and the Medical Invention of Sex.* Cambridge, MA: Harvard University Press, 2000.

Ehrenreich, Barbara, Elizabeth Hess, and Gloria Jacobs. *Re-Making Love: The Feminization of Sex.* New York: Anchor Press, 1986.

Epstein, Barbara. "Family, Sexual Morality, and Popular Movements in Turn-of-the-Century America." In *Powers of Desire: The Politics of Sexuality*, edited by Ann Snitow, Christine Stansell, and Sharon Thompson. New York: New York University Press, 1983.

Erzen, Tanya. *Straight to Jesus: Sexual and Christian Conversions in the Ex-Gay Movement.* Berkeley and Los Angeles: University of California Press, 2006.

Fahs, Breanne. "Daddy's Little Girl: On the Perils of Chastity Clubs, Purity Balls, and Ritualized Abstinence." *Frontiers: A Journal of Women's Studies* 31, no. 3 (2010): 116–142.

———. *Performing Sex: The Making and Unmaking of Women's Erotic Lives*. Albany: State University of New York Press, 2011.

Fausto-Sterling, Anne. *Sexing the Body: Gender Politics and the Construction of Sex*. New York: Basic Books, 2000.

Fessenden, Tracy, Nicholas F. Radel, and Magdalena J. Zaborowska, eds. *The Puritan Origins of American Sex: Religion, Sexuality, and National Identity in American Literature*. New York: Routledge, 2001.

Foster, Lawrence. *Religion and Sexuality: The Shakers, The Mormons, and the Oneida Community*. Champaign, IL: University of Illinois Press, 1984.

Foster, Thomas A. "Deficient Husbands: Manhood, Sexual Incapacity, and Male Marital Sexuality in Seventeenth-Century New England." *William and Mary Quarterly* 56, no. 4 (October 1999): 723–744.

Foucault, Michel. *The History of Sexuality*. Vol. 1, *An Introduction*. Translated by Robert Hurley. New York: Vintage, 1980.

Frankfurter, David. *Evil Incarnate: Rumors of Demonic Conspiracy and Satanic Abuse in History*. Princeton: Princeton University Press, 2008.

Frederick, Marla F. *Between Sundays: Black Women and Everyday Struggles of Faith*. Berkeley and Los Angeles: University of California Press, 2003.

Freitas, Donna. *Sex and the Soul: Juggling Sexuality, Spirituality, Romance, and Religion on America's College Campuses*. New York: Oxford University Press, 2008.

Gallagher, Sally K. *Evangelical Identity and Gendered Family Life*. New Brunswick, NJ: Rutgers University Press, 2003.

Gardella, Peter. *Innocent Ecstasy: How Christianity Gave America an Ethic of Sexual Pleasure*. New York: Oxford University Press, 1985.

———. "Sex and Submission in the Spirit." In vol. 2 of *Religions of the United States in Practice*, edited by Colleen McDannell, 173–193. Princeton: Princeton University Press, 2001.

Gardner, Christine J. *Making Chastity Sexy: The Rhetoric of Evangelical Abstinence Campaigns*. Berkeley and Los Angeles: University of California Press, 2011.

Gerber, Lynne. *Seeking the Straight and Narrow: Weight Loss and Sexual Reorientation in Evangelical America*. Chicago: University of Chicago Press, 2011.

Gibbs, Nancy. "The Pursuit of Teen Girl Purity." *Time*, July 17, 2008. http://www.time.com/time/magazine/article/0,9171,1823930,00.html.

Godbeer, Richard. *Sexual Revolution in Early America*. Baltimore, MD: Johns Hopkins University Press, 2004.

Good Morning America. "Daughter–Dad Pledge of Chastity." June 28, 2007. http://abcnews.go.com/GMA/story?id=3325449&page=1.

Gordon, Michael. "From an Unfortunate Necessity to a Cult of Mutual Orgasm: Sex in American Marital Education Literature, 1830–1940." In *Studies in the Sociology of Sex*, edited by James M. Henslin, 53–77. New York: Appleton-Century-Crofts, 1971.

———. "Sex Manuals: Past and Present." *Medical Aspects of Human Sexuality* 5, no. 9 (September 1971): 20–37.

Gordon, Michael, and M. Charles Bernstein. "Mate Choice and Domestic Life in the Nineteenth-Century Marriage Manual." *Journal of Marriage and the Family* 32, no. 4 (November 1970): 665–674.

Gordon, Michael, and Penelope J. Shankweiler. "Different Equals Less: Female Sexuality in Recent Marriage Manuals." *Journal of Marriage and the Family* 33, no. 3 (August 1971): 459–466.

Griffith, R. Marie. *Born Again Bodies: Flesh and Spirit in American Christianity*. Berkeley and Los Angeles: University of California Press, 2004.

———. *God's Daughters: Evangelical Women and the Power of Submission*. Berkeley and Los Angeles: University of California Press, 2000.

Hall, Donald. *Muscular Christianity: Embodying the Victorian Age*. Cambridge: Cambridge University Press, 1994.

Hendershot, Heather. *Shaking the World for Jesus: Media and Conservative Evangelical Culture*. Chicago: University of Chicago Press, 2004.

Howard, Jay R. "Vilifying the Enemy: The Christian Right and the Novels of Frank Peretti." *The Journal of Popular Culture* 28, no. 3 (1994): 193–206.

Hubbard, Ruth. *The Politics of Women's Biology*. New Brunswick, NJ: Rutgers University Press, 1990.

Ingersoll, Julie. *Evangelical Christian Women: War Stories in the Gender Battles*. New York: New York University Press, 2003.

Irvine, Janice M. *Disorders and Desire: Sex and Gender in Modern American Sexology*. Philadelphia: Temple University Press, 1990.

Jakobsen, Janet, and Ann Pellegrini. *Love the Sin: Sexual Regulation and the Limits of Religious Tolerance*. New York: New York University Press, 2003.

Jenkins, Kathleen. "Genetics and Faith: Religious Enchantment through Creative Engagement with Molecular Biology." *Social Forces* 85, no. 4 (2007): 1693–1712.

Joyce, Kathryn. *Quiverfull: Inside the Christian Patriarchy Movement*. Boston: Beacon Press, 2009.

Laipson, Peter. "'Kiss Without Shame, For She Desires It': Sexual Foreplay in American Marital Advice Literature 1900–1920." *Journal of Social History* 29, no. 3 (Spring 1996): 507–525.

Lennon, Patricia M. "Bible Believers Have Better Sex: Popular Sexology and Gender Ideology in Biblical Marriage." MA thesis, Indiana University, 1993.

Luhrmann, T. M. *When God Talks Back: Understanding the American Evangelical Relationship with God*. New York: Knopf, 2012.

Mansfield, C., et al. "Termination Rates after Prenatal Diagnosis of Down Syndrome, Spina Bifida, Amencephaly, Turner and Kleifelter Syndromes." *Prenatal Diagnosis* 19, no. 9 (1999): 808–812.

Marty, Martin E. "Fundies and the Fetishes." *The Christian Century*, December 8, 1976, 1111.

Maynard, Joyce. "The Liberation of Total Woman." *New York Times Magazine*, September 28, 1975, 47.

McLaren, Angus. *Twentieth-century Sexuality: A History*. Malden, MA: Wiley-Blackwell Publishers, 1999.

McMahon, Michael. "Come, All Ye Faithful." *The Spectator*, December 15–25, 1999, 18–19.

Medical News Today. "Many Teens Who Take 'Virginity Pledges' Substitute Other High-Risk Behavior for Intercourse." http://www.medicalnews today.com.

Melody, M. E., and Linda M. Peterson. *Teaching America about Sex: Marriage Guides and Sex Manuals from the Late Victorians to Dr. Ruth*. New York: New York University Press, 1999.

Miller, Albert J. "The Rise of African American Evangelicalism in American Culture." In *Perspectives on American Religion and Culture*, edited by Peter W. Williams. New York: Blackwell Press, 1999.

Moore, David. "(It Seems) Mark Driscoll Thinks Wives Are Only Good for Sex." January 4, 2012. http://theburnerblog.com/arts/books/mark-driscoll-thinks-wives-are-only-good-for-sex/.

Morgan, David. "The Masculinity of Jesus in Popular Religious Art." In *Men's Bodies, Men's Gods: Male Identities in a (Post) Christian Culture*, edited by Björn Krondorfer, 251–266. New York: New York University Press, 1996.

Moslener, Sara. "By God's Design? Sexual Abstinence and Evangelicalism in the United States, 1979–Present." PhD dissertation, Claremont Graduate University, 2009.

———. "Don't Act Now! Selling Christian Abstinence in the Religious Marketplace." In *God in the Details: American Religion and Popular Culture*, edited by Eric Mazur and Karen McCarthy, 197–218. New York: Routledge Press, 2009.

Moultrie, Monique. "After the Thrill Is Gone: Married to the Holy Spirit but Still Sleeping Alone." *Pneuma* 33 (2011): 237–253.

Neuhaus, Jessamyn. "The Importance of Being Orgasmic: Sexuality, Gender, and Marital Sex Manuals in the United States, 1920–1963." *Journal of the History of Sexuality* 9, no. 4 (October 2000): 447–473.

Oppenheimer, Mark. "An Evolving View of Natural Family Planning. *New York Times*, July 8, 2011. http://www.nytimes.com/2011/07/09/us/09beliefs.html?_r=0.

———. "In the Biblical Sense: A Guide to the Booming Christian Sex-Advice Industry." *Slate*, November 20, 1999. http://www.slate.com/articles/briefing/articles/1999/11/in_the_biblical_sense.html.

Regnerus, Mark D. *Forbidden Fruit: Sex and Religion in the Lives of American Teenagers*. New York: Oxford University Press, 2007.

Reis, Elizabeth. *Damned Women: Saints and Sinners in Puritan New England*. Ithaca, NY: Cornell University Press, 1999.

Robb, Amanda. "Father Knows Best." *Marie Claire*, August 7, 2007. http://www.marieclaire.com/sex-love/relationship-issues/articles/father-marriage.

Rosenbaum, Janet E. "Patient Teenagers?: Virginity Pledges as a Marker for Lower Sexual Activity." *Pediatrics* 123, no. 1 (January 2009): 110–120.

Rusbridger, Alan. *A Concise History of the Sex Manual, 1886–1986.* London: Faber and Faber, 1986.

Safran, Claire. "Can the Total Woman 'Magic' Work for You?" *Redbook*, February 1976, 90.

Schaeffer, Frank. *Sex, Mom, and God: How the Bible's Strange Take on Sex Led to Crazy Politics—and How I Learned to Love Women (and Jesus) Anyway.* Cambridge, MA: Da Capo Press, 2011.

Schmidt, Leigh Eric. *Hearing Things: Religion, Illusion, and the American Enlightenment.* Cambridge, MA: Harvard University Press, 2002.

Shively, Beth. "'Can-Do' or 'Set-Apart'?: Contemporary Christian Courtship and the Rejection of Girl Power." Rock Island, IL: Midwest American Academy of Religion, 2010.

Stephens, Walter. *Demon Lovers: Witchcraft, Sex, and the Crisis of Belief.* Chicago: University of Chicago Press, 2002.

Taves, Ann. *Fits, Trances, and Visions: Experiencing Religion and Explaining Experience from Wesley to James.* Princeton: Princeton University Press, 1999.

Thompson, Roger. *Sex in Middlesex: Popular Mores in a Massachusetts County, 1649–1699.* Amherst: University of Massachusetts Press, 1986.

TLC. *Purity Balls.* Nov. 2008.

The Today Show. "Purity Balls." September 16, 2008. http://video.google.com/videoplay?docid=4762184037273160599.

Vance, Carole S., ed. *Pleasure and Danger: Exploring Female Sexuality.* Boston: Routledge and Kegan Paul, 1984.

Vance, Norman. *The Sinews of the Spirit: The Ideal of Christian Manliness in Victorian Literature and Religious Thought.* Cambridge: Cambridge University Press, 1985.

Wacker, Grant. *Heaven Below: Pentecostalism and American Culture.* Cambridge, MA: Harvard University Press, 2001.

Walton, Jonathan. *Watch This! The Ethics and Aesthetics of Black Televangelism.* New York: New York University Press, 2009.

Weinberg, Martin S., Rochelle Ganz Swensson, and Sue Kiefer Hammersmith. "Sexual Autonomy and the Status of Women: Models of Female Sexuality in U.S. Sex Manuals from 1950–1980." *Social Problems* 30, no. 3 (February 1983): 312–324.

Wilcox, W. Bradford. *Soft Patriarchs, New Men: How Christianity Shapes Fathers and Husbands*. Chicago: University of Chicago Press, 2004.

Woodward, Kenneth L. "The Bible in the Bedroom." With Eloise Salholz. *Newsweek*, February 1, 1982, 71.

Worthen, Molly. "Not Your Father's L'Abri." *Christianity Today*, March 2008. http://www.christianitytoday.com/ct/2008/march/36.60.

———. "Who Would Jesus Smack Down?" *New York Times Magazine*, January 6, 2009. http://www.nytimes.com/2009/01/11/magazine/11punk-t.html?pagewanted=all&_r=0.

Zika, Charles. *Exorcising Our Demons: Magic, Witchcraft, and Visual Culture in Early Modern Europe*. Leiden: Brill, 2003.

INDEX

Frigidity, *45, 56*
A Full Quiver: Family Planning and the Lordship of Christ (Hess & Hess), *118*

Gardella, Peter, *64*
Gardner, Tim Allen, *74, 75*
Garth, Lakita, *38*
Gender differences, *53*
Gender roles, *93–128*; in evangelical sex manuals, *2–3, 43*; and fairy-tale narratives, *27, 107–110*; and female knowledge, *110–112*; female ordination, *104, 105*; and feminism, *102–107*; Jakes on, *139, 144–145*; motherhood as sacred vocation, *96, 99*; and purity rituals, *40*; in Quiverfull Movement, *5, 115–126*; wife's role in marriage, *61, 65, 70, 97–102, 112–115*
Generational curses, *18, 88*
Generations of Light Purity Ball, *10–11*
Genetics, *73, 88–89, 90, 171n8*
Genital pleasuring. *See* Masturbation
The Gift of Sex (Penner & Penner), *52*
Gigi, God's Little Princess (Walsh), *15*
"Girls Gone Wise" blog, *102, 176n18*
Glamour magazine on purity balls, *13*
Glimpses of the Devil: A Psychiatrist's Personal Accounts of Possession, Exorcism, and Redemption (Peck), *78*
Gothard, Bill, *179n54*
Gresh, Dannah, *32, 34, 36, 161n35, 164n70*
Griffith, R. Marie, *172n12*
G-Spot, *51*

Haggard, Ted, *71–72, 83, 170n1*
Hammond, Frank & Ida, *76, 78–79, 80, 81, 88*
Harris, Alex, *159n7*
Harris, Brett, *159n7*
Harris, Josh, *35, 159n7*

Hayford, Jack, *170–171n3, 170n1*
Healing (MacNutt), *76*
Healing the Family Tree (McAll), *76, 88*
Helpmeet literature, *101, 107–110, 136, 139, 144*
He-Motions (Jakes), *140*
Hendershot, Heather, *30*
"Her-meneutics" blog, *150*
Hess, Rick & Jan, *118, 119, 120, 121, 122*
The Hidden Art of Homemaking (Schaeffer), *100*
High risk pregnancies, *120*
The Hite Report, *64*
Holmes, Andy, *16*
Holy pregnancy, *86, 87*
Holy Sex (Wier & Carruth), *72, 75–76, 82–85*
Holy Spirit: baptism in, *77*; demons vs., *74, 79–80, 82, 85–88*; gifts of, *132*; healing via, *78*; and purity rituals, *133*; sexualization of, *85–88*; as spiritual marriage component, *75*
Homemaking, *99*
Homeschooling, *178–179n54*
Homosexuality, *3, 8, 57, 170n2*
Houghton, Craig, *118*
Howard, Jay, *174n24*
How to Be Happy Though Married (LaHaye), *61*
Human Sexual Response (Masters & Johnson), *44*
Hunt, Susan, *103*
Hymen, *55*
Hysterectomies, *119*

I'd Be Your Princess (O'Brien), *15*
Ideal Marriage: Its Physiology and Technique (Van De Velde), *44*
Illustrations in sex manuals, *46–47, 57–60*
Impotency, *56*
Infertility, *117–118, 164n75*
Institute of Basic Life Principles, *179n54*